AFTER CAPITALISM

New Critical Theory
General Editors:
Patricia Huntington and Martin J. Beck Matuštík

The aim of *New Critical Theory* is to broaden the scope of critical theory beyond its two predominant strains, one generated by the research program of Jürgen Habermas and his students, the other by postmodern cultural studies. The series reinvigorates early critical theory—as developed by Theodor Adorno, Herbert Marcuse, Walter Benjamin, and others—but from more decisive post-colonial and post-patriarchal vantage points. *New Critical Theory* represents theoretical and activist concerns about class, gender, and race, seeking to learn from as well as nourish social liberation movements.

AFTER CAPITALISM
Second Edition

David Schweickart

ROWMAN & LITTLEFIELD PUBLISHERS, INC.
Lanham • Boulder • New York • Toronto • Plymouth, UK

Published by Rowman & Littlefield Publishers, Inc.
A wholly owned subsidary of The Rowman & Littlefield Publishing Group, Inc.
4501 Forbes Boulevard, Suite 200, Lanham, Maryland 20706
www.rowmanlittlefield.com

Estover Road, Plymouth PL6 7PY, United Kingdom

British Library Cataloguing in Publication Information Available

Library of Congress Cataloging-in-Publication Data

Schweickart, David.
After capitalism / David Schweickart.—2nd ed.
    p. cm.—(New critical theory)
 Includes bibliographical references and index.
 ISBN 978-0-7425-6497-8 (cloth : alk. paper)—ISBN 978-0-7425-6498-5 (pbk. : alk.
paper)—ISBN 978-0-7425-6499-2 (electronic)
 1. Democracy. 2. Capitalism. 3. Socialism. I. Schweickart, David.
 JC423.S387 2011
 320.53'1—dc22   2011016193

∞™ The paper used in this publication meets the minimum requirements of American
National Standard for Information Sciences—Permanence of Paper for Printed Library
Materials, ANSI/NISO Z39.48-1992. Printed in the United States of America

For
Anita and Karen
Lauryn and Carrie and Liam and Gracie
the next generation
and the next

Contents

Figures

Preface to the Revised Edition

Who now can use the words of socialism with a straight face? As a member of the baby boomer generation, I can remember when the idea of revolution, of brave men pushing history forward, had a certain glamour. Now it is a sick joke. . . . The truth is that the heart has gone out of the opposition to capitalism.[1]

That's Paul Krugman, Nobel laureate in economics, writing in 2009. But in truth, it's capitalism that is "a sick joke," isn't it? Our version of capitalism, at any rate. Two years earlier, the Great Recession had begun. The staggering excesses of the financial elite had finally brought the system to the verge of collapse. Suddenly those elites, who had been agitating for decades, with great success, to "get government off our backs," were clamoring for assistance. And of course they got it. Suddenly all concern about fiscal responsibility, deficits, etc., were set aside and hundreds of billions of taxpayer dollars were funneled to the banks. As Joseph Stiglitz, another Nobel laureate, remarked at the time:

> Some have called this new economic regime "socialism with American characteristics." But socialism is concerned with ordinary individuals. By contrast, the United States has provided little help for the millions of Americans who are losing their homes [or] workers who lose their jobs. . . . America has expanded the corporate safety net in unprecedented ways, from commercial banks to investment banks, then to insurance and now to automobiles, with no end in sight.[2]

"But," he says, "this new form of ersatz capitalism, in which losses are subsidized and profits privatized, is doomed to failure."

Is it? As I write this, the recession has long been declared over; the stock market has rebounded, the Dow Jones Industrial Average from its 6710 low in 2008 not quite to its 14,093 peak in bubble 2007, but not too far below it. Productivity is way up. Corporations are wracking up record profits, and sitting on mountains of cash. The Wall Street banks and hedge funds are back, with the multimillion-dollar bonuses flowing again. (In 2009 the average income of the top twenty-five hedge fund operators was $1 billion—that's 2,500 *times* the salary of the president of the United States.)

The recession is certainly over for the rich, who have just received yet another reward: an extension on the income tax bonanza President Bush had given them. However: The millions who have lost their homes haven't gotten them back; indeed foreclosures continue to mount. Official unemployment is still close to 10 percent, real unemployment much higher. Job prospects for graduating college students remain bleak. But we can't do anything about these things, we are told. We don't have the money. Look at the federal deficit! Look at our national debt! We have to *cut back* our social programs, not expand them or create new ones.

This is a joke, right? A sick joke.

In fairness to Krugman—whose excellent work will be cited often in this book—it must be noted that he follows his "sick joke" remark with this:

> Capitalism is secure, not only because of its successes—which have been very real—but because no one has a plausible alternative. This situation will not last forever. Surely there will be other ideologies, other dreams, and they will emerge sooner rather than later if the current economic crisis persists and deepens.[3]

After Capitalism is an exercise in "other ideologies, other dreams"—other than capitalism, that is. (It is unabashedly socialist.) The first edition of *After Capitalism*, as I explain in the preface to that edition, was the fourth incarnation of a set of ideas I had begun to develop as a graduate student in philosophy in the early 1970s. This edition is the fifth.

Some background: I had returned to graduate school, having had a crisis of conscience of sorts that prompted me to resign my position as an assistant professor of mathematics at the University of Kentucky. Although I had completed my PhD in mathematics, I had come to realize that I was not as passionate about that subject as were some of my colleagues. "Moreover," so I thought to myself, "I'm spending a lot of time teaching differential equations to engineering students, many whom will head off to defense industries and use the skills I'm helping them develop to build better bombs."

I didn't want to do that. I had become politicized, involved first in the civil rights movement, then in the antiwar movement. I loved teaching, but I wanted to teach something more meaningful (in my eyes) than mathematics. "You get only one turn on this earth," I said to myself. "Don't waste it."

In fact, my training in mathematics turned out to be exceedingly useful to me in pursuing the topic that became the subject of my dissertation. For shortly after deciding to leave mathematics, I encountered Marx. I thought I knew what Marxism was all about—some kind of atheistic, totalitarian utopianism that didn't take into account human nature—but I had never read any of Marx's actual writings. The summer between my leaving mathematics and my beginning again as a graduate student, this time in philosophy, I read Marx's *Capital* (vol. 1). I read it very carefully—as a mathematician—reading all the footnotes, working through all the equations.

I've not yet recovered from the experience. I had been involved in antiracist and antiwar activities, but it had never occurred to me until that time that there might be something fundamentally wrong with our *economic* system, something *really* wrong, not amenable to this or that liberal reform. Marx persuaded me that capitalism is irredeemably exploitative and ultimately irrational—and I remain persuaded still.

But there was a problem. Marx's critique of capitalism, which acknowledges its accomplishments while laying bare its exploitative underpinnings and irrational dynamic, remains just that: critique. Marx offers no model for an alternative economic order, no "recipes for cookshops of the future," in his disdainful phrase.[4] I don't fault Marx for this omission. He was trying to be a *scientific* socialist. Although there were sufficient data available to him to ground his critique of capitalism, there was little upon which to draw regarding alternative economic institutions. No "experiments" had been performed. But this omission, when coupled with the failure of the Soviet model, left later socialists vulnerable to Krugman's implied critique: "capitalism is secure . . . because no one has a plausible alternative."

"We no longer have Marx's excuse," I thought to myself. "The twentieth century has been thick with economic experimentation at both the macro and micro levels. We know far more now about what works and what doesn't than Marx could possibly have known." Hence my dissertation project, which involved reading widely in economics (thus the utility of my mathematics background—those curves and equations didn't intimidate): to specify and defend "a plausible alternative" to the prevailing economic order.

The present edition is a rewrite of the 2002 incarnation of this project with the data updated and new material added. The most significant additions are new sections on the economic instability of capitalism, the current crisis, and China, and more material on the ever-vexing transition question: how to get from here to there. I've also restructured the presentation somewhat. In the original version, chapter 4 was my multicount indictment of capitalism, and chapter 5 my demonstration that Economic Democracy (the proposed alternative) will not suffer these defects, at least not to the degree that they are present under capitalism. In the revised edition, we now consider, for each of the seven specific topics taken up—inequality, unemployment, overwork, poverty, economic instability, ecological degradation, and lack of democracy—why it is endemic to capitalism, and then, right away, how it would be different under Economic Democracy. Chapter 4 treats the first four topics; chapter 5 the latter three. (It is an easier read, I think, if you get point-counterpoint in succession, rather than the whole critique of capitalism followed by a lengthy analysis of Economic Democracy.)

This version, like the original, was written for the general reader but it is more heavily endnoted than the first. Unlike the first version, the endnotes sometimes take up issues relevant, although not central, to the main text. They are not, as they are in the original, merely documentations of facts or quotes, or suggestions for further reading. Still, you can read through without looking at the endnotes, and you won't miss much.

Why a new edition? Above all, because debate about the desirability of capitalism is more widespread now than it has been in decades, and I want my contribution to that debate to be as current as possible. Also—because the world has changed significantly since 2002, and I want my analysis to reflect those changes. In 2002 pundits, politicos, and a coterie of "neoconservative" intellectuals were speaking of a "New American Century." Influential economists were telling us that economic crises, at least here in the United States, were a thing of the past. The United States looks very different today.

Another big change: the word "socialism" is being used again—in the United States most often to scare people (those for whom "socialism" remains a scary word), but more importantly, in Latin America, where governments calling for "a socialism for the twenty-first century" have come to power, and have done so not via guerilla insurrection but via free and fair *democratic* elections.

Mainstream economists remain loath to use the *s*-word (Joseph Stiglitz, as quoted above, an exception), but more and more are expressing deep reservations about the current economic order. One very prominent one, another Nobel laureate, had already expressed these reservations in a book published more than a decade ago, going so far as to raise doubts about capitalism itself:

> The big challenges that capitalism now faces in the contemporary world include issues of inequality (especially that of grinding poverty in a world of unprecedented prosperity) and of "public goods" (that is, goods people share together,

like the environment). *The solution to these problems will almost certainly call for institutions that take us beyond the capitalist market economy.*[5]

Amartya Sen hinted at that earlier remark of his more recently, while commenting on the European conference on "A New Capitalism," hosted by Nicolas Sarkozy and Tony Blair. "Should we search for a new capitalism," he asks, "or for a 'new world' . . . that would take a different form?"[6] This book will argue: a new world!

Special thanks to two persons who were immensely helpful with this revision. Some months ago, Todd Wilson, chair of the computer science department at California State University, Fresno, a person I've never met in person, e-mailed me about my work. When I told him that I was working on a revised edition of *After Capitalism*, he immediately volunteered his services. He subsequently read every chapter, corrected numerous typos, and made invaluable suggestions as to form and content. I am deeply grateful. The other person is Patsy Schweickart, who also did some major editing—and so many other things that have made my spirit soar. I should also thank Loyola University Chicago for granting me a semester's research leave to bring this project to fruition and Eric Graff for compiling the index.

Chicago, January, 2011

Preface to the First Edition

This book is the fourth incarnation of a set of ideas I began to develop nearly thirty years ago, as a graduate student, during those heady days in the early 1970s when anything seemed possible. I was less sanguine than many of my peers about the imminent collapse of capitalism or a revolutionary upsurge here at home—"in the belly of the beast," as we called it then. Moreover, it was pretty clear to me that even if capitalism should collapse and a revolutionary government come to power, that government would not have the slightest idea as to how to restructure the economy. "Power to the people," sure, but *how* is economic power to devolve to them? What institutions would replace those of capitalism? The Soviet system had long ceased to inspire, and although great things seemed to be happening in Mao's China (not so great, we later learned), the Chinese economic model had little relevance to an advanced industrial society such as our own.

So my project became to determine how an advanced industrial economy might be structured to be economically viable, while, at the same time, embody the great ethical ideals of the democratic socialist tradition. My dissertation, "Capitalism: A Utilitarian Analysis," was its first incarnation. Although there is no mention of an economic alternative in the title, such an alternative had to be presented in the text, since "utilitarianism" requires that comparisons be made. If you are going to critique capitalism from a utilitarian perspective, you have to show that some other economic system would provide a greater amount of happiness for more people.

That dissertation was later revised and published (in 1980) as *Capitalism or Worker Control? An Ethical and Economic Appraisal.* Here the alternative is named: "worker-control socialism." (In the next book and in this one, I call it "Economic Democracy.") A model is presented that features worker self-managed enterprises competing with one another in a market environment, but with new investment "socially controlled." Although I've refined and adjusted the model over the years, you will see it has retained the same basic features. (Political philosopher Isaiah Berlin famously characterized thinkers as foxes or hedgehogs. "A fox," he says, "knows many things. A hedgehog knows one big thing."[1] I probably belong among the hedgehogs, for I do know one big thing: what a viable, desirable alternative to the present, pernicious economic order would look like.)

In 1993 I published *Against Capitalism.* The world had changed enormously since 1980. Most significantly, the Soviet empire had collapsed. First, its satellite states in Eastern Europe broke free of Soviet domination and repudiated their socialist heritage; then the Soviet Union itself disintegrated. These were gloomy days for those of us on the Left. Not that we were admirers of the Soviet Union; few of us were. But most of us felt, consciously or unconsciously, that the persistence of communism (indeed its steady expansion) in the face of violent hostility on the part of the vastly richer and more powerful capitalist states, led by the United States, indicated that history was on our side. In due course the Soviet Union and other socialist states would democratize, figure out how to run their economies efficiently, and, in the meantime, capitalism would enter into terminal crisis. So we thought.

History had other ideas. And yet I couldn't help thinking we were right. Morally we were right—whatever history's verdict. Capitalism *is* a ruthless, predatory system, and there *is* a better way. It made me almost crazy to hear otherwise smart and decent thinkers (the philosopher Richard Rorty, for example) proclaim that we are "going to have to stop using the term 'capitalist economy' as if we knew what a functioning non-capitalist economy looked like."[2] We *do* know what a functioning, noncapitalist economy would look like. I wrote *Against Capitalism* to show once again—with suitable revisions to the model and additional material added—that the problem is not that we don't know what a humane economy would look like, but that forces of immense power are blocking its emergence. If intellectuals are supposed to "speak truth to power," as it was fashionable to say in those days, we ought to at least say *that.*

Here I am again, writing another book on the same theme. It's at once the same book that I've written before—data updated, of course—and a rather different book. Let me highlight some of the differences. When I began writing this book, nearly four years ago, I had in mind a simple plan. I would rewrite *Against Capitalism* in a more popular key. *Against Capitalism* and its predecessors had been written for professional philosophers and economists. There were numerous footnotes and fairly esoteric discussions of technical matters, sometimes within those footnotes, sometimes in the text itself. This book was to be more "user friendly"—and I believe that it is. The footnotes remain—notes at the end of chapters, actually—but they simply source my quotes and data and occasionally suggest further reading. You can skip over them and miss nothing of substance. I've included in the text (as parenthetical remarks) side comments that I would have put in footnotes had I been writing for an academic audience. I've omitted all references to the technical debates.

I don't mean to suggest that I've "dumbed down" my presentation. Not at all. What I'm offering here is as intellectually rigorous as anything I've written. It won't be a quick and easy read. It's just that the person I have in mind as I write, with whom I am conversing, is an intelligent and concerned ordinary reader, not a scholar with philosophical or economic expertise. I want to be comprehensible to the nonexpert reader.

The original plan was simply to produce a more popular version of *Against Capitalism*, but as the writing progressed, two things changed. My earlier works focused on capitalism as a way of organizing a national economy and on providing an alternative national model. But, as everyone knows, "globalization" has become the name of the capitalist game. Therefore, this book more carefully treats capitalism as an international phenomenon (which, of course, it always has been), and more carefully specifies how a nation whose economy was structured as an Economic Democracy would interact with other nations.

A second, even more important, change occurred without my being aware of it at first. Looking back, I see that *Against Capitalism* and its predecessors were theoretical works aimed at establishing a theoretical point: those who have argued (and there are many) that a viable democratic socialist economy is impossible, given the kinds of creatures we are, are wrong. Democratic socialism, properly structured, is not contrary to human nature. It does not require extraordinary altruism on the part of its citizenry. It does not run counter to deep-seated human impulses. While the present work remains theoretical, it has become theory with a more practical intent. The point here is not simply to undercut arguments advanced by various philosophers and economists against the possibility of a viable socialism, but to help ordinary people—those who will form the basis of the next great challenge to capitalism—to understand how the world works, and what can be done to make it work better.

The shift from theory with theoretical intent to theory with practical intent marked a subtle change in my thinking. I have become convinced—as

I was not in 1993—that there will indeed be another sustained challenge to the capitalist world order, and that that challenge needs a clearer vision as to what is possible.

Why this shift in my thinking? Two sorts of factors were responsible. The first was of a personal nature, having to do with the reception of my work. In 1997 a Spanish translation of *Against Capitalism* appeared, published by the Jesuit-affiliated publishing house Sal Terrae of Santander, Spain, in conjunction with the social action network *Cristianisme i Justícia*. The latter arranged a book tour for me in early 1998, which took me to Barcelona, Bilbao, Tarragona, and Zaragoza. Suddenly I found myself speaking not to exclusively academic audiences but to ordinary people committed to social change. I also gave numerous interviews to local newspapers. Later that year, while in the Philippines, I was asked to speak to the Cooperative Foundation of the Philippines, Inc. Back home I was approached by the Eighth Day Center for Justice, a Chicago-based Catholic social action group, and asked to make a presentation. I was also invited to speak to the Midwest Center for Labor Research (now the Center for Labor and Community Research). During this same period, I began trying out chapter drafts of my new book on students, both undergraduate and graduate. As a result of these interactions, it became clear to me that there is a hunger on the part of a great many people of good will, particularly those with an activist bent, for a more concrete and comprehensive vision of present historical possibilities than is currently available. Many people are aware of injustice and want to change things, but, although sensitive to many instances of social evil and working to alleviate them, they are unclear as to long-term, permanent solutions. They want to believe such solutions exist, but most have doubts. This book is intended to remove (or at least reduce) those doubts.

The other factors influencing the shift in my project toward the practical have been the changes in the world itself since 1993. A number of things have happened (or not happened) that have dampened the giddy triumphalism of capitalism's op-ed apologists so evident back then.

First, communist governments did not collapse everywhere—as was almost universally expected. All non-European communist states have remained intact. All are experimenting with market reforms—some with considerable success—but none has broken officially with its socialist past. Of course most commentators see market reforms as leading inevitably to capitalism, but, as we shall see, that view is mistaken. There is nothing inevitable about such a transition. Markets (I argue) do not imply capitalism. Indeed, they are essential to a healthy *socialism*.

Second, what have collapsed since 1993 are not the economies claiming to be socialist, but the economies of many of the ex-socialist societies that have tried consciously to restore capitalism. Here's a recent evaluation of the Russian experience:

> The result has been an unmitigated disaster. In the first year of reform, industrial output collapsed by 26 percent. Between 1992 and 1995, Russian GDP fell 42 percent and industrial production fell 46 percent—far worse than the contraction of the U.S. economy during the Great Depression. . . . Real incomes have plummeted 40 percent since 1991. By the mid to late nineties, more than forty-four million of Russia's 148 million people were living in poverty (defined as living on less than thirty-two dollars a month); three quarters of the population live on less than one hundred dollars a month. Suicides doubled and deaths from alcohol abuse tripled in the mid-nineties. Infant mortality reached third world levels, while the birthrate plummeted. After five years of reform, life expectancy fell by two years (to seventy-two) for women and by four years (to fifty-eight) for men—lower than a century ago for the latter.[3]

Or consider this *cri de coeur* circulated via e-mail by a Bulgarian woman in the aftermath of NATO's war against Yugoslavia. It warns the Serbian "Democratic Opposition" about what will be in store for them. Here's an excerpt:

> We, here in Bulgaria, have had US-style democracy since 1989. For ten years already.
> My Ten Most Awful Years
> What happened during that most awful period of my life on Earth?
> Through the ardent UDF leaders in power, the International Monetary Fund and the World Bank are successfully devouring Bulgarian industry, destroying the social fabric, and opening national boundaries. (Our national boundaries, mind you, never those of the U.S. or Germany.)
> Three ways they devour Bulgarian industry:
>
> —privatizing the Bulgarian plants and factories and liquidating them afterwards;
> —directly liquidating them;
> —selling them for twopenny-halfpence to powerful foreign corporations. For instance, the Copper Metallurgical plant near the town of Pirdop, producing gold and platinum as well as electrolytic copper, was sold in 1997 to Union Miniere, Belgium, for next to nothing.
>
> Conclusion: Bulgarian industry and infrastructure (the roads for instance) have been most successfully demolished—and this WITHOUT bombing—in less than ten years. All this, just from doing what the Serbian opposition is saying the Serbs should do.
> A popular joke here during the U.S. war on Yugoslavia: two Turkish pilots, flying over Bulgaria, are looking down at the Bulgarian landscape. One of them says, "I wonder? Have we dropped bombs here?" "Don't be silly," answers the other. "It is Bulgaria! It looks like that without bombing."

Side results: hordes of unemployed, as you can well imagine.
Beggars in the streets.
Children dying in the street from drugs and malnutrition.
Old people digging in the rubbish containers for some rags or moldy pieces of bread.
    Yesterday my brother-in-law told me he had seen the former headmistress of his son's school digging in a rubbish container.[4]

The third change that affected my thinking has been the sharp increase in global instability in recent years. In 1995 the Mexican "tequila crisis" came close to bringing down the entire global financial superstructure. According to Michel Camdessus, then head of the International Monetary Fund, who, with U.S. treasury secretary Robert Rubin and a handful of other powerful insiders, launched an unprecedentedly large rescue plan, they had to act, whatever the cost, or else "there would have been a real-world catastrophe."[5] Two years later financial panic gripped Southeast Asia, bringing to its knees even the vaunted South Korean economy; the panic spread to Russia, which had to default on its internal debt, then to Brazil. Since then crises of varying magnitudes have broken out throughout Latin America, while Africa continues its downward spiral. Capitalism, freed from constraints, seems to have run amok, littering the globe with wreckage.

Fourth, and above all, there has been *resistance*. On January 1, 1994, the day that the famed North American Free Trade Agreement went into effect, armed revolt broke out in the poor Mexican state of Chiapas, led by a movement taking its name from the legendary Mexican revolutionary of nearly a century ago, Emiliano Zapata. This unorthodox, imaginative movement, although itself renouncing violence while being subjected to harsh governmental oppression, refuses to go away. (In March 2001, members undertook a well-publicized "caravan of peace and dignity" from Chiapas to Mexico City, drawing support along the way, then staged a huge rally in Mexico City and entered the National Congress to speak to the politicians present.)

In the spring of 1995 the trade union federations of Italy called a general strike to oppose the right-wing Berlusconi government's plan to roll back pension gains. This strike shut down the country for several days, and brought 1.5 million workers, by the trainloads and busloads, to Rome. (I happened to be living in Rome at the time, teaching at Loyola University's Rome Center. Never in my life had I witnessed anything like this. My wife and I walked out of our apartment in Monte Mario, an upper-middle-class section of Rome, to find everything closed: grocery stores, fruit stands, wine shops, barber shops, newsstands, restaurants, even the gas stations. We stared in disbelief, trying to imagine something like this happening at home: the unions put out a call, and every business, everywhere—in every city, town and neighborhood—shuts down.) In the fall of that year French students and workers, 5 million plus, also took to the streets, in a similar, even larger action.

Protests and demonstrations began to pop up everywhere, although almost always focusing on specific issues of local or national concern. Then came Seattle, November 1999—"Five Days that Shook the World," as writers Alexander Cockburn and Jeffrey St. Clair termed them[6]—thousands of protesters, young and old, First World and Third World, labor unions, environmentalists, anti-sweatshop activists and many more, converged on the city to disrupt the high-profile meeting of the World Trade Organization.

Even closer to home—here in Chicago, seven Loyola students were arrested for unfurling an anti-sweatshop banner at Niketown, a downtown store selling Swoosh products, and are scheduled to go on trial at the end of this month (August 2001).

Everywhere you look these days, people are resisting the ravages of our "new world order." It is impossible to predict how strong this resistance will become, or how serious the economic crises that doubtless will continue to break out (perhaps in unexpected places) will be, but it seems to me that whatever I write at this point in time should contribute in some small way to that resistance. That's what this book hopes to do.

I owe thanks to many people for assisting me in refining the ideas in this book. Two of my graduate assistants, Kory Schaff and Jason Barrett, helped a lot in tracking down data. I've profited from student reactions—graduate and undergraduate—to earlier drafts of this material. Particularly memorable were discussions with three honors students—Dan Hoyne, Kate Henderson, and Peter Gianopulos—at the Rome Center (one of whom refused to be convinced). Appreciation should be extended to Juan Manuel Sinde, of the Caja Laboral in Mondragon for a useful meeting, and to Dan Swinney of the Center for Labor and Community Research for extended conversations as to the applicability of the model of Economic Democracy to concrete reform efforts now. I've been stimulated by ongoing debates with Al Campbell and Bertell Ollman. Although we disagree strongly on a central issue—the necessity of markets in a viable socialism—our discussions have been non-rancorous and productive. I've benefitted from the commentaries on an earlier version of this book by Patricia Mann, Frank Thompson, and Justin Schwartz, given at the Radical Philosophy Association Conference in the fall of 2000. I owe a lot to discussions with Michael Howard, with whom I agree on (almost) everything. I've also benefitted from the written comments of Allen Hunter, Robert Heilbroner, Bruno Jossa, David Chandler, and an anonymous referee. (If the referee is who I think it is, he has been thanked by name in this paragraph.)

There are many more I should also thank. I've had the good fortune to be able to present papers based on this book to various conferences and meetings: in Havana, Holguin, and Camaguey, Cuba; at the Universidad de Centroamerica in El Salvador; at the University of the Philippines; at El Escorial and Gandia, Spain; at the Università di Bergamo in Italy; at the Université de Paris, Nanterre; and at numerous campuses in the United States. My thanks to all the organizers and inviters.

Special thanks also to my Cuban friends, Humberto Miranda, Raul Rodriguez, and Gilberto Valdez, whose courage and commitment to a humane socialism never faltered, even during the darkest days of the "Special Period," when Cuba's principal trading partner collapsed and the U.S. tightened its ruthless embargo. They—and so many other Cubans I've had the good fortune to meet—have been inspiring. (I've had occasion to visit Cuba six times during the past decade, almost always in conjunction with the annual Conference of North American and Cuban Philosophers and Social Scientists. I owe a debt of gratitude to Cliff DuRand, of the Radical Philosophy Association, the indefatigable organizer of the North American delegation, for facilitating these visits.)

Special thanks to two other people. More than anyone else's, it was the work of Jaroslav Vanek, which I encountered while working on my dissertation, that put me on the intellectual trajectory I've since followed. I was privileged to make a presentation at a conference in his honor at Columbia University in 1999, which allowed me to express my gratitude. Let me express it again.

Finally, special thanks to Patsy—*sine qua non*.

Chicago, August 2001

Postscript

This manuscript was submitted to the publisher in August 2001, so obviously no mention was made of the September 11 terrorist attacks. However, given the significance of these events, the production schedule has been modified so as to allow for a short postscript:

"Everything has changed." This refrain was repeated constantly in the aftermath of the attacks. Is it true?

From the perspective set out in this book, the answer is "No." Not everything has changed. (As I write, widespread rioting in Argentina has brought down a neoliberal government trying to impose yet another International Monetary Fund austerity package.) The big things have not changed—

although the attacks of September 11 do highlight a factor to which I paid little attention as I wrote this book.

After Capitalism documents and analyzes the destructive tendencies of capitalism, and it predicts a renewed challenge to this system. Among other things, it argues that the unrestrained capitalism that is now dominant will further widen the gap between the global haves and the global have-nots, while making life increasingly precarious for ordinary people, even in rich countries. What the book does not do—apart from an occasional aside—is consider nonprogressive reactions to economic stress and dislocation.

Yet, as the history of European fascism makes clear, modern mass movements based on ruthless, atavistic ideologies thrive under such conditions. Indeed, they are often cultivated by wealthy interests to deflect discontent and to destroy challenges from the Left. In recent times, with the socialist project in disarray, such movements have proliferated: neo-Nazi revivals in the West, the ethnic nationalisms that tore Yugoslavia to shreds and have wreaked havoc in many other poor countries, and, perhaps most significant of all, the various flavors of what I'm inclined to call "theocratic fascism"—faith-based fundamentalist movements that seek political power and do not shy away from terror.[7] Christian fundamentalists blow up abortion clinics. Jewish fundamentalists dream of a "final solution"—the ethnic cleansing in Greater Israel of "Palestinian lice" (as they were called by the recently assassinated leader of Israel's ultra-right National Union Party).[8] Islamic fundamentalists set off bombs in shopping malls, and commandeer aircraft full of people, which they fly into buildings full of people.

We need to be clear about several matters.

1. The cause of extremist activities is not religion, per se. The vast majority of Christians, Jews, and Muslims of the world are anything but fundamentalists and are sickened by the slaughter of innocents. It is not even fair to brand all fundamentalists as theocratic fascists, although the intense *ressentiment* characteristic of most contemporary forms of religious fundamentalism point them in that direction.
2. Nor is the cause poverty, per se. Poverty inevitably breeds resistance, but that resistance can take various forms. Recall that not once during the Cold War era did indigenous Marxist forces fighting directly against the United States (as in Korea and Vietnam) or against U.S.-backed dictatorial regimes ever engage in terror against U.S. civilians. These forces were overwhelmingly poor workers and peasants struggling for a better life, who could see clearly that the United States opposed their efforts. But Marxism as an ideology has always distinguished between the government of a country, seen to be acting on behalf of that country's

ruling class, and the ordinary citizens of the country. Fascist ideologies make no such distinction.

3. We should also be clear that terror is not confined to fascist movements. By any objective measure the nation now leading the charge in the "war against terror" has committed more acts of violence against innocent people—either directly or via its support for murderous client regimes—than has any other nation of the post–World War II era. As I argue in chapter 5, had the United States been concerned to promote democracy in the world rather than capitalism, the body-count of the postwar period would be many millions lower. (As I also argue, there has been very little public support for the policies that have had such horrendous consequences. Successive administrations have had to expend considerable effort to keeping the American people in the dark as to the exact nature of their endeavors.)

4. Finally, we should remember that although wealthy interests often bankroll fascist movements, using them for their own ends, these efforts often have disastrous consequences. Wealthy landowners and industrialists backed Mussolini and Hitler to counter the Left. Saudi Arabia has funded fundamentalist movements throughout the Islamic world so as to legitimize its own corrupt regime. The United States gave enthusiastic (if covert) support to mujahideen fighters eager to overthrow the secular Marxist government of Afghanistan—and to drive out the Russians when they later invaded. That fascist movements often bite the hands that have fed them should come as no surprise. These movements are as cynical about their financial backers as the backers are about them. (Consider the recently published comments of President Carter's national security advisor, Zbigniew Brzezinski, interviewed before September 11, about the United States having given arms and advice to future terrorists: "What is more important to the history of the world? The Taliban or the collapse of the Soviet empire? Some stirred up Moslems or the liberation of Central Europe and the end of the Cold War?"[9])

What follows? The brutal events of September 11 call sharp attention to the virulence of movements that embrace terror as a "weapon of the weak" and to the threat they pose not only to innocent civilians everywhere but to domestic civil rights and liberties. Conservative forces can be counted on to exploit these events to further their own agenda. Indeed, they already have.

At a deeper level the events of September 11 demonstrate how desperately the world needs a *progressive* alternative to the ideology of global capitalism. Capitalist globalization breeds resistance, which, when progressive responses are cut off, turns murderously ugly. Without a progressive vision—and a global movement animated by that vision—we are left with only capitalism and terror—McWorld versus Jihad.[10] This book hopes to demonstrate that these alternatives, which are in fact two faces of the same coin, do not constitute our only possible future.

Chicago, January 2002

The form of association, however, which, if mankind continues to improve, must be expected in the end to predominate, is not that which can exist between a capitalist as chief, and work-people without a voice in the management, but the association of the labourers themselves on terms of equality, collectively owning the capital with which they carry on their operations, and working under managers elected and removable by themselves.

—John Stuart Mill, *Principles of Political Economy* (1848)

But there was in store a still greater victory of the political economy of labor over the political economy of property. We speak of the co-operative movement, especially the co-operative factories raised by the unassisted efforts of a few bold hands. The value of these great social experiments cannot be over-rated. They have shown that production on a large scale, in accord with the behests of modern science, may be carried on without the existence of a class of masters employing a class of hands.

—Karl Marx, "Inaugural Address of
the Working Men's International Association" (1864)

Our ideal as cooperativists must be the achievement of authentic human solidarity, as wanted by God, and through which people progress in every aspect. . . . Our cooperatives must primarily serve those who see them as bastions of social justice and not those who see cooperatives as refuges or safe places for their conservative spirit.

—Don José María Arizmendiarrieta, *Pensamientos* (1978)

The General Assembly, recognizing that cooperatives, in their various forms, promote the fullest possible participation in the economic and social development of all people, including women, youth, older persons, persons with disabilities and indigenous peoples, are becoming a major factor of economic and social development and contribute to the elimination of poverty, . . . proclaims the year 2012 the International Year of Cooperatives.

—United Nations General Assembly, December 18, 2009

1

Counterproject, Successor-System, Revolution

A specter is haunting Europe—the specter of Communism.
So wrote Marx and Engels in 1848. They were right. Over the course of the next century and a half, this specter would indeed haunt Europe. Not only Europe. It would stalk the entire planet. Millions of people—workers, peasants, intellectuals, and assorted "class traitors"—began to dream of a new economic order and commit themselves to action. The world polarized into two great camps. Atrocities mounted on both sides. Vast quantities of nuclear weapons were readied for use. Humanity found itself staring into the abyss of MADness—"mutually assured destruction."

Now, at least for the time being, the ghost of communism has been exorcised. Capitalism has emerged victorious. It is this spirit, arrogant and triumphant, that now stalks the earth. It appears to us in various forms.

It appears as "consumer society"—vaguely disquieting but infinitely alluring. More astonishing than grace, invisible waves project the sounds and images of commodity happiness to all but the remotest regions of the globe. Great temples to this spirit—shopping malls that dwarf in size (and attendance) the cathedrals and mosques of earlier epochs—have spread from capitalism's heartland to almost every country of the world. Smaller shrines—from fast-food franchises to dot.com websites—have sprung up everywhere. Not everyone has access to these holy places, but few remain who have not felt the power of their attraction. In poor countries, armed guards screen those pushing to enter the local McDonalds and Pizza Huts.

The specter of capitalism appears to us in another form, this one more distant, more shrouded in mystery, less benevolent, but even more powerful. Global financial markets pass judgments, create and destroy fortunes, make or break countries. A hierarchy of priests—financial advisors, brokers, bankers, traders, journalists, and economists—serves the subdeities of currencies, commodities, stocks, and bonds. These clergy grasp the mysteries of finance better than the laity, but they remain servants of the specter. The markets themselves decide who will succeed, who will fail—and when. One day all is well. The next day the markets plunge. Shortly thereafter, more mysterious still, people start losing their jobs, their homes, their self-respect. What happened? There was no war, no pandemic, no climate change—and yet catastrophe. (The most exalted of priests are sometimes humbled. Readers may recall the saga of Myron Scholes and Robert Merton, Nobel laureates in economics, who teamed up with some other financial wizards to form the hedge fund Long-Term Capital Management—which was saved from complete collapse in 1998 only because the Federal Reserve decided it was too important to go under.[1])

Capitalism appears to us not only as an alluring consumer society and as mysterious financial markets. Its cruelest manifestation is its savage inequality. We have all heard the statistics, although they are too numbing to remember for long. In 2007, for example, the combined wealth of the richest 500 people equaled the combined income of the bottom 60 percent of the world's population.[2] (Roughly, the average wealth of each one of these individuals is equal to the combined incomes of 8 million people earning the average income of the bottom 60 percent of humanity.) Nations are also divided as to rich and poor, those at the bottom having per capita incomes one-twentieth or even one-fiftieth of those at the top. Life expectancy in rich countries now exceeds eighty; in poor countries, it is often under fifty-five. Infant mortality, malnutrition, and literacy rates are comparably disparate.

Even within rich countries, the inequalities are staggering. In the United States, the upper 1 percent of the population owns more wealth than the bottom 90 percent. More than *43 million* families live below the poverty line (the largest number since the census bureau began collecting such data fifty years ago), including some 20 percent of our children, whereas corporate CEOs often make $30 million or more per year, and successful hedge fund managers make thirty times that much. (Top dog David Tepper, managing the Appaloosa Fund, took home $4 billion in 2009, about 200,000 *times* as much as a family of four living at the poverty line.[3])

It was once believed by most respectable academics and policy makers that capitalism would even out these inequalities over time, bring up the bottom faster than the top, reduce the income disparities among nations, until, sooner or later, everyone consumed like a middle-class American. Nobody believes that anymore. Now we simply build more prisons and more gated communities. If we happen to be in the upper-middle ranks of a rich country, we give thanks for our good fortune, and maybe buy a newspaper from a homeless person or write a small check to a favorite charity. If we are rich in a poor country, we might have to write a larger check to a death squad should the peasants or workers get unruly.

The fourth manifestation of our specter is less often noted, but no less evident: the deep irrationality of its overall functioning. How can it be that the amazing technologies we keep developing tend to intensify, not lessen, the pace of work, and make our jobs and lives less, not more, secure? How can it be that in a world of material deprivation, we must worry about industrial overcapacity and crises of overproduction? (How can there be too much stuff, when so many have so little?) Conversely, how can it be that the health of the global economy requires what ecological common sense knows is impossible—ever increasing consumption? (Economist Kenneth Boulding has remarked, "Only a madman or an economist could believe that exponential growth can go on forever in a finite world."[4]) To invoke Marx's term, how can we be so "alienated" from our products? How can it be that our own creations turn against us?

The specter of globalized capitalism: infinitely alluring, mysteriously powerful, savagely unequal, and profoundly irrational—has this spirit triumphed definitively? Have we indeed reached "the end of history," as Francis Fukuyama has proclaimed? Even on the Left, many seem to think so. Jeffrey Isaac, writing in *The New Left Review*, endorses Anthony Giddens's claim that "no one has any alternatives to capitalism:"[]

> Now we might not like this, but Giddens is alas correct. To say this is not to regard contemporary capitalism as a "trans-historical feature of human existence" or "second nature." It is simply to remark that given the history we have inherited and the world that human beings have created, there exists no credible wholesale alternative to capitalism. The same could be said of water purification, modern medicine, electronic communication, industrial technology with all its wastes and hazards, and also civil liberties and representative government of some sort. These are all historical achievements we cannot imagine transcending.[5]

1.1 The Counterproject

These are strong claims: Capitalism as the end of history; capitalism as a historical achievement we cannot imagine transcending. Are they true?

This book will demonstrate that the latter claim is false. We can well imagine transcending capitalism. As to the former—let me suggest something different: humanity's project for the twenty-first century will be to exorcise the ghost that now haunts us. If the contradictions of capitalism are as serious as I argue they are, and if they become more, not less, acute, as almost surely they will, then we will witness another sustained challenge to this most peculiar economic order. The challenge may not succeed. The forces arrayed against it are immense. (Not in numbers, but in wealth and power.) But since it is becoming ever clearer that getting beyond capitalism is the best hope for our species, the attempt will be made.

In fact, a new challenge to global capitalism has already begun. On the morning of July 21, 2001, as I was making final revisions to the manuscript that became the first edition of this book I glanced at the newspaper. The headline of the *Chicago Tribune* blared: "Riots turn Genoa into a war zone." The subhead added, "One killed, hundreds injured." While George W. Bush and other leaders of the G-8 (the seven leading industrial nations plus Russia—the latter added, presumably, out of respect for its nuclear missiles, not for its wrecked economy) met behind huge barricades and mouthed platitudes, at least 100,000 demonstrators, invited mainly via the Internet by an Italian network, the Genoa Social Forum, converged on the city. I checked my e-mail. Waiting for me was a first-person account, part of which reads as follows:

> I think I am calm, that I am not in shock, but my fingers are trembling as I write this. We were just up at the school that serves as a center for media, medical and trainings. We had just finished our meeting and we were talking, making phone calls, when we heard shouts and sirens and the roar of people yelling, objects breaking. The cops had come, and they were raiding the center. . . . We watched for a long time out the windows. They began carrying people out on stretchers. One, two, a dozen or more. A crowd was gathering and were shouting, "Assassini! Assassini!" They brought out the walking wounded, arrested them and took them away. We believe they brought someone out in a body bag. . . . Finally the cops went away. We went down to the first floor, outside, heard the story. They had come into the room where everybody was sleeping. Everyone had raised up their hands, calling out, "*Pacifisti! Pacifisti!*" And they beat the shit out of every person there. There's no pretty way to say it. We went into the other building. There was blood at every sleeping spot, pools of it in some places, stuff thrown around, computers and equipment trashed. We all wandered around in shock, not wanting to think about what is happening to those arrested, to those they took to the hospital. We know that they've taken people to jail and tortured them. One young Frenchman from our training, Vincent, had his head badly beaten on Friday in the street. In jail they took him into a room, twisted his arms behind his back and banged his head on the table. Another man was taken into a room covered with pictures of Mussolini and pornography, and was alternately

slapped around and stroked with affection in a weird psychological torture. Others were forced to shout, "Viva Il Duce!"

Just in case it isn't clear, this is fascism, Italian variety, but it is coming your way. It is the lengths they will go to defend their power. It is a lie that globalization means democracy. I can tell you, right now, tonight, this is not what democracy looks like. . . .

Please, do something![6]

Welcome to the counterproject!

This renewed challenge to capitalism—let us call it the *counterproject*, since it opposes the project of globalizing capital—had already been brewing for some years. It burst into full public view in November 1999, where, in Seattle, union members, environmentalists, Third World activists, students, and thousands of other people fed up with watching the globalization juggernaut rampage unimpeded, decided to protest. They did so with considerable effect. In the face of massive and violent police retaliation, they shut down the World Trade Organization's opening ceremony, prevented President Clinton from addressing the WTO delegates, and compelled the WTO to cancel its closing ceremonies and adjourn in disorder and confusion.[7]

Suddenly, protests, self-consciously linked to the Seattle upheaval and to each other, began to erupt all over the world: in Quito, Ecuador (January 2000), Washington, D.C. (April 2000), Bangkok (May 2000), South Africa (May 2000), Buenos Aires (May 2000), Windsor/Detroit and Calgary (June 2000), Millau, France (June 2000), Okinawa (July 2000), Colombia (August 2000), Melbourne (September 2000), Prague (September 2000), Seoul (October 2000), Davos, Switzerland (January 2001), Quebec City (April 2001), then Genoa (July 2001).

In November 2001 (post 9/11) a sizable contingent of protestors trekked to far-off Qatar, where nervous WTO ministers decided to hold their post-Seattle meeting, while tens of thousands more rallied in their own countries— some thirty countries in all—to analyze and criticize the WTO agenda. In New York City in February 2002 some 15,000 rallied against the World Economic Forum being held there. Thousands more went to Porto Alegre, Brazil, for a "World Social Forum," billed as a counter-WEF—signaling something new.

Protests have continued—Florence (2002), Miami and Cancun (2003), Monterrey (Mexico) and Dublin (2004), Melbourne (2006), Rostock (Germany), and Montebello (Quebec) (2007)—but increasingly the point has become, not simply to protest, but to develop positive solutions to the global problems that global elites are either unwilling or unable to solve.

The World Social Forum has continued to meet, the venue shifting around the world—Mumbai, Caracas, Nairobi, Belem, Porto Alegre. (Some 150,000 people attended the 2005 Porto Alegre forum). National "Social

Forums" have also sprung up. Ten thousand activists and academics met in Atlanta in June 2007 for the first U.S. Social Forum; fifteen thousand met in Detroit in July 2010.

The counterproject, this broad-based movement for social justice, is still quite young, although its roots extend deep into the past. Its growth has been remarkable—and largely under the mainstream radar. The subtitle of environmentalist Paul Hawken's *Blessed Unrest* points to a startling thesis: *How the Largest Movement in the World Came into Being and Why No One Saw It Coming.*[8] Having given nearly a thousand talks during the previous fifteen years to a wide range of environmental and social justice groups, Hawken began to wonder about the size of the movement he was addressing.

> So, curious, I began to count. . . . I initially estimated a total of 30,000 environmental organizations around the globe; when I added social justice and indigenous peoples' rights organizations, the number exceeded 100,000. I then researched to see if there had ever been any equals to this movement in scale or scope, but I couldn't find anything, past or present. The more I probed, the more I unearthed, and the numbers continued to climb, as I discovered lists, indexes, and small databases specific to certain sectors or geographical areas. . . . I soon realized that my initial estimate of 100,000 organizations was off by at least a factor of ten, and I now believe there are over one—and maybe even two—million organizations working toward ecological sustainability and social justice.[9]

That is to say, a movement has come into being that dwarfs even the far more visible antiwar movement of the 1960s to 1970s. This is as it should be, for that earlier movement was focused on ending just one war. The current movement is trying to change the world and save the planet.

Let us consider the general contours of this new movement. This counterproject is a dialectical synthesis of the great *anticapitalist* movements of the nineteenth and twentieth centuries and the *other* emancipatory movements of these centuries, especially the ongoing gender revolution, the struggle for racial equality, the fight against homophobia, the mobilizations against nuclear madness, and the efforts to halt ecological devastation and to preserve indigenous cultures. Participants in all these struggles are beginning to see themselves as part of a larger project, the huge, global effort to put an end to structural oppression everywhere and to ensure each and every human being a fair chance at self-realization and happiness.

In many (perhaps most) quarters, this counterproject, as it develops, will be called "socialist" or "communist." If it is anticapitalist—which it must be if it is to address the deep structures of economic injustice that pervade the world—it will certainly be so labeled by powerful entrenched interests.

It is pointless to contest these labels, which can in fact be worn with dignity. The counterproject should draw on the rich theoretical legacy of the socialist-communist tradition, and take sustenance from the many heroic struggles waged by committed individuals identifying themselves with this tradition.

There is a tendency on the part of many on the left today to distance themselves from this tradition, which has been thoroughly demonized and pretty much effaced from current memory. This is a mistake. The counterproject needs to recover this part of its past. We cannot afford to forget Karl Marx, Friedrich Engels, Rosa Luxemburg, Antonio Gramci, Bertolt Brecht, the Frankfurt School, C. L. R. James, Raya Dunayevskaya, Paul Sweezy, and many, many more. We owe it to ourselves—and to them—to keep this tradition alive. For as Walter Benjamin has noted (another person who should not be forgotten), "Even the dead will not be safe from the enemy if he wins."[10]

The counterproject must keep the tradition alive without denying the shortcomings and failures—sometimes horrific—of individuals, parties, and governments that have called themselves socialist or communist. This is not so strange. Consider the parallel with Christianity. Progressive Christians draw strength and inspiration from the Christian tradition without denying the inquisitions, religious wars, corruption, and abuse that are also a part of Christianity's history. There are values, and lives committed to those values, in both traditions (essentially the same values—as liberation theologians have demonstrated) that continue to inspire.[11]

The counterproject, as it develops, will have to be a dialectical socialism, not a nihilistic socialism.[12] Its aim is not to negate the existing order, wipe everything out and start over, but to create a new order that preserves what is good in the present while mitigating its irrationality and evil. The counterproject will not be what Marx decried as "crude communism," a communism animated by envy, which wants to level down and destroy whatever cannot be enjoyed by all.[13] It will be a project that builds on the material and cultural accomplishments of past centuries. It will embrace the political ideals of liberty, democracy, and the rule of law. It will endorse and promote such values as generosity, solidarity, and human creativity, and also self-discipline, personal responsibility, and hard work. It will not sneer at any of these ideals or values as "bourgeois." They will be regarded as indispensable to the construction of a new and better world.

Although it may eventually call itself socialist or communist, the counterproject will extend well beyond the confines of that tradition. It will not make the mistake made by earlier anticapitalist movements of assuming that the struggle against capitalism is more urgent than other emancipatory movements, or that these other struggles are somehow reducible to the struggle against capital. Theoreticians of the counterproject will be clear on this point.

It will not be claimed (because it is not true) that the struggle against the power of capital is more fundamental than, for example, the struggle against patriarchy or against the deep and bloody oppressions sanctioned by racism. It will not be claimed (because it is not true) that the dispositions and structures that sustain sexism, racism, militarism, and homophobia are less deeply rooted than those that sustain capitalism or less in need of being rooted out.

Counterproject theory will make it clear that all people everywhere who are working to overcome structural oppression are participating in a common project. Counterproject theory will allow individuals who have committed themselves to contesting some specific evil to identify with the hopes and fears, accomplishments and failures of other individuals struggling against other evils. To invoke another Marxian term, it will allow us a sense of our *species-being*: the connection each of us has to all others.

1.2 Successor-System Theory

In addition to illuminating the relationships among past and present emancipatory movements and among individuals committed to different aspects of what can be considered a common project, counterproject theory must also enable us to envisage, with some degree of precision, an economic order beyond capitalism. It must theorize a *successor system* to capitalism.

The concept of a successor system is conspicuously missing among the "practical Left" today—people engaged in concrete struggles against specific forms of structural oppression. Almost all the progressive struggles being waged at present are taking place within the imaginative and conceptual horizon of capital. There is much discussion of reforming this or that aspect of capitalism or even capitalism itself, but there is little talk of *transcending* capitalism—at least not in the rich countries of the world.

In the global North progressive struggles are mostly aimed at preserving and extending earlier gains; for example, strengthening antidiscrimination and environmental legislation, increasing the minimum wage, shortening hours of work. On economic issues, the struggles are largely defensive. Reactionary forces cite "global competition" or, more recently, the need to "live within our means" as the rationale for dismantling the welfare provisions of social democracy. Workers go on strike and, sometimes with students, take to the streets to block government rollbacks of hard-won gains. We call for more *regulation* of those private financial institutions that have wreaked such havoc recently—but not their *abolition*.

The importance of these struggles should not be minimized, but it is hard not to notice that in none of these cases do we find articulated a specific conception of a qualitatively new way of organizing an economy—a new "mode of production." Even when activists converge to protest the policies of the WTO, International Monetary Fund (IMF), World Bank, or G-8, their concrete demands are for debt relief, tougher environmental laws, an end to "structural adjustment policies" that bleed poor countries, stricter labor laws to block the race to the bottom, and so forth—worthy demands, to be sure, and well worth pressing, but demands that don't contest capitalism at its root. Even among those protestors who denounce capitalism by name—still a distinct minority, although a rapidly growing one—the lack of a concrete economic alternative is palpable.

The situation is more complicated in the global South. The most dynamic economy in the world today, namely that of the People's Republic of China, claims to be socialist. But is it? Mainstream Western opinion, and even most theorists and activists on the Left, consider "a socialist market economy with Chinese characteristics" to be just another name for authoritarian capitalism. Is this true? Maybe not. (The case of China will be discussed more fully in chapter 6.)

And what is going on in Venezuela? Hugo Chavez came to power in a landslide election in 1998, was reelected under a new constitution in 2000, then survived a U.S.-backed coup attempt in 2002. On January 30, 2005, while addressing the Fifth World Social Forum at Porto Alegre, Chavez, to the apparent surprise of almost everyone, announced his support for a "new socialism for the twenty-first century," and began forming alliances with other Left governments in the region (Cuba, Brazil, Argentina, Bolivia, Chile, Ecuador, Nicaragua).[14]

Without successor-system theory it is difficult to make sense of these developments. Without successor-system theory, we see the world through the lens of the dominant ideology, which tells us that capitalism is the only game in town. We are blind to the significance of new institutional experiments that may well be pointing to a world beyond capitalism.

The counterproject needs successor-system theory. To change the world, we need to act concretely, but we also need, both as a guide and inspiration to action, theoretical illumination as to what is possible. So long as capitalism remains the horizon, all emancipatory efforts remain unduly circumscribed.

The fact of the matter is we now have sufficient theoretical and empirical resources to construct such a theory. We are vastly better situated than was Marx or even Lenin in this respect, for we have accessible to us not only a century of unprecedented socioeconomic experimentation but also data and conceptual tools that were unavailable to the founding theoreticians of socialism. We can now say with far more warranted confidence than they ever could what will work and what will not. There is a certain irony here. At precisely the moment when capitalism appears to have triumphed most completely, we can assert with more evidence-backed conviction than ever before that an efficient, dynamic, democratic alternative to capitalism is possible.

This book will offer a nontechnical sketch of such an alternative. As such, it is a contribution to successor-system theory, and hence a contribution to the counterproject. The model should not be thought of as a rigid blueprint, but as a rough guide to thinking about the future. It is meant to be an antidote of sorts to the paralyzing "bankers' fatalism" (French sociologist Pierre Bourdieu's apt term) that has such a hold on the contemporary imagination.[15] The fashionable mantra, TINA, TINA, TINA (There Is No Alternative) is not a reasoned statement. It is a poison designed to kill off a certain kind of hope. This book is an attempt at poison control.

1.3 Historical Materialism

Successor-system theory may be viewed as a supplement to Marx's famous historical materialism. Historical materialism asserts that the human species is a pragmatic, creative species that refuses to submit passively to the perceived difficulties of material and social life. Through a process of technological and social innovation, often proceeding by means of trial and error, we reshape the world over time to make it more rational, more productive, and more congenial to our capacity for species solidarity. The process is not smooth. Change involves losers as well as winners, so there is often bitter struggle. There are setbacks as well as advances, but, the theory asserts, human history exhibits a directional intelligibility that may be reasonably called "progress." We, as a species, are gaining ever more conscious control over our world and over ourselves.

It should be noted that, anticommunist rhetoric notwithstanding, historical materialism implies nothing whatsoever about the existence of God. Marx, it is true, was an atheist, influenced by Feuerbach and other militantly atheistic young Hegelians, but the "materialism" of historical materialism refers to social and economic structures, not to a denial of divinity. *Historical* materialism is not *metaphysical* materialism. Historical materialism does imply that the particular form a religion takes at a particular time is shaped by the economic structure and class configuration of the period, but as to whether the socioeconomic progress historical materialism posits is part of God's plan or simply the result of unaided human effort, it has nothing to say. (Anticommunist ideology has always stressed the atheism of "godless Communism," since the abolition of religion is far more threatening to most people's sense of self than is the abolition of private ownership of the means of production.

The dominant economic class has always feared—as well it should—that the latter proposal, to most people, who in fact own no means of production, might seem worth a try.)

Historical materialism is a philosophy of hope. When applied to the modern world, historical materialism claims that capitalism, the dominant economic system of Marx's day and our own, will be superseded by a more rational order. This successor system has been traditionally called "socialism," and has been viewed as itself a stage on the way to a higher "communism."[16]

But as anyone who has studied Marx knows, there is a blank page at precisely this point in his theory. Marx says almost nothing as to what this "socialism" would look like. Virtually no attention is given to the institutional structures that are to replace those of capitalism and thus define an economic order genuinely superior to capitalism.

When socialism descended from theory to practice, it had to write something on this blank page. Lenin, on the eve of the Russian Revolution, thought it would be a simple matter to replace capitalism with something better:

> It is perfectly possible, immediately, within twenty-four hours of the overthrow of the capitalists and bureaucrats, to replace them in the control of production and distribution . . . by the armed workers. . . . All citizens are here transformed into hired employees of the state. . . . All that is required is that they should work equally, should regularly do their share of the work, and should receive equal pay. The accounting and control necessary for this have been simplified by capitalism to the utmost, till they have become the extraordinarily simple operations of watching, recording and issuing receipts, within reach of anyone who can read and write and knows the first four rules of arithmetic.[17]

He soon learned otherwise. Since there was nothing in the Marxian corpus to provide guidance, the Bolsheviks had to improvise. They tried a very radical War Communism, abolishing private property, wage labor, even money—which got them through the Civil War but then broke down. They backtracked to Lenin's New Economic Policy (NEP), which reinstituted money, reintroduced the market, and allowed for some private ownership of means of production. Russia even sought (unsuccessfully) foreign investment.

The NEP was successful but not wildly so. Following Lenin's death, Stalin opted for something more drastic. Agriculture was collectivized (at terrible human cost), all enterprises were nationalized, market relations were abolished, and an immense central planning apparatus was put in place to coordinate the economy. What is now known as "the Soviet economic model" came into being.

For a rather long while, well over half a century, it looked as if this radically new way of organizing an economy was the wave of the future. The Soviet

Union industrialized while the West collapsed into the Depression—as Marx had predicted it would. The Soviet Union survived a German invasion, broke the back of the Nazi military machine, and then, without any Western help, rebuilt its war-ravaged economy. Next came Sputnik, and a deep concern in Western circles that this new economic order might indeed "bury us" (economically) as Soviet premier Nikita Khrushchev proclaimed it would. Numerous Western economists looked at relative growth rates and nervously plotted the point at which the Soviet economy would surpass that of the United States. (My 1973 edition of Paul Samuelson's *Economics*—by far the most widely used undergraduate economics textbook of the time—includes a graph, based on "plausible assumptions," showing the Soviet economy overtaking our own by 1990.[18])

Leaders of the capitalist West scrambled to contain this dynamic giant, whose example was proving contagious. In 1949, the world's most populous nation declared itself a "People's Republic." A few years later the communist forces of Vietnam drove out their French colonial masters. In 1959, Fidel Castro, at the head of a guerilla army, forced the Batista dictatorship from power, and shortly thereafter proclaimed "Socialismo o Muerte." By 1975, the Vietnamese had defeated the vastly more powerful Americans (who had replaced the French), and began reconstructing their economy along noncapitalist lines. In 1979, a guerilla movement toppled the U.S.-backed Somoza dictatorship in Nicaragua, and, although declining to call themselves communists, looked to Cuba and the Soviet Union for aid and inspiration. The course of history seemed clearly marked.

But, as we all know, a funny thing happened on the way to the future. In the 1980s, Soviet economic growth ground to a halt. The economy didn't collapse—that would come only with the attempted capitalist restoration—but the Soviet model hit its limits. It proved unable to generate new technologies or even exploit effectively those developed in capitalist countries. People became increasingly discontented. Thus, as historical materialism would predict, with existing "relations of production" inadequate to new "forces of production," (that is to say, when existing economic structures cannot take advantage of new technologies) there occurred a decisive shift in class power, which led to, to use Marx's words, "the transformation of the whole, immense superstructure."[19] (The West did not sit by idly during this historical upheaval, but intervened with considerable success to ensure that the class it favored—the one committed to restoring capitalism—came out on top.[20])

Does the collapse of the Soviet model, not only in Russia but also throughout Eastern Europe, mean that Marx has been proven wrong? Elementary logic says no, unless it is assumed that every attempt at constructing a successor system must necessarily succeed. Such an assumption doesn't fit with historical materialism's basic premises. Historical materialism regards the human species as a practical species, groping to solve the problems that confront it. There is no reason to expect success right away. It is more probable to see only partial successes at first, or outright failures, with subsequent attempts learning from these experiences—until finally a transformation takes hold that is superior enough to the old order to be irreversible.

Neither I nor anyone else can prove that historical materialism is the correct theory of history. It is a hopeful, optimistic theory. It aims to be "scientific," but it clearly embodies elements that do not lend themselves to scientific validation. Still, it is a plausible theory, made even more plausible when supplemented by an adequate successor-system theory. That, at any rate, is what I hope to show.

1.4 Criteria

Let me specify more precisely what I take to be the essential criteria for an adequate successor-system theory.

- The theory should specify an economic model that can be cogently defended to professional economists and ordinary citizens alike as being both economically viable and ethically superior to capitalism. Although necessarily abstract, the model should be concrete enough for us to foresee how it would likely function in practice when animated by the finite, imperfect human beings that we are.
- This model should enable us to make sense of the major economic experiments of the past century, which have been numerous and diverse. If the human species is indeed groping toward a postcapitalist economic order, successor-system theory should illuminate that process.
- The model should clarify our understanding of the various economic reforms for which progressive parties and movements are currently struggling, and it should be suggestive of additional reform possibilities. It is a tenet of historical materialism that the institutions of new societies often develop within the interstices of the old. Successor-system theory should help us locate the seeds and sprouts of what could become a new economic order, so that they might be protected and nourished.
- Successor-system theory should enable us to envisage a transition from capitalism to the successor system. It should specify a set of structural modifications that might become feasible under certain plausible historical conditions that would transform a capitalist economy into an economy qualitatively different and unequivocally better.

Having said what an adequate successor-system theory should be, let me underscore what it is *not*. Successor-system theory is *not* the whole of counterproject theory. It is not even the whole of the economic component of this theory. Successor-system theory is centered on a rather abstract economic model. It does not concern itself with the actual history of capitalism and its development from feudalism, its relationship to slavery and colonialism, its curious mix of progressive ideals and brutal practices. It does not address, except indirectly, such Marxian concepts as alienated labor, fetishism of commodities, the labor theory of value, or the falling rate of profit. It does not concern itself with the ways in which the economic "base" of society manifests itself in other areas of society.

Nor does successor-system theory address in a sustained or systematic fashion the issues of racism, sexism, homophobia, and other forms of structural oppression. These issues are quite important to the counterproject, but they lie outside the purview of successor-system theory, at least as it will be sketched in these pages.

Successor-system theory is further restricted in that it is not a theory about Marx's "higher stage of communism," that moneyless, stateless form of society governed by the principle, "from each according to ability, to each according to need." It is concerned with what is both possible and necessary now—the immediate next stage beyond capitalism, a stage that will be marked by its origins within capitalism. One can speculate as to the evolution of a postcapitalist society such as the one I will describe, but such speculations extend beyond the range of the theory itself.[21]

1.5 Revolution

Successor-system theory must address the transition question. Successor-system theory is meant to be theory with practical intent. If it cannot offer a plausible projection as to how we might get from here to there, successor-system theory remains an intellectual exercise in model building, interesting in its own right perhaps, and capable of providing a theoretical rejoinder to the smug apologists for capitalism, but useless to people trying to change the world.

The successor-system theory marked out in these pages will not offer a full-blown "theory of revolution," where, by "revolution" I mean a process by which the power of a dominant economic class is broken and new socio-economic institutions put in place that significantly enhance the prospects and power of the subordinated classes at the expense of the dominant class. I am not sure that the time is ripe for such a theory. At any rate, I don't have one. Nonetheless, I do think it is possible to sketch some plausible transition scenarios. This will be done in chapter 6. I also think it possible to discern the general direction a new theory of revolution should take.

- A new theory of revolution will recognize that the old models of social revolution, drawing their inspiration from the French, Russian, Chinese, and Cuban revolutions, are largely inappropriate to the world today, certainly to advanced capitalist societies, perhaps even to poor countries. The question of armed insurrection will have to be reexamined. The masses are never going to storm the White House, nor is a people's army ever going to swoop down from the Appalachian Mountains and march up Pennsylvania Avenue. A revolutionary transition to socialism will almost certainly be a *democratic* transition.
- The new theory will recognize the need for a more concrete vision of structural alternatives than has been customary in the past. It is not enough to say, "Seize state power and establish socialism." Blind faith in the laws of history or in an omniscient party has been justly discredited. The intelligence of ordinary people must be acknowledged and respected. Most workers, certainly those in rich countries, have far more to lose now than just their chains.
- The theory will emphasize the need for reform struggles now, before the conditions are right for a truly fundamental socioeconomic transformation. What we get, if and when space opens up for revolutionary structural change, will depend crucially on what we have already gotten—and on who, during the course of many struggles, we have become. (In struggling to change the world, we change ourselves as well.) As we shall see, radical structural transformation will involve a substantial deepening of democracy. But democracy, while a necessary ingredient of the kind of world we want, is not sufficient in and of itself. The output of a democratic procedure depends on the quality of the input. Hence the importance *now* of struggles against racism, sexism, and homophobia, against senseless violence, rampant consumerism, and environmental destruction. Hence the importance *now* of trying to figure out better ways of living with one another and with nature and changing our lives accordingly.
- The new theory will also emphasize the need for diverse strategies and diverse aims. The transition to a genuinely democratic socialism will likely vary, depending on whether the country is rich or poor, on whether or not the country has undergone a socialist revolution in the past, and on various other historical and cultural contingencies. Although there will be commonalities of vision, there will be differences as well—of tactics,

transitional strategies, and ultimate goals. Unlike the program of neo-liberal capitalism, one size does not fit all. The counterproject does not envisage all nations aiming for the same patterns of development, or adopting the same technologies, values, and consumption habits. The counterproject calls for a halt to the McDonaldization of the world.

- Finally, an adequate theory of the transition from global capitalism to democratic, sustainable socialism will stress the need for an *international* social movement, not in the sense of a unified, centrally directed party, but in the sense of a common consciousness that recognizes a kind of unity in diversity and allows for cross-national cooperation and inspiration. The counterproject is nothing less than the project of our species.

1.6 A Note on Gender

The most significant revolution of the twentieth century was not the Russian Revolution or the Chinese Revolution (although the impact of each has been immense) but the irreversible transformations, still underway, in the ways men and women live with one another. We are currently living through one of the most significant moments in the history of *Homo sapiens*. We are in the midst of a revolution that should be called by its proper name, *the feminist revolution*.

The feminist revolution, where it is most advanced, has touched virtually every facet of human life—family structure, child rearing, sexuality, work, play, love, war, our grand ambitions, and our innermost identities. It is, moreover, a worldwide revolution, far from finished but hardly confined to the relatively affluent portions of the globe. It is more advanced in some places than others, but there is no country on earth where women have not come together to think collectively about their common problems and about strategies for emancipation. In some countries, such strategizing is extremely dangerous, but in every such place, there are women braving the danger. In most countries, thinking is accompanied by action—from the microlevel of individual relationships to the macrolevel of national policy.

Despite the importance and pervasiveness of the as yet unfinished feminist revolution, the successor-system theory offered here does not address the issue of gender explicitly and systematically. Certainly, gender concerns and feminist theorizing are germane to many of the issues to be discussed here, but in a short book such as this, these cannot be treated adequately. Still, it is worth pointing out a number of areas where gender concerns and feminist theorizing raise questions that need to be addressed to do full justice to the concerns of successor-system theory.

- *Ethics.* The question "Capitalism or socialism?" is widely held to be a dispute about values, but this view is mistaken, at least with respect to the version of socialism we will be discussing here. Any sensible ethical theory, when the facts are properly presented, will find in favor of Economic Democracy, the successor-system I propose. (In my earlier writings I have demonstrated this with respect to utilitarianism, Rawlsian "justice as fairness" and a social ethic based on the value of "participatory autonomy."[22])

  But ethics is about more than principles and values, as various philosophers, particularly feminist philosophers, have pointed out. Ethics is also about cultivated moral capacities, styles of moral reasoning, and concepts of self-identity. Building on the pioneering work of Carol Gilligan, various feminist philosophers have articulated a sophisticated "ethic of care" (contrasted with an "ethic of rights), centered less on principles and abstract values, more on cultivating empathy and attentiveness to the concrete, to difference, to interconnectedness. This ethic may be particularly appropriate to the counterproject. It is not so much needed to ground the argument for Economic Democracy, although it can serve that purpose—as can most other contemporary ethical theories. But successor-system theory is also about transition, about actually getting beyond capitalism to a better world. An ethic of care, with its emphasis on our responsibilities to others and on our deep interconnectedness, not only to those closest to us, but to that ever-enlarging circle of human beings with whom our fate is ever more concretely tied and to nature itself, has a motivational appeal that more abstract theories often lack.[23]
- *Poverty.* I will consider the question of poverty, both in affluent societies and poor countries. I will propose a full-employment policy as the basic solution to poverty in both rich and poor countries—a policy (as we shall see) that cannot be enacted under capitalism. I couple this with "fair trade," so that poor countries do not have to devote a disproportionate amount of their resources to catering to rich-country consumers. I recommend that poor countries engage in broad-based, labor-intensive public programs of health and education.

  Well and good—but clearly, any realistic attempt to eradicate poverty must take into account the gender dimension of the problem. How do we ensure that women as well as men have the requisite opportunities and skills for meaningful work? Should all women be encouraged to seek paid employment? What about those with young children? What about those caring for aging parents? These latter questions lead to deeper questions: Should women continue to do most of the care work in society? How should we, collectively, care for our children, for those among us with disabilities, and for our elderly? These questions, at some point, will have to be addressed.

- *Leisure.* I argue that under capitalism, there is a structural tendency toward overwork. But as everyone knows (or should know), women in paid employment tend to be more overworked than are men, since in most cases women must bear the brunt of "the second shift"—the unpaid labor of daily domestic life. In the successor-system we will have far more choices concerning consumption-leisure tradeoffs at work. What sorts of changes in domestic relationships are in order to insure that this leisure is fairly apportioned? I argue that ecological sustainability requires we opt increasingly for leisure over consumption. What sort of family re-structuring will be needed for people to view leisure as unambiguously attractive? (As Berkeley sociologist Arlie Hochschild has documented, many men prefer the structure and clear lines of responsibility they experience at work to the chaos and unpleasantness they claim to encounter at home.[24]) There is a large gender dimension to this issue that should be explored.

- *Community.* It is possible under Economic Democracy to redesign local communities to make them more "user-friendly." Each year funds will be available for public capital expenditures so that new public amenities may be instituted. Would the priorities advanced by women be the same as those advanced by men? Who would likely be most active in deciding these priorities? (A striking feature of the "Bolivarian circles" and various neighborhood councils promoted in Venezuela, which focus on community issues, is the overwhelming preponderance of women in these organizations.[25])

- *Democracy.* The successor system to be proposed entails a large advance in democracy. Citizens will have far more opportunity than they do now to discuss, debate, and decide issues of common concern. Feminist theory has been much involved with the question of preconditions for real democratic dialogue. What is the role of argument in democratic decision-making? How do we do justice to the "difference" of those with whom we engage when we talk across the borders of race, gender, class, and sexual orientation? How do we develop the ability to listen to the other? These and related questions are of profound importance to a movement that raises high the banner of democracy.[26]

- *Revolution.* The relationship between feminism and anticapitalist revolution is complex and offers much ground for further research. Several issues stand out.
  o The feminist revolution does not fit the model of revolution that usually comes to mind when we think of moving beyond capitalism.

The feminist revolution has been, above all, a nonviolent revolution. Moreover, it has not been marked by decisive, watershed events that clearly mark a "before" and "after" the revolution. A new theory of revolution must pay careful attention to what has been learned from the millions (quite literally) of small and large battles fought, lost, and won as women have moved to redefine the world and their place in it.

o The worst excesses of political revolutions have often been marked by masculinity. Angry young men have contributed courageously to revolutionary struggle, but they have also been involved in nonproductive and sometimes gratuitous violence. (Those of us who were active in the 1960s can recall the macho posturing that sometimes pushed us in directions we shouldn't have gone.) Masculine excess has not been confined to Western societies. The Chinese Great Leap Forward and Cultural Revolution were marked by similar excesses, as were many other radical upheavals and movements. There is a gender component to revolutionary struggle that bears analysis.

o Women have played a huge role in virtually all the progressive struggles of the past several decades. Women have often constituted the majority of the participants, not only in struggles related to gender but those concerning human rights, nuclear disarmament, ecology, solidarity with the people of El Salvador or Nicaragua, sweatshops, and so forth. If the counterproject comes to have revolutionary potential, it will almost certainly count as many women as men among its activists, quite likely more, and thus will have a different character and ethos from classical revolutionary movements. How different? What are the implications for organizational theory and practice?

The above listing is not exhaustive. As with race, which I address briefly in chapter 4, theoretical and practical issues regarding gender inevitably impinge on theoretical and practical issues regarding economic structures. I regret not being able to do justice to these various intersections in this work.

1.7 An Outline of the Argument

Successor-system theory claims that capitalism is no longer justifiable as an economic order because there now exists a better alternative. Since this claim is comparative, the argument for it must spell out this "better alternative" in some detail so that the two systems can be evaluated side by side. However, before considering this alternative, which we will call "Economic Democracy," we must be clear about the nature of capitalism itself. A serious critique of capitalism cannot be content with merely noting the negative features of the contemporary world. It must show a causal connection between these features and the structures that characterize capitalism.

Chapter 2 specifies precisely the defining characteristics of capitalism and clarifies such key concepts as capital, capitalist, entrepreneur, savings, and investment. As it turns out, these terms are closely connected to certain "noncomparative" justifications for capitalism, that is, arguments that make no reference to alternatives. These are worth considering carefully, to see how they hold up, and for the light they shed on the inner workings of the system. Chapter 2 proceeds to deconstruct these justifications.

It doesn't follow that capitalism as such cannot be justified. It may be that capitalism, however unfair, is the best that we poor, finite human beings can do. To refute this claim, an alternative must be specified. Chapter 3 does this. First, the institutions of the "basic model" of Economic Democracy are set out; then evidence is marshaled in support of the claim that Economic Democracy is an economically viable system. Among the important pieces of evidence is the remarkable success of a most unusual economic experiment occurring in the Basque region of Spain.

Chapter 3 then offers an "expanded model" of Economic Democracy, one less pure than the basic model, but consistent with its spirit. The expanded model adds a mechanism that will insure full employment and institutions that allow savers to earn interest on their savings. It also opens up the possibility for entrepreneurial individuals to become true capitalists. These allowances can be made, as we shall see, without jeopardizing the radically different principles according to which the economy as a whole functions.

The institutions of both the basic and expanded models of Economic Democracy are defined within the context of a nation-state. However, given the economic interdependency of nations in an ever more globalized economy, principles of interaction must be specified. Chapter 3 does this also. Economic Democracy will insist that "fair trade," not "free trade," should be the governing principle, and hence will adopt a policy of "socialist protectionism."

Chapters 4 and 5 constitute the heart of the argument—the head-to-head confrontation of capitalism and Economic Democracy. Chapter 4 analyzes four fundamental defects of capitalism (massive inequality, unemployment, overwork, and poverty in the midst of plenty) and examines the degree to which these problems would be less severe in a democratic economy. Chapter 5 analyzes three more: economic instability, environmental degradation, and lack of real democracy.

Chapters 3 through 5 are concerned with satisfying the first criterion of an adequate successor-system theory, namely the presentation and defense of an alternative model. Chapter 6 addresses the remaining three criteria. We see that Economic Democracy as a model allows us to form a coherent account of the major economic experiments of the twentieth century. We see that the model is suggestive of a reform agenda that can and should be worked for now. Several scenarios are then offered for a final transition out of capitalism and into a full Economic Democracy. By way of conclusion, we return to the *Communist Manifesto* (a quote from which opened this chapter). It is proposed that something like a "New Communism," taking its cue at least in part from the original manifesto, would be highly desirable. We then consider, briefly, several "visions of a new world" and the question, "What should I do?"

2

Justifying Capitalism

If we ask how capitalism has been, and continues to be, justified by its legions of supporters, the justification that most immediately comes to mind is the "comparative justification": capitalism works—not perfectly by any means, but better than any other system we humans can devise. So popular is this argument that it has been given a name: TINA—There Is No Alternative (at least no alternative that can give us both freedom and prosperity). TINA, of course, cannot be refuted without specifying an alternative system to which capitalism can be compared.

There are other justifications for capitalism—"noncomparative" justifications—that are also significant. They constitute an important part of the intellectual armor of capitalism, protection against a question that cannot fail to occur to any decent, thoughtful person who looks at the world with open eyes: How can it be right that under capitalism some people have so much while others have so little? In particular, what do capitalists *do* to merit their stupendous wealth? That is to say, what is it that they do that entitles them, morally, to so large a slice of the economic pie?

This chapter, after defining the key terms, will consider four such answers:

- The capitalist provides the capital necessary for economic development.
- The capitalist exhibits entrepreneurial creativity.
- The capitalist risks his capital.
- The capitalist defers personal consumption for the benefit of society.

These justifications are noncomparative in that they do not refer to alternatives to capitalism. They appeal implicitly to a commonly accepted ethical standard: it is right that people be rewarded for actions that contribute to the common good. They implicitly assert that the rewards accruing to capitalists are more or less proportional to their contributions. As we shall see, none of these answers can withstand critical scrutiny. In seeing why not, we will come to a better understanding as to how this system in which we live actually works. We will then be in better position to address TINA, capitalism's most formidable defense.

2.1 What Is "Capitalism"? What Is a "Capitalist"?

In any economic system human beings interact with nonhuman nature to produce the goods and services that human beings desire. Human labor utilizes nonhuman means of production to generate products. The laws and customs that govern the relationships among these three entities (human labor, means of production, and products) constitute the economic structure of a given society. A *capitalist* society is characterized by three basic features:

- *The bulk of the means of production are privately owned, either directly or by corporations that are themselves owned by private individuals.*
  Marx and the socialists of his day called this feature "private property." This may have been an unfortunate choice of terminology, since calling for the abolition of private property, which Marx does, conjures up images of communal food, clothing, shelter, and (who knows what those radicals will do?) maybe even communal toothbrushes. In fact, these things are not at issue. Items purchased for one's own use are, for Marx, "personal property," not private property. Your toothbrush, your clothes, your car, and your home remain yours under socialism.
- *Most products are exchanged in a "market." That is to say, goods and services are bought and sold at prices determined by competition and not by some governmental pricing authority. Individual enterprises compete with one another in providing goods and services to consumers, each enterprise trying to make a profit.*
  The term "free market" is often used as a defining characteristic of capitalism, but this is misleading, since some degree of price regulation—via differential product taxes, subsidies, tariffs, or outright price controls—is present in most capitalist societies. A capitalist economy must be a market economy, but the market need not be wholly free of governmental regulation or, for that matter, wholly free of private-sector price fixing either.

- *Most of the people who work for pay in this society work for other people who own the means of production. Most working people are "wage laborers."* Whether the income is called a wage or a salary is immaterial. In order to gain access to means of production (without which no one can work), most people must contract with people who own (or represent the owners of) such means. In exchange for a wage or a salary, they agree to supply the owners with a certain quantity and quality of labor. It is a crucial characteristic of the institution of wage labor that the goods or services produced do not belong to the workers who produce them but to those who supply the workers with the means of production.

There are several things to note about this definition. First of all, it defines capitalism as an economic system, not a political system. Whether or not a society has a free press or allows its citizens to vote in competitive elections is irrelevant as to whether it is a capitalist society. Fascist Italy, Nazi Germany, white supremacist South Africa, and most of the almost-too-many-to-count military dictatorships of this century were capitalist societies.

The name or nature of the government that comes to power is also irrelevant. All postwar Western European countries have remained capitalist, even when socialist or social democratic parties have been elected, even when these parties have nationalized certain industries and/or instituted various public welfare programs. So long as most productive assets are privately owned, most economic exchanges take place through the market, and most people work for wages or a salary, a society is capitalist. (Sweden, for example, is very much a capitalist country. Privately owned firms account for 90 percent of its industrial output.)

All three of these defining structures must be present for a society to be capitalist. A society of small farmers and artisans, for example, is not a capitalist society, since wage labor is largely absent. A society in which most means of production are owned by the central government or by local communities is not a capitalist society. Contemporary China, for example, is not capitalist since private ownership of the means of production—if we include land as a means of production—is not (yet?) dominant. (More on China in chapter 6.)

It must be emphasized that using the market to allocate goods and services does not make a society capitalist. Almost everywhere today the term "market economy" is employed as a synonym for (and usually instead of) "capitalism." This is a serious conceptual mistake. As we shall see, it is perfectly possible—and indeed desirable—to have a market economy that is socialist. Competition is not the antithesis of socialism. "Market socialism" is not an oxymoron. A viable successor system will not be as ruthlessly competitive as contemporary capitalism, but it will by no means abandon market competition altogether.

To use "market economy" as a synonym (indeed, euphemism) for "capitalism" is not merely an analytical mistake; it is an ideological distortion. The term "market economy" highlights the least objectionable defining feature of capitalism while directing attention away from the really problematical institutions, namely, private ownership of means of production and wage labor. For example, the "privatization" reforms so insistently prescribed for Russia and the countries of Eastern Europe following their turn away from communism were not "market reforms." Market reforms, fully compatible with socialism, were well under way in most of these countries. The Western-advocated reforms were attempts (largely successful) to establish *private ownership of the means of production.*

If capitalism as an economic system is defined by the three institutions listed above, what is a "capitalist"? It is a curious fact that in our capitalist society there is no commonly agreed-upon definition of this key term. In fact, the term is rarely used in the mass media or even in scholarly circles. We hear of industrialists, businessmen, entrepreneurs, and shareholders—but almost never of "capitalists"—perhaps because the word still has unsavory connotations (robber barons calling on the Pinkertons to break strikes and beat up protesting workers). Capitalists don't like to be called capitalists, at least not in public; they prefer to remain invisible, or at least be called by some other name.

If we are to understand capitalism, we need some sort of definition that picks out the class of people who constitute the system's driving force. For our purposes, a reasonable definition of "capitalist" is someone who owns enough productive assets that he can, if he so chooses, live comfortably on the income generated by these assets. A capitalist is not someone who merely believes in capitalism, nor are you a capitalist just because you happen to own a few stocks or bonds. To be a capitalist you must own enough income-generating assets that you can live comfortably without working. You may work—you probably do—but you don't have to. (The capitalist class in the United States, by this definition, comprises roughly 1 percent of the population, owners of productive assets of $2 million or more. A 5 percent return on these assets would generate an income of $100,000 per year.)

The capitalist class derives its wealth from its ownership of productive wealth, that is, from "capital." A capitalist receives income because he "contributes" his capital to production. But what exactly is the nature of this "contribution"? Indeed, what exactly is "capital"? These questions are more difficult to answer than one might think. Answering them carefully will allow us to see through a number of spurious justifications for capitalism itself.

2.2 Neoclassical Shenanigans: Marginal Product as Contribution

To the question "What is capital?" Marx offered a straightforward answer: capital is "embodied labor"—the material result of past labor. The machine the worker is using, which so greatly enhances her productivity, is the product of other people's labor. The food the worker eats, purchased with her wages, is the product of other people's labor. When you think about it, says Marx, every conceivable good we consume comes from human beings working with and on nonhuman nature. These are the only "factors of production"— human labor (mental as well as physical) and nonhuman nature.

This is a dangerous thought. If the factors of production are only labor and nature, where does "the capitalist" enter the picture? It is clear that labor should be rewarded for its contribution to production. It is equally clear that nonhuman nature need not be. (It must be replenished or conserved, but that's a separate matter.) The capitalist also demands a reward, a "fair return on his investment"—but on what basis?

The standard answer, taught in every introductory economics course, is that goods are the product of *three* factors of production—land, labor, and capital—and that the owners of these factors are rewarded on the basis of their contributions. Well, land is clear enough—that's shorthand for natural resources (i.e., nature)—and labor is labor. But what is "capital"? Tools? Technology? Money? Congealed time? Embodied labor? What?

Marx devoted the bulk of his greatest work (called, appropriately, *Capital*) to pursuing the implications of *his* answer, which were utterly unacceptable to the capitalist class but not so easy to refute. Marx constructed his argument using "classical" value theory, the standard theory of his day as developed from Adam Smith through David Ricardo—the "labor theory" of value.

To avoid the uncomfortable implications of this particular theory, it became necessary to reconstruct economic theory on a new foundation. A new economics, a "neoclassical" economics, thus came into being, which zeroed in on this labor theory of value, criticized it, and offered an alternative theory, a "marginalist" theory of value. This new theory quickly replaced the treasonous old theory in all respectable quarters, and has remained to this day the dominant paradigm in the economics profession.

We needn't pursue the value controversy here, which is normally (if wrongly) presented as a controversy as to how best to understand prices. (Is the price of a commodity determined by the amount of labor it took to produce it or by the "marginal utility" of the commodity, that is, the satisfaction that one more unit of that commodity would give to the consumer?) This celebrated controversy is a smoke screen. The real heart of the "neoclassical revolution" is its theory of distribution.

The fundamental problem confronting post-Marxian economic theory is the problem of explaining (and justifying) the profits of the capitalist. If a commodity, say corn, is the product of three factors, land, labor, and capital (as the neoclassical account has it), how can we determine how much of the final product should be distributed to each of the claimants: landowners, laborers, and capitalists? To be sure, a free market will set a rental rate, wage rate, and interest rate, and so bring about a distribution—but what grounds do we have for saying that this is a *just* distribution? (Lurking in the background here is that uncomfortable Marxian question: if labor is the source of all value, why should the landowners or capitalists get *anything*?)

Let's forget about the capitalist for the moment and concentrate on the remaining two factors. Clearly, it takes both land and labor to produce corn. How should the product be divided between landlords and laborers? The neoclassical economist answers: it should be divided according to *contribution*. Each factor should get what it contributes.

Fine. That seems fair—but how do we know how much each factor contributes? At the end of the harvest, we have Z bushels of corn. How can we say that the workers contributed X bushels and the land contributed Y bushels? You can't just say that the competitive market will take care of the distribution. Why should we think this "invisible hand" distribution has anything to do with respective contributions? Why not just say that the workers did all the work, the landowner is a parasite, and be done with it?

John Bates Clark, one of the pioneers of neoclassical economics, acknowledges the seriousness of this question.

> The welfare of the laboring class depends on whether they get much or little; but their attitude toward other classes—and therefore the stability of society— depends chiefly on the question of whether the amount they get, be it large or small, is what they produce. If they create a small amount of wealth and get the whole of it, they may not seek to revolutionize society; but if it were to appear that they produce an ample amount and get only a part of it, many of them would become revolutionists and all would have the right to do so.[1]

Surprisingly enough, Clark and his neoclassical colleagues were able to answer the question in a noncircular manner. This is no mean feat. Here we have sacks of corn, the result of the harvest. Without making any question-begging references to competitive markets, you cannot say, can you, how much of that corn is due to labor and how much due to land? The neoclassical economist smiles and replies, "But I can. . . . Not only that. I can prove to you that, in a competitive capitalist economy, the market will set the wage rate at exactly the contribution of the laborer and the rent at exactly the contribution of the land. I can also show that if we allow monopoly—either of laborers or landowners—the market will not distribute in accordance with contribution but will return to the monopolists more than they contribute. That is to say, if we assume that justice entails giving to each what he contributes, I can prove to you that monopolies will generate injustice, but a thoroughly competitive capitalist economy will be a just economy."

The argument is technical, but worth understanding, for it has had enormous ideological impact and has done much to give neoclassical economics an aura of scientific respectability. Let me explain it by means of an example. Suppose we have five acres of land and ten workers. We will assume that the land is of uniform quality and that the workers are equally skilled. At the end of harvest, we have one hundred bushels of corn. How many were contributed by the land, and how many by labor? (The restless reader may want to say, "This is silly. Obviously each and every bushel required both land and labor. You can't say that some were produced by the land and others by labor." But wait. . . . There's a clever story coming.)

Let us calculate the "marginal product" of labor. Suppose one worker were to work the five acres and suppose the yield is twelve bushels. Now let two workers work the land. Because there is plenty of land, and because they can cooperate and take advantage of economies of scale, they will likely produce more than twenty-four bushels. Let us suppose they produce twenty-six. In this case, we will say that the "marginal product" of the second worker is fourteen—the gain in total production brought about by adding that second worker to the workforce. (In reality, no one is going to conduct this experiment. The point is simply that these marginal products have scientific validity because they can, in principle, be calculated experimentally.)

Now use three workers. If there are still economies of scale to be had, this third worker's marginal product might be even higher, perhaps fifteen bushels. Sooner or later, however, economies of scale give way to "diminishing returns," that basic, beloved law of neoclassical economics. After a while, the laborers begin to crowd one another. Adding a new laborer will increase production, since the land can be cultivated more intensively, but the extra output you get by adding another laborer, his marginal product, is less than what you got from the last one. If we graph the marginal product of each laborer, we have a step curve that rises for a while, but then steadily declines. (See figure 2.1.)

Suppose we define the "contribution" of *each* worker to the total output of ten workers working five acres (in our example, one hundred bushels) to be the marginal product of the *last* worker. Suppose this is six bushels. In that case, the *total* contribution of labor is sixty bushels (ten times the marginal product of that last laborer). Graphically, this is the shaded portion of the area under the step curve in the top graph.

Chapter 2

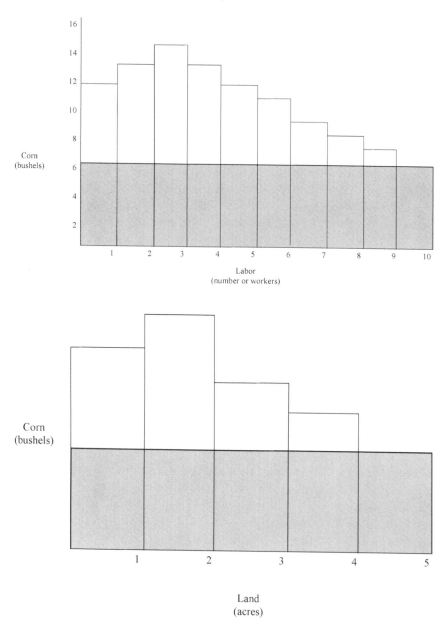

Figure 2.1   Marginalist Calculation of the Contributions of Labor and Land

This might seem to be a wholly arbitrary definition. Why should the contribution of each worker be defined as the marginal contribution of the last worker? To be sure, we have assumed them all to be equally skilled, and it is true that if we pulled any one of them from production, the total product would decline by exactly the marginal product of the last worker, but so what? If we removed two workers, the total product would decline by more than their combined "contribution." If we removed them all, there would be no product at all. What is so special about the marginal product of the last worker?

Well, consider the following. Suppose we reverse our procedure and calculate the marginal product of the land. Suppose we hold our labor force constant, and have them work first one acre, then two acres, then three, four, and five, each time calculating the marginal product of the land. We will see a similar phenomenon to what we observed with labor. At first, there will be increasing returns to scale, so the marginal product of land will go up, but then, after a while, diminishing returns will set in. Adding an additional acre will always increase total production, but adding that fifth acre won't increase the output by as much as adding the fourth, because the workers will have to spread themselves ever more thinly. Suppose we define the "contribution" of each acre of land to be the marginal product of the last acre—just as we defined the contribution of each worker to be the marginal product of the last worker. Thus, the total contribution of the land is the shaded area of the lower graph.

Notice, we have derived both the contribution of labor and the contribution of land from purely technical considerations. We have made no assumptions about ownership, competition, or any other social or political relationship. No covert assumptions about capitalism have been smuggled into the analysis. Notice, too, we have a technical problem on our hands. We have determined, by means of a rather esoteric definition, both the contribution of labor and the contribution of land—but what makes us think these contributions are going to add up to the total product? What grounds do we have for thinking that the shaded area of the top graph will equal the white area of the bottom graph and vice versa? If they don't, then we cannot claim to have separated our hundred bushels of corn into the respective contributions of labor and land.

But they do add up! That is the mathematical result that gave neoclassical economics its intellectual respectability. In fact, the portions don't always add up. In an example such as I've given, they probably wouldn't. But if the numbers are large—of workers and acres—and if you make enough assumptions about homogeneous fertility and skills, substitutability of land and labor, and diminishing returns, then Euler's Theorem (first proven by the great eighteenth-century mathematician Leonard Euler) can be invoked—a purely mathematical result having nothing to do with economics per se—to demonstrate that the total product will in fact be equal to the contribution of labor (defined as the marginal product of the last laborer multiplied by the number of laborers) plus the contribution of land (defined as the marginal product of the last acre multiplied by the number of acres).[2]

A remarkable result that, moreover, can be extended to include capital. If we allow capital into our story, it can be shown that our corn harvest subdivides neatly into the contribution of land, labor, and capital. Moreover—as mentioned above—it can be further demonstrated (again with appropriate simplifying assumptions) that a free competitive market will set the land rent at the marginal product of land, the wage rate at the marginal product of labor, and the interest rate at the marginal product of capital. (Actually, the argument concerning capital is a whole lot murkier and more controversial than the argument for land and labor, since it is not at all clear how, in this analysis, capital is to be understood.[3] We needn't go into that here, since even the two-factor argument is fatally flawed.)

What we have here is a remarkable technical accomplishment: separating out quantities associated with each separate factor in such a way that they all add up to the total output. *But it is utterly bogus as an ethical argument.* Our original objection was correct: there is something arbitrary in defining the contribution of *each* laborer to be the marginal product of the *last* laborer. Actually "deceptive" is a better word than "arbitrary." To call the marginal product of the last laborer the "contribution" of each laborer is to invoke an ethical category suggesting entitlement. Since each worker "contributed" that amount, each is entitled to that amount, right? And, lo and behold, that's exactly what the free market gives the worker. In a competitive free market economy, wages are what they should be, rent is what it should be, interest is what it should be. Monopolies generate injustice, but pure competitive capitalism is fair capitalism. Workers get precisely what they contribute—and hence have no right to "become revolutionists."

But this conclusion, so much more comforting to landlords and capitalists than Marx's conclusion, in no way follows from the technical premises of the argument. Suppose our ten workers had cultivated the five acres as a worker collective. In this case, they would receive the entire product, all one hundred bushels, instead of sixty. Is this unfair? To whom should the other forty bushels go? To the land, for its "contribution"? Should the collective perhaps burn forty bushels as an offering to the Land-God? (Is the Land-Lord the representative on Earth of this Land-God?)

We can see that a moral sleight-of-hand has been performed. A technical demonstration has passed itself off as a moral argument by its choice of terminology, namely, by calling a marginal product a "contribution." The "contribution = ethical entitlement" of the landowner has been identified with the "contribution = marginal product" of the land. Had we not called that marginal product "contribution," it would have been impossible to conclude that our original question had been answered. We wanted to know why we should think that what the market gives the landlord has anything to do with his actual contribution. To say that the market gives him sacks of corn equal to the marginal product of his last acre multiplied by the number of acres he owns in no way answers the question. Why should that amount count as his *contribution*?

At issue here is something more than just a quantitative problem, our inability to specify the magnitude of the landowner's contribution. We have a quantitative problem because we have a qualitative problem. What is the exact nature of the landowner's "contribution" here? We can say that the landlord contributed the land to the workers, but notice the qualitative difference between his "contribution" and the contribution of his workforce. He "contributes" his land—but the land remains intact and remains his at the end of the harvest, whereas the labor contributed by each laborer is gone. If the laborers do not expend more labor during the next harvest, they will get nothing more, whereas the landowner can continue to "contribute" year after year (lifting not a finger), and be rewarded year after year for doing so. Labor and land (and capital) are not so symmetrical as the neoclassical tale makes them appear to be. Our "factors of production" do not meet as equals on a level playing field. The owners of one of the factors must expend their physical and mental energy year after year to continue their "contribution," whereas the owners of the other two factors need do nothing at all.

The great iconoclastic economist John Kenneth Galbraith put the matter this way:

> No grant of feudal privilege has ever equaled, for effortless return, that of the grandparent who bought and endowed his descendants with a thousand shares of General Motors or General Electric. The beneficiaries of this foresight have become and remain rich by no exercise of intelligence beyond the decision to do nothing, embracing as it did the decision not to sell.[4]

I am not saying that in actuality landlords and capitalists do nothing. Sometimes they too expend physical and mental energy during the process of production (although often they do not). What is interesting, indeed paradoxical, about the neoclassical argument is that in making enough simplifying assumptions to be able to invoke so elegantly a mathematical theorem, it assumes away everything the landlord or capitalist might actually be doing to justify his reward. In the neoclassical story landlords and capitalists are wholly passive. They don't supervise workers; they don't invent anything; they don't make any decisions as to what to produce or what technologies to employ. They are wholly absent from the production process. They merely grant permission for their land and capital to be used—in exchange for a healthy cut of the proceeds.

But "granting permission" is not an activity that can be defined technically without regard to specific laws or institutions. (If the workers owned the land collectively, we wouldn't say that part of their contribution to production is their labor, while another part is their granting permission to themselves to use the land.) So Marx's question retains its bite. To produce material goods, we need human labor and we need nonhuman raw materials. But why do we need landlords? Why do we need capitalists?

2.3 Capitalism's White Knight: The Entrepreneur

It is precisely to distract attention from its theoretically inert landlords and capitalists that neoclassical economics complicates its initial story by introducing another character into the drama: the entrepreneur. Here is an economic actor par excellence. The entrepreneur sees an opportunity, rushes to take advantage of it, thereby benefiting not only himself but society at large. The entrepreneur develops a new product, invents a new technology, comes up with a new and more efficient way of producing or marketing. Or, more modestly, he replicates in a new location what others have done elsewhere—develops another strip mall, opens another coffee shop or dollar store or fast food restaurant. The entrepreneur is the creative principle of capitalism, celebrated, emulated, envied. Surely no one will deny that the entrepreneur makes a productive contribution to society—and hence is deserving of reward.

No one can doubt that the entrepreneur makes a productive contribution. One can question the long-range value of specific contributions, but any society, if it is to be at all dynamic, needs people who are economically creative and willing to initiate new projects. Entrepreneurial activity is vital for capitalism *and* for successor-system socialism. Socialism will need entrepreneurs—but not passive capitalists.

The entrepreneur under capitalism makes a productive contribution, but there is a problem with appealing to the entrepreneur in order to justify capitalist income. *Most income derived from capital has nothing to do with ongoing entrepreneurial agency.* Once again, a sleight-of-hand is performed in order to justify a return to the capitalist. The entrepreneurial function has been identified with the capitalist function. To be sure, some capitalists are entrepreneurs, and some entrepreneurs become capitalists. Nonetheless, theoretically and in practice, the two categories, capitalist and entrepreneur, are distinct. Neoclassical economic theory acknowledges this distinction. It defines the entrepreneur to be the agent who brings together land, labor, and capital, paying to the owners of each the market rate of rent, wage, and interest, respectively. That is to say, she rents land from the landowner, borrows capital from the capitalist, and hires workers. If the entrepreneur's project is successful, she reaps a profit.

We observe that the entrepreneur's profit is quite distinct from the "return to capital," that is, the interest paid on the funds borrowed from the capitalist. The entrepreneur is rewarded for her activity; the capitalist is rewarded for "providing capital." The real issue in justifying capitalism is not justifying profit per se. (Profit will, in fact, remain an important category in our socialist successor system.) The real issue is justifying the income that flows to the capitalist simply by virtue of his ownership of real or financial assets. (It should be noted that neither depositing money in a savings account, nor purchasing shares of stock, nor buying government or corporate bonds or any of Wall Street's more esoteric financial concoctions—mortgage-backed securities, collateralized debt obligations, credit default swaps, etc.—requires that the agent receiving the reward develop a new product, invent a new technology, or create a more efficient way of producing an existing product. Entrepreneurs do these things, not those who simply put money in the bank or have their broker "invest" their excess cash.)

The precise amount of money flowing to those who simply "provide capital" is difficult to calculate, but it is worth noting that in 2009, personal interest income totaled $1.2 trillion. Another $705 billion was paid out as dividend income to shareholders for their (wholly passive) "contributions" to production.[5] This is a mind-boggling total. If this $1.9 trillion had been distributed equally, every household in the United States would have received $16,000 from these sources that year—which would virtually eliminate poverty in America. (The poverty line for a family of four is $22,600.)

To recapitulate the argument of this section: The specific function of the capitalist qua capitalist is to "provide capital"—a function unrelated to entrepreneurial activity. The capitalist qua capitalist remains the passive figure of the preceding section, who engages in nothing that can be reasonably regarded as "productive activity." Workers produce and distribute goods and services. Salaried managers coordinate production. Entrepreneurs and other creative personnel develop new products and techniques of production. The capitalist qua capitalist does none of these things. As an individual, he might also be an entrepreneur or a manager, but these productive functions are quite distinct from "providing capital"—the function that, in a capitalist economy, legally entitles him to his (often huge) slice of the economic pie. In short, not all entrepreneurs are capitalists; not all capitalists are entrepreneurs. You can't justify the income of one by appealing to the function of the other. The entrepreneurial justification for *capitalist* income is specious.

2.4 Risk and Reward: Playing Reverse-Lotto

It will be objected that we have failed to take seriously the most important justification for capitalist income: the capitalist—indeed any investor—puts his money at risk. It is this risk that entitles the investor to a reward.

This is also a bad argument, as we shall see, but why this is so is not so obvious. It is reasonable to ask, what's wrong with rewarding people who take risks if such risk-taking is socially beneficial? If a wealthy person, instead of simply spending his money on personal consumption, chooses to back a project that ultimately enhances consumer satisfaction, society benefits, does it not? And since the investment could have failed, do we not owe this person something for the risk he ran on our behalf?

A response to this line of argument can begin by noting that we cannot propose, even tentatively, that capitalism rewards *in proportion to* risk. We cannot say that riskier investments earn a higher return. We can only say that riskier investments, *if they succeed*, tend to do so. If they don't succeed—and the riskier they are, the more likely it is that they won't—the investments may earn nothing at all. We can't say that because he took the risk, an investor deserves a return on his investment. If such risk-taking conferred entitlement, then an investor whose investment failed would have grounds for demanding compensation. But a bankrupt investor cannot sue the government, saying, "I took a risk, so I deserve a reward."

A more appropriate ethical standard for judging the rewards to risk is that of "pure procedural justice," a technical concept from game theory, deriving from the concept of a "fair game." The principle is straightforward: if everyone plays by the rules, and if the rules of the game are fair, then the results are just, no matter what they are.

With *pure procedural justice* there is no independent standard of justice regarding outcome. The fairness of the procedure is determined by direct examination. If the procedure is fair, then the outcome is just, whatever it may be. Tossing a coin to decide which football team should kick off is an example of pure procedural justice, as is a poker game among (noncheating) friends. A trial by jury is not, since, even when the rules are followed scrupulously, innocent people are sometimes found guilty and guilty people innocent.[6] With pure procedural justice, no independent standard for evaluating the outcome exists, even theoretically. So long as no one cheated, what I win or lose at poker, no matter how much or how little, is just.

A pure procedural defense of capitalism asks us to think of capitalist investment as a game. The ethical question then becomes: are the rules fair? An objection comes at once to mind. Not everyone can play. You can play the investment game only if you have money to invest. That's one of the rules.

A defender of capitalism will protest that no one is legally excluded from the game, but two points must be borne in mind. First of all, the obvious point: whatever the law may say, large numbers of people simply do not have any discretionary funds to invest. They can't play at all. Secondly, among those who can play, some are better situated than others. Wealth gives access to information, expert advice, and opportunities for diversification that the small investor often lacks. Since the rules of the capitalist investment game not only exclude many potential players but also favor some players over others, we would seem to have good grounds for questioning the justice of even "clean" capitalism, that is, capitalism without insider trading, market manipulation, and so forth.

A defender of capitalism will protest: Small investors can invest in mutual funds and so take advantage of diversification and expert judgment. This may not have been so easy to do in the past, but it is not difficult now. Moreover—and more importantly—these investors have *freely chosen* to enter the game. They don't have to play. Surely we don't want to prohibit people from putting their money at risk if they so desire.

These points are not without merit. Capitalist financial markets need some regulation if they are not to produce chaos (as the recent financial meltdown has made clear), and small investors may be in need of special protection, but these shouldn't be too hard to provide.

Moreover, the capitalist investment game is a positive-sum game. The small investor, although perhaps disadvantaged vis-à-vis the large investor, is still likely to make money on his investment, particularly if he is not too greedy. Certainly there are schemes and scams aplenty to detach the unwary small investor from his savings, but there are also lots of legitimate opportunities. The stock market, for example, may not be a magic carpet ride (however much it sometimes seems to be), but neither is it a fraud. Most investors over the years, small as well as large, have made money on the stock market—a lot more than they have ever made playing poker.

The game-theory concept just introduced, "positive-sum game," is a useful concept for understanding certain key features of capitalism. A game is *positive sum* if the total expected gain from playing, computed according to probability theory, is positive. More simply put: a positive-sum game is one in which more money is won than is lost. A *zero-sum* game is one in which gains and losses match. In such a case, being excluded does not disadvantage you (at least not financially), since the expected gain from playing is zero. On balance, you are no better off playing than not playing. A game is *negative sum* (for example, any gambling game where the house gets a cut) when your expected gain is negative. If monetary gain is your only reason for playing the slot machines, you are better off passing them by.

The capitalist investment is a positive-sum game. Let me call the capitalist investment game "Reverse-Lotto," since, unlike Lotto itself, this game pays out far more than it takes in. (Lotto and other state lotteries are among the worst of the negative-sum gambling games, paying out barely half of what they take in. Not surprisingly, lottery outlets are far more prevalent in poor communities than in those where there are other, vastly more favorable, games to play.[7])

If the capitalist investment game is positive sum, then people who are excluded are disadvantaged. As we have already noted, many people are indeed excluded—anyone who lacks sufficient discretionary income to play. If capitalist investment were a zero-sum game, such people would have little reason to complain—unless they were more skilled at picking winners than the professionals with whom they would be competing. If the investment game were negative sum (like a state lottery), such people could count themselves lucky for being kept out.

Is the capitalist investment game really a positive-sum game? One proxy for investment income is what shows up in the national accounts as "property income." This figure is usually about one-quarter of the national income. It is never negative. The fact of the matter is, those who play the investment game usually gain by doing so, for they are playing a game where, except in times of major crisis, the net gain (interest, dividends, capital gains) is massively positive. To be sure, there are losers, but overall, far more money is won than lost.

But how is this possible? How is it possible for the investment game to be positive sum? Negative-sum games, like Lotto, are easy to understand. More money is lost than is won because the house takes a cut. But how can more money be won at Reverse-Lotto than lost? Where does that extra money come from?

This question takes us to the heart of capitalism. Let us address it by first detouring through another question. What is the point of the capitalist investment game? That is to say, what is the purpose of stock markets, bond markets, currency markets, investment banks, and other institutions that allow those with surplus money to risk it in hopes of seeing it grow? What is the point for society? It is no mystery why individuals would want to play a positive-sum game, but what's in it for society at large?

The point of the investment game is to encourage socially beneficial behavior of two distinct sorts. The *primary* purpose is to foster entrepreneurial activity: actions by talented people that lead to new products, new techniques of production, and so on. Any society that wishes to be reasonably dynamic must find ways of encouraging such activity.

But in order to actualize a new idea, an entrepreneur needs *the labor of other people.* Notice, I did not say "money." It is important to realize that money is not an essential condition. What an entrepreneur needs is labor—the past labor of other people (in the form of buildings, equipment, and raw materials) and present labor (her own and that of her employees). At bottom, what an entrepreneur needs is *authority,* the authority to command the labor of others.

In a capitalist society one can command the labor of others if one has the money to purchase the products of past labor and to hire those who will utilize those products. (It is here that money enters the picture.) Where does the entrepreneur lay hold of such money? In a capitalist society, partly from her own savings, but mostly from individuals who have money to spare. Thus we have the *secondary* purpose of the capitalist investment game: to encourage those with money to spare to make it available to those who can use it effectively to mobilize the labor of others.

We can now understand how it is that the investment game is positive sum, and why it is the case that the players' overall net gain is (largely) at the expense of the nonplayers. One gets something for nothing because someone else gets nothing for something. Investment income, the reward to those who have "risked" their money by channeling it into financial institutions—banks, stock markets, real estate trusts, venture capital consortia, hedge funds, and the like—is possible *only because those who produce the goods and services of society are paid less than the value of the goods and services they produce.* If capitalist distribution were really in accord with the principle of contribution, the investor would get nothing. The entrepreneur (the person with the innovative idea) would still be rewarded, as would workers and managers, but there would be nothing left over for the person who merely "provided the capital."

What I am saying here may be rather hard to swallow, particularly if you have made a little money with your investments. Let me illustrate more concretely. Let's take the case of the stock market. How do you make money in the stock market? Basically, there are two sources of income. When you buy a share of stock in Company X, you are entitled to a portion of Company X's profits. That's your *dividend* income. You can also make money from *capital gains.* If, over time, the value of your share appreciates, you can sell it and pocket the difference.

In the first case, the analysis is straightforward. Dividend payments come from net profit, and net profit derives from surplus value—the difference between the monetary value added to the raw materials by the workers (including management) and what they are paid. As any economist will confirm (since it is an analytical truth), unless labor costs are less than the value added by labor, there will be no profit.

What about capital gains? Here the situation is less transparent. Some part of your capital gain may be due simply to speculation. If enough investors think that a stock will rise in value, their buying it will cause it to rise, thus fulfilling their expectations. If you happen to have purchased a share of that stock prior to the speculative surge, and you sell it while the price is high, you realize a "magic" profit.

Of course, if you buy near the top of a bubble, you can lose big, but as a general rule overall capital gains are positive—because the real basis for stock appreciation lies not in investor psychology but elsewhere. Part of a company's net profit is paid out to the shareholders in the form of dividends, but a good portion of the remainder is reinvested in the company. These "retained earnings" increase the real value of the company, and hence the value of the stock itself. So the capital gains portion of stock income also derives from profit, hence from surplus value—hence from what Marx called the "exploitation" of labor.

(Speculation gives stock markets a volatility that obscures what is really going on. People win big and lose big, depending on price movements that often have nothing do to with the real value of the firm, suggesting that a stock market is just a gaming parlor. A stock market is, to be sure, a casino that makes a lot of money for the "house"—that is, for the traders and brokers who execute the deals—but the Wall Street casinos are almost always positive sum, whereas their Las Vegas counterparts are always negative sum. Collectively, players lose more than they win in Las Vegas; they win more than they lose on Wall Street.)

"But wait!" you will surely say. "In buying shares of stock I supplied the company with investment capital. Without me, the company would have made fewer profits."

In most cases, this assertion is flat-out false. In the vast majority of cases, when you buy stock, you give your money not to the company but to another private individual. You buy your share of stock from someone who is cashing in his share. Not a nickel of your money goes to the company itself. The company's profits would have been exactly the same, with or without your stock purchase. (Venture capitalists fund many start-ups, but they don't operate via the stock market.)

It is true that once in a while a company will offer a new issue of stock, to be sold to the public for cash. This dilutes the value of the existing shares, so shareholders aren't enthusiastic about new issues, but sometimes new funds are acquired this way. But even here, there's a problem. The stock purchaser keeps getting "repaid" long after the value of his contribution has been reimbursed. So long as the company endures as a profitable enterprise, dividend checks keep coming, and the reinvested profits of the company—no longer connected in any way to the original investment—keep adding to your stock's value. You—and your descendents—keep getting paid (unless the company goes under) forever.

Let me be clear as to what has been shown thus far. I have explained how it is possible that the capitalist investment game (as a whole and usually in its various parts) is positive sum. In most years more money is made in the financial markets than is lost. How is this possible? It is possible only because those who engage in real productive activity receive less than that to which they would be entitled were they fully compensated for what they produce. The reward, allegedly for risk, derives from this discrepancy.

Notice: my argument thus far does not imply that rewarding risk in this manner is immoral or even socially harmful. The entrepreneur engages in productive activity of an important nature. An entrepreneur must have access to funds to enact her vision. In a capitalist society, these funds come from private investors. But the entrepreneur's gamble poses a risk to an investor. Since an investor can lose, he must be enticed to take the risk. This, remember, is the secondary function of the capitalist investment game. I have shown that this part of the game is unfair because it is a positive-sum game from which many are excluded. Still, it could be argued (and often is) that unless the secondary goal of the investment game is satisfied, the primary goal, the encouraging of entrepreneurial activity, cannot be satisfied either, at least not adequately. The game might not be fair, but it serves so important a function that, all things considered, it is justified.

Consider an analogy. A peasant community is in thrall to a theocracy. Every year the peasants turn over a portion of their harvest to the priests, who pray to the Land-God for a good harvest next year. The priests also exhort their flock to work hard, informing them that they will offend the Land-God if they do not. Thus motivated, the peasants do work hard, and do in fact produce more than they did in pretheocratic days.

Ideologically, the system is based on a lie. The productivity of the land is not due to the prayers of the priests but to the hard work of the peasants themselves. But perhaps this is a Noble Lie—justified by its consequences.[8] Without it, the people would in fact be worse off.

Perhaps people need Noble Lies—that the Land-God must be appeased, that providing capital is a productive activity, that capitalists are mostly creative entrepreneurs, that financial markets are fair.

Or perhaps we've outgrown the need for such lies. What if there exists an alternative—a mechanism for providing authority to entrepreneurs that does not involve people with wealth compounding their wealth without engaging in any sort of productive activity?

This question moves us from the noncomparative justification to the comparative one. We see that it is not risk per se that justifies a capitalist's income, but the assumption that there is no better mechanism for generating sufficient entrepreneurial energy than capitalist positive-sum Reverse-Lotto. The comparative case for Economic Democracy will challenge this assumption.

2.5 The Utility (and Disutility) of Deferred Consumption

Before taking up the comparative argument, we need to consider one final noncomparative justification. To understand more fully how capitalism actually works, we need to consider a concept that has been absent from the discussion so far, the concept of "saving."

Like capital, this concept might seem to be so commonplace that no analysis is necessary. To save is to defer consumption. I put away a part of my income now so that I might spend it later. Nothing mysterious here.

There is something a little peculiar about these savings, however. In a capitalist economy, there are places for me to deposit my savings that will pay me for doing so. This is odd, isn't it? The bank is protecting my savings. It is performing a service for me. Shouldn't I be paying the bank for this service? But no, that's not how it works. In fact, the bank pays me.

Let us ask the ethical question. Why should I receive interest on my savings? I put money in a bank. There is no question of risk here. My savings account is fully insured by the federal government. There is no question of entrepreneurial activity on my part. I have not the slightest idea what the bank does with my money. All I know is, so long as I leave my money in the bank, it will "grow."

Interest may seem to be a simple thing, but interest, particularly when compounded, is remarkable. John Maynard Keynes, somewhat whimsically, calculated that the entire foreign investment of Britain, some £4 billion in 1928, could be derived from the portion of the treasure Sir Francis Drake stole from the Spanish that Queen Elizabeth invested in the Levant Company—some £40,000, compounding at a very modest 3.25 percent each year. "Thus every £1 which Drake brought home in 1580 has now become £100,000. Such is the power of compound interest."[9]

One pound grows to be a hundred thousand pounds. Again we must ask, how is this possible? Population growth is easy enough to understand. If every couple has four children who live to adulthood, the population will double every generation. That's easy to see. No mystery. If I invest $1,000 at 6 percent, my investment will double every twelve years. How did *that* procreation take place? From whom did that extra $1,000 come?

Superficially, the answer is simple enough. It is possible for a bank to pay its savers interest because it charges interest to its borrowers—a higher rate, in fact, so that it can make a profit. If we ignore the bank's profit (which we may do, since it is irrelevant to the argument at hand), and if we imagine the loan to be a consumer loan, then clearly nothing more is going on than a redistribution of income. Lenders gain at the expense of borrowers. In order to consume now, before you have saved up the full price of the item you wish to purchase, you agree to pay me for the privilege of doing so. I lend you $1,000; you repay me $1,060 a year from now. That year I can spend $60 more than I could have if I hadn't waited, whereas you must spend $60 less than you otherwise could. This is a nice arrangement for me, to be sure, but you have no grounds for complaint, do you? You also gained something, namely, the ability to enjoy a product before you had saved enough to purchase it.

Of course, background assumptions are important here, since this process is not always benign. It is not a particularly startling fact that those who lend money typically have more of it than those who borrow. In a class-polarized society, institutions that facilitate the transfer of funds from rich to poor, to be repaid *with interest*, will likely make inequality worse. Ancient and medieval philosophers had a point when they condemned the charging of interest as "that most hateful sort of wealth getting, which makes a gain out of money itself."[10]

Nevertheless, in a modern society, so long as the practice does not get out of hand, consumer loans seem harmless enough. Paying for the privilege of consuming before saving need not be prohibited. Indeed, a network of savings and loan associations to facilitate home buying and other consumer purchases can be part of a well-organized socialist society—as we shall see in the next chapter.

However, this sort of saving and lending is not the saving and lending that forms the cornerstone of capitalism. This sort of saving and lending redistributes income, but it has no direct effect on production. I can consume $60 more a year from now than I otherwise could, but you must consume $60 less. Total consumption remains the same. Ancient and medieval philosophers may have found the transfer of wealth from poor to rich repugnant. We may appreciate the convenience of being able to buy on credit. Neither of these judgments has anything to do with the economic function of saving under capitalism. Neither draws any connection between savings and *economic growth*.

We smile now at the railings of Aristotle or Thomas Aquinas (the latter proclaiming, "It is by its very nature unlawful to take payment for the use of money lent, which payment is known as usury, and just as a man is bound to restore other ill-gotten goods, so is he bound to restore the money he has taken in usury.["]11) They failed to realize, we tell ourselves, how interest can function as a mechanism for enhancing production, so that in the long run, everyone's consumption goes up. Consumer loans are a sideshow. What are crucial under capitalism are business loans—savings loaned out, not for consumer gratification, but for the purpose of productive investment.

We all know the story that Aristotle and Aquinas did not know. Frugal savers put money in the bank. The bank loans it out to entrepreneurs who use these loans not for personal consumption but to open new businesses or otherwise expand production. From their profits the loans can be repaid with interest. Everybody benefits—lenders, borrowers, workers, and consumers. The economy grows. The best of all possible worlds!

This is the *standard story*, the basic story meant to explain the social utility of interest. We need savers to supply funds to entrepreneurs so that the economy can grow. The well-known schema is: savings → investment → growth.

John Maynard Keynes, the most influential economist of the twentieth century, stared at the wreckage of the Great Depression and realized that the standard story had it backwards. For society as a whole, the causal sequence runs: investment → growth → savings. The implications of this story are dramatic and unsettling. You don't need savings for growth. So you don't need to pay people interest to encourage them to save.

The *Keynesian counterstory* is counterintuitive. Someone must save, must defer consumption, to provide funds for investment, right? "Wrong," says Keynes. Consider a simple variation on the standard story. Suppose we have an enterprising entrepreneur with a project in mind. Suppose, instead of waiting for a frugal saver to accumulate the funds to finance it, the government simply prints the money and lends it to her. She can now do exactly what she would have done had there been a frugal saver willing to lend her money—hire workers, increase production, make a profit, then repay the loan with interest. As in the standard story, everyone is better off—the entrepreneur, workers, consumers. (Won't the government's printing money lead to inflation? Not necessarily. Not if there is some slack in the economy, that is, less than full employment of workers and resources—which is almost always the case under capitalism.)

The crucial thing to note about this counterstory is that production was increased without anyone doing any prior saving. No one deferred consumption. Therefore, no one has to be rewarded for doing so.

I am not suggesting here that a society should rely on governmental printing presses to generate its funds for investment. (Where these funds should come from will be discussed in the next chapter.) The fundamental point is this: business credit is necessary for a healthy economy—but personal savings are not. A person who wants to start a new business, or a business that wants to expand, needs to command the labor of others. Money is a convenient and effective mechanism for exercising this authority. In capitalist societies, for historical reasons, most business credit comes from financial institutions that accumulate funds from private savers. But this credit need not come from private savers. It could come from public sources. Therefore, the payment of interest to private savers is not necessary for economic growth.

The Keynesian counterstory makes it clear that private savings are not essential to a modern economy. In fact, it points to an even more shocking conclusion. In a capitalist society, saving rather than consuming can be *detrimental* to the economy. Saving, rather than spending, can be an antisocial act.

Keynes was the first to make theoretically explicit what should now be a commonplace: the key to a healthy capitalist economy is effective demand. The deep economic crises of capitalism are rarely supply-side crises. The recurring problem is insufficient demand for all the goods the system has produced or could produce. If demand is strong, businesses make healthy profits, and hence have plenty of money to reinvest. But when demand is weak, profits decline, investment is cut back, and workers are laid off—which compounds the problem, since laid-off workers buy less, depressing demand still further: the familiar downward recessionary spiral.

From the point of view of the economy as a whole, the personal decision to save rather than consume *decreases* aggregate demand, thus increasing the likelihood of unemployment, and exacerbating the tendency toward economic stagnation. (Remember George Bush's exhortation to the country in the aftermath of September 11: "Be patriotic! Go shopping!" Or the *Newsweek* cover of March 23, 2009: Uncle Sam pointing his finger at the reader, saying, "I want YOU to start spending! Invest in America before it is too late!" These gestures mimic Keynes himself, who, in a 1931 radio broadcast, had urged, "Oh patriotic housewives, sally out tomorrow early into the streets and go to the wonderful sales which are everywhere advertised. You will do yourselves good . . . and have the added joy that you are increasing employment, adding to the wealth of the country."[12])

To be sure, the decision to save does not always have negative consequences. If the money saved is loaned out to an entrepreneur who uses it to buy raw materials and hire workers, then aggregate demand is not reduced. However, as Keynes so forcefully pointed out, there is no reason to suppose that the demand for investment loans will be sufficient to absorb the supply of savings. When it is not, the whole economy suffers. We get recession, unemployment—and the eventual disappearance of those excess savings.

It should be noted that this strange irrationality—the propensity of an economy to slump because of too much saving—becomes ever more acute the richer and/or more unequal the society becomes, since wealthy people tend to save more than poor people. It should also be noted that banks are not the only institutions that encourage people to save. So do stock markets, bond markets, real estate trusts, mutual funds, and all the other financial institutions that offer "investment" opportunities. "Investing" in these institutions is not investing in the Keynesian sense, but *saving*. Investing, for Keynes, means "real" investing: building new facilities, purchasing new equipment, expanding production capabilities. Financial markets enhance effective demand only to the degree that, when buoyant, those "invested" in these markets feel richer, hence inclined to spend more than they otherwise would. Of course, when these markets begin to tumble, they have the opposite effect.

2.6 TINA

But there is no alternative, is there? That's the mantra: TINA, TINA, TINA. Of course there are always alternatives, but are there better alternatives, more desirable alternatives?

We must now confront what is surely the strongest argument in favor of capitalism. The reader can grant all that has been so far demonstrated:

- Providing capital isn't really a productive activity.
- Most capitalists aren't entrepreneurs.
- Those with money to risk in the financial markets tend to gain at the expense of working people.
- Private savings are not necessary for an economy to grow.
- Saving can be harmful to the economy.

The reader can grant all this and still doubt that any other set of institutions could produce better overall results than those that define capitalism. To be sure, the history of capitalism is full of sound and fury—imperial conquest, slavery, systematic violence against working people, internecine wars of almost unimaginable destructiveness—but now that the institutions of liberal democracy seem to have taken firm root, at least in the advanced capitalist countries, and now that the Soviet and Eastern European socialist experiments have collapsed, the comparative case for capitalist supremacy is strong. If we want efficiency and growth along with freedom and democracy, shouldn't we stick with capitalism? Wouldn't any attempt at fundamentally altering the basic institutions, as opposed to softening their rough edges, kill the goose that is laying all these golden eggs? These are the hard questions we must now address.

3

Economic Democracy: What It Is

A serious critique of capitalism cannot be content with merely noting the negative features of the contemporary world. It must show a causal connection between the structures that define capitalism and these features. Otherwise, the negatives can simply be written off as either the inevitable effects of human nature or the consequences of some reformable aspects of capitalism. A serious critique must show that these negative features would not be present, or would at least be far less prominent, if certain structural elements of capitalism were altered and that such alterations would not have other worse consequences.

Hence, we must specify precisely not only the defining characteristics of capitalism, which was done in the previous chapter, but also the structural features of an alternative to capitalism. Such a specification, even in rudimentary form, is necessarily complicated, since a modern economy is a complicated affair. But if we want to do more than simply denounce the evils of capitalism, we must confront the claim that there is no alternative—by proposing one.

3.1 Economic Democracy: The Basic Model

The model to be elaborated here and defended in subsequent chapters does not originate simply from economic theory, nor is it a stylized economic structure of some particular country or region. The model is a synthesis of theory and practice. What we are calling "Economic Democracy" is a model whose form has been shaped by the theoretical debates that have taken place over the past half century concerning comparative economic systems, by the empirical studies of modes of workplace organization, and by the records of various historical "experiments" of the twentieth century, notably the Soviet Union, postwar Japan, Tito's Yugoslavia, China before and after Mao, and (smaller in scale, but extremely important) a most unusual "cooperative corporation" in the Basque region of Spain.

The model also derives from an analysis of two sources of felt discontent with capitalism, discontent already acute in many quarters and likely to intensify. Both sources may be regarded as "democratic deficits"—lack of democratic control over conditions that affect us profoundly.

The first concerns workplace democracy. It is a striking anomaly of modern capitalist societies that ordinary people are deemed competent enough to select their political leaders—but not their bosses. Contemporary capitalism celebrates democracy, yet denies us our democratic rights at precisely the point where they might be utilized most immediately and concretely: at the place where we spend most of the active and alert hours of our adult lives. Of course, if it could be demonstrated that workplace democracy is too cumbersome to be efficient or workers too ignorant or shortsighted to make rational decisions, this would be a powerful counterargument to extending democracy in so logical a direction. But, as we shall see, the evidence points overwhelmingly to the opposite conclusion: workplace democracy works—in fact, as a general rule, workplace democracy works better than owner-authoritarianism, that is, the capitalist form of workplace organization.

The other disconcerting feature of contemporary capitalism is capital's current "hypermobility." The bulk of capital in a capitalist society belongs to private individuals. Because it is theirs, they can do with it whatever they want. They can invest it anywhere and in anything they choose, or not invest it at all if profit prospects are dim. But this freedom, when coupled with recently enhanced transfer capabilities (both money and goods move faster than ever before), gives capital a mobility that now generates economic and political insecurity around the globe. Financial markets now rule, however "democratic" our political systems purport to be, and this rule is often capricious, often destructive.

Let us consider a socialist alternative to capitalism that addresses these democratic deficits. (I use the term *socialist* to refer to any attempt to transcend capitalism by abolishing most private ownership of means of production.) It is a socialism quite different in structure from the failed models of the past, but Economic Democracy shares with them the conviction that private ownership of the means of production must be curtailed if the human species is to flourish.

Recall that capitalism is characterized by three basic institutions: private ownership of means of production, the market, and wage labor. The Soviet economic model abolished private ownership of the means of production (by collectivizing all farms and factories) and the market (by instituting central planning), but retained wage labor. Economic Democracy abolishes private ownership of the means of production and wage labor, but retains the market. To be more precise, Economic Democracy, like capitalism, can be defined in terms of three basic features, the second of which it shares with capitalism:

- *Worker self-management*: Each productive enterprise is controlled democratically by its workers.
- *The market*: These enterprises interact with one another and with consumers in an environment largely free of government price controls. Raw materials, instruments of production, and consumer goods are all bought and sold at prices largely determined by the forces of supply and demand.
- *Social control of investment*: Funds for new investment are generated by a capital assets tax and are returned to the economy through a network of public investment banks.

This basic model, which will be elaborated more fully below, is necessarily stylized and oversimplified. In practice, Economic Democracy will be more complicated than the version presented here. Later in this chapter I will specify a number of additional institutions that a viable, desirable Economic Democracy would likely want to adopt. However, to grasp the nature of the system and to understand its essential dynamic, it is important to have a clear picture of the basic structure. (The same is true of capitalism. Economists must use simplified models to explain the basic laws of the system.)

3.1.1 Worker Self-Management

Each productive enterprise is controlled by those who work there. Workers are responsible for the operation of the facility: organization of the workplace, enterprise discipline, techniques of production, what and how much to produce, what to charge for what is produced, and how the net proceeds are to be distributed. Enterprises are not required to distribute the proceeds equally. Most firms will likely award larger shares to more highly skilled workers, to those with greater seniority, and to those with more managerial responsibility. Decisions concerning these matters will be made democratically. Disgruntled members are free to quit and seek work elsewhere, so egalitarian considerations must be balanced against the need to motivate and retain good workers—including good managers.

In a firm of significant size, some delegation of authority will be necessary. The usual solution to this general problem of democracy is representation. Most enterprises elect a workers' council, which appoints the chief executive officer and perhaps other members of upper management. Management is neither appointed by the state nor elected by the community at large nor, since this is not a capitalist corporation, selected by a board of directors elected by shareholders. There are no shareholders in Economic Democracy.

An important practical issue emerges at this level—getting the right balance between managerial accountability and managerial autonomy. Accountability without autonomy risks managerial timidity and paralysis; autonomy without accountability risks despotism. Managers need sufficient autonomy to manage effectively, but not so much that they can exploit the workforce to their own advantage. Various enterprises will handle this issue differently, the more successful models being emulated. (As we shall see, highly successful models already exist.) But whatever internal structures are put in place, ultimate authority rests with the enterprise's workers, one person, one vote.

Although workers control the workplace, they do not "own" the means of production. These are regarded as the collective property of society. Workers have the right to run the enterprise, to use its capital assets as they see fit, and to distribute among themselves the whole of the enterprise's net profit. Societal "ownership" of the enterprise manifests itself in two ways.

- All firms must pay a tax on their capital assets, which goes into society's investment fund. In effect, workers lease their capital assets from society.
- Firms are required to preserve the value of the capital stock entrusted to them. This means that a depreciation fund must be maintained. Money must be set aside to repair or replace existing capital stock. This money may be spent on whatever capital replacements or improvements the firm deems fit, but it may not be used to supplement workers' incomes.

If an enterprise finds itself in economic difficulty, workers are free to reorganize the facility or to leave and seek work elsewhere. They are not free to sell off their capital assets and use the proceeds as income. If a firm is unable to generate even the nationally specified minimum per capita income—Economic Democracy's equivalent to the minimum wage—then it must declare bankruptcy. Control of the firm's capital assets reverts to the state; its workers must seek employment elsewhere.

In essence, a firm under Economic Democracy is regarded not as a thing to be bought or sold (as it is under capitalism) but as a community. When you join a firm, you receive the rights of full citizenship, that is, full voting rights. When you leave one firm and join another, these rights transfer. With rights

come responsibilities, in this case the responsibilities of paying the capital assets tax and maintaining the value of the assets you are using.

3.1.2 The Market

Economic Democracy is a market economy, at least insofar as the allocation
of consumer and capital goods is concerned. Firms buy raw materials and
machinery from other firms and sell their products to other enterprises or
consumers. Prices are largely unregulated except by supply and demand, although in some cases price controls or price supports might be employed—as
they are in all real-world forms of capitalism.

Enterprises in our economy strive to make a profit. *Profit* is not a dirty
word in this form of socialism—but profit is calculated differently in a democratic firm than it is in a capitalist firm. Market-economy firms, whether
capitalist or worker self-managed, strive to maximize the difference between
total sales and total costs. However, for a capitalist firm, labor is counted as
a cost; for a worker-run enterprise, it is not. In Economic Democracy, labor
is not another "factor of production" on technical par with land and capital.
Instead, labor is the residual claimant. Workers get all that remains once
nonlabor costs, including depreciation set-asides and the capital assets tax,
have been paid. (As we shall see, this seemingly small structural difference
will have far-reaching consequences.)

"Market socialism" remains a controversial topic among socialists. I have
long argued that centralized planning, the most commonly advocated socialist alternative to market allocation, is inherently flawed, and that schemes
for decentralized, nonmarket planning are unworkable. Central planning,
as theory predicts and the historical record confirms, is both inefficient and
conducive to an authoritarian concentration of power. This is one of the great
lessons to be drawn from the Soviet experience. Without a price mechanism
sensitive to supply and demand, it is extremely difficult for a producer or
planner to know what and how much to produce and which production and
marketing methods are the most efficient. It is also extremely difficult in the
absence of a market to design a set of incentives that will motivate producers
to be both efficient and innovative. Market competition resolves these problems (to a significant if incomplete degree) in a nonauthoritarian, nonbureau-
cratic fashion. This is an achievement indispensable to a serious socialism.[1]

3.1.3 Social Control of Investment

This is the most technically complex feature of our model. It is vastly simpler
than the institutions that comprise the investment mechanisms of capitalism,

that is, those mysterious, omnipotent "financial markets" with their stocks, bonds, futures, derivatives, swaps, collateralized debt obligations, structured investment vehicles, and so on, but it is more complicated to specify than is worker self-management or the market. (Paul Krugman reports that the system is now so hard to understand that Ben Bernanke, when he took over as Federal Reserve chairman in 2007, required a face-to-face refresher course from hedge fund managers.[2])

In any society that wants to remain technologically and economically dynamic, a certain portion of society's labor and natural resources must be devoted to developing and implementing new technologies and to expanding the production of the goods and services in high demand. In a modern society, this allocation of resources is effected through monetary investment. In a capitalist society, these investment funds come largely from private savings, either the direct savings of private individuals or the retained earnings of corporations, that is, the indirect savings of shareholders. These savings are then either invested directly, or deposited in banks or other financial institutions, which lend them out to businesses or entrepreneurs.

In Economic Democracy, investment funds are generated in a more direct and transparent fashion. We simply tax the capital assets of enterprises— land, buildings, and equipment. This tax, a flat-rate tax (essentially a property tax) may be regarded as a leasing fee paid by the workers of the enterprise for use of social property that belongs to all.

Revenues from the capital assets tax constitute the national investment fund, all of which is earmarked for new investment. ("New investment" is simply investment over and above that financed by enterprises directly from their own depreciation funds.) All new investment derives from this fund. In stark contrast to capitalism, Economic Democracy does not depend on private savings for its economic development.

Since investment funds are publicly, not privately, generated, their allocation back into the economy is a public, not private, matter. Society must decide on procedures that are both fair and efficient. Here we have options. There is no set of procedures that can guarantee perfect efficiency and perfect fairness, but there do exist various mechanisms that can be employed to produce more rational, equitable, and democratic development than can be expected under capitalism.

At one extreme, a democratically accountable planning board could allocate all the funds according to a detailed plan. This would not be a plan for the entire economy, à la Soviet central planning, but only for new investments (in a country like the United States, roughly 10 to 15 percent of GDP), so it would not run up against the insurmountable difficulties inherent in the Soviet model. Such planning would be more akin to the "market-conforming" investment planning practiced by Japan and South Korea during their periods of rapid development. For a country in which developmental priorities are relatively clear and widely accepted, such planning might be appropriate.[3]

At the other extreme, these funds could simply be distributed to a network of public banks that would then lend them out using precisely the same criteria that capitalist banks would use. This would be a kind of laissez-faire socialism: let the market decide investment allocation. Banks would be charged a centrally determined interest rate on the funds they receive. They would be expected to make a profit, that is, to charge more than the base-rate interest, adjusted according to risk. Banks would compete, as they do now, trying to balance the riskiness of their loans against the interest rates they charge. As under capitalism, managers of successful banks (i.e., the most profitable) would be rewarded, managers whose banks performed poorly would be sacked. In all cases, bank profits are returned to the national investment fund.

In my view, the optimal mechanism, at least for a rich country, lies between these extremes. Decision making is more decentralized than in the first alternative; the market is more constrained than in the second. Concerns for justice and efficiency are balanced by using a mix of market and nonmarket criteria. The basic idea is to allocate the centrally collected funds according to a *principle of fairness* first, and then to bring in competition to promote *efficiency*.

The principle of fairness pertains to regional and communal distribution: each region of the country and each community within each region is entitled to its *fair share* of the national investment fund. "Fair share" is understood to be, prima facie, its *per capita* share; that is to say, if Region A has x percent of the nation's population, it gets x percent of the money available for new investment. The central implication of this principle is that regions and communities do not compete for investment funds. They do not compete, as they must under capitalism, for capital. Each region and each community gets its share, each and every year, as a matter of right.

Why should "fair share" be per capita share? Clearly it would not be fair simply to return to each region the investment funds collected (via the capital assets tax) from that region, since that amount merely reflects the quantity of capital assets in that region. The fact that one region has a larger capital base than another is not due to the greater effort on the part of the people in that region, or to their greater intelligence or moral worth. The discrepancy is due to the region's specific history. It would hardly be fair to base present capital allocation on past history. Doing so would give a greater-than-per-capita share to the regions that are already more capital intensive, thus exacerbating, rather than mitigating, regional inequalities.

This, of course, is precisely what happens under capitalism. New investment tends to flow to where the capital base is already large. Cities attract

more capital than rural areas. Prosperous areas suck investment funds from
the rest of a country. Capital tends to move to where capital is already plentiful, because that is where new investment opportunities are easiest to find.
Workers must then follow, migrating to where new jobs are being created.
(To be sure, there are countermovements. An industrial region may decline
if shifting patterns of demand or new technologies or low-wage foreign competition adversely affect the market for their products, or if labor unions get
too strong, or if social or infrastructure problems make a desirable region less
desirable. But this simply means that capital will flow elsewhere, and workers
must, if they can, chase after it.) Under Economic Democracy workers have
the right to relocate to any region of the country, but they will not be compelled to move because capital is no longer flowing into their region.

The pattern of industrialization and capital density that an Economic
Democracy has inherited from its capitalist past cannot be regarded as enti-
tling a capital-intensive region to even more capital. If one wants a positive
justification for the principle of per capita capital allocation, one can appeal
to Marx's insight that labor, not capital, is the source of value, and hence of
the surplus value that constitutes the investment fund. If this is so, then the
investment fund ought to be distributed to regions in proportion to the size of
their workforces, that is (essentially), on a per capita basis. Or, if one prefers
a non-Marxian justification, allocating investment funds to regions may be
regarded as providing a public service. Hence, the allocation of investment
funds should follow the principle used in the allocation of such public services
as education and health care (at least in those parts of the world where education and health care are publicly funded and rationally distributed)—namely,
per capita share.[4]

These justifications do not give the per capita principle absolute force. The
right of a region or community to its per capita share of the investment fund
is a prima facie right only, which can be overridden by other ethical or economic considerations. The green-modernization of an outmoded industry in
a particular region might require that it receive more than its per capita share
for a period of time. It might be desirable to allocate a larger-than-per-capita
share to an underdeveloped region or community for a number of years, to
aid it in catching up. These decisions will have to be made publicly, by the
democratically elected national or regional legislature, with full weight being
given to the fact that if some regions get more than their per capita share,
others will get less.

The principle of fair share governs the allocation of the national investment
fund to regions and communities. When this share reaches a community, it
is then distributed to public banks within the communities. These banks then
make the funds available to local enterprises wanting to expand production or

introduce new products or enter new lines of business or upgrade technologies—anything requiring capital in excess of what has accumulated in their depreciation funds.

Each bank receives a share of the investment fund allocated to the community, but this allocation is no longer governed by the principle of fair share. A bank's share is determined by the size and number of firms serviced by the bank, and by the bank's success at making economically sound loans, creating employment, and satisfying other community-determined goals.[5] Unlike banks under capitalism, these banks are not themselves private, profit-maximizing institutions. They are public institutions charged with effectively allocating the funds entrusted to them in accordance with at least two criteria: profitability and employment creation. A region or community may impose additional criteria to better control its pattern of development. It may, for example, offer loans at lower rates to businesses creating green jobs, or retooling to use more ecologically sound technologies.

The income the bank itself receives, to be distributed among the bank's employees, comes from general tax revenues. The amount of income depends on how successful the bank has been at managing its loan portfolio and meeting its community-determined goals.

If a community is unable to find sufficient investment opportunities to absorb the funds allocated to it, the excess must be returned to the center, to be reallocated to where investment funds are more in demand. Thus communities have a strong incentive to seek out new investment opportunities in order to keep the allocated funds at home. Banks have a similar incentive, so it is reasonable to expect that communities and their banks will set up entrepreneurial divisions—agencies that monitor new business opportunities and provide technical and financial expertise to existing firms seeking new opportunities and to individuals interested in starting new worker self-managed enterprises. These agencies might go so far as to recruit prospective managers and workers for new enterprises.

One further element of the investment mechanism needs to be considered. In a market economy, two kinds of capital investment take place: "public" investment related to the provision of free (or heavily subsidized) goods and services (e.g., roads, bridges, harbors, airports, schools, hospitals, basic research facilities, and the like) and "private" investment related to goods and services to be sold competitively on the market. Under capitalism, these funds are separately generated: public investment is financed from general tax revenues; private investment comes from private savings. (The separation is not so clean in practice. Governments turn to the private financial markets to finance budget deficits. They also use public money—often large amounts—to subsidize favored private industries.[6])

Under Economic Democracy, all capital investment comes from the same source, namely, the national investment fund. Thus, key decisions must be made at each level of government as to how much of the investment fund should be allocated for public capital investment and for what projects, and how much should be left for the market sector. (Note: public "capital investment" is investment in durable physical assets. Thus, funds for school construction would come from the investment fund whereas salaries of teachers and operating expenses come from general tax revenues.)

Decisions as to the allocation of investment between the public and market sectors are made democratically by the legislative bodies at each level—national, regional, and local. Investment hearings are held, as budget hearings are currently held; expert and popular testimony is sought. The legislature then decides the nature and amount of capital spending on public goods appropriate to its level, sets these funds aside, then passes the remainder to the next level down.

For example, the national legislature decides, in accordance with the democratic procedures just described, on public capital spending for projects that are national in scope (e.g., an upgrading of rail transport) and then transfers funds to the appropriate governmental agency (e.g., the Department of Transportation). The remainder of the national investment fund is distributed to regions on a per capita basis. Regional legislatures now make similar decisions concerning regional capital spending, then pass the remainder of their investment funds to local communities on a per capita basis. The communities, in turn, make decisions about local public investment, then allocate the remainder to their banks, which make them available to local enterprises.

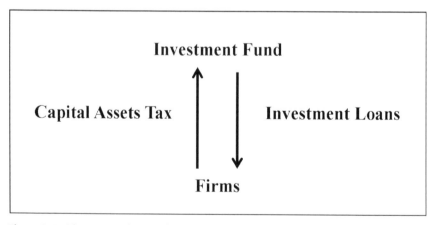

Figure 3.1   Flows To and From the Investment Fund

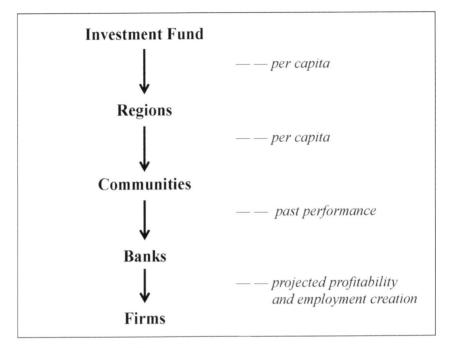

Figure 3.2   Investment Allocation Criteria

(It should be noted that there is considerable countervailing power in the system to prevent "excessive" public spending—most immediately, from the enterprises that might want to apply for bank funding, and more generally, from most citizens, who know that a thriving community requires thriving local businesses. Democratically accountable legislative bodies must weigh the benefits to their constituents of more public spending against the need for market-sector development. There would seem to be no systematic bias here one way or the other.)

We now have before us the basic structure of "social control of investment." To summarize: A flat-rate tax on the capital assets of all productive enterprises is collected by the central government, all of which is plowed back into the economy, assisting those firms needing funds for purposes of productive investment. These funds are dispersed throughout society, first to regions and communities on a per capita basis, then to public banks in accordance with past performance, then to those firms with profitable project proposals. Profitable projects that promise increased employment and/or further other democratically decided goals are favored over those that do not. At each level—national, regional, and local—legislatures decide what portion

---

Figure 3.3   Investment Fund Decisions

The National Legislature
- Determines the capital assets tax rate.
- Decides how much of the investment fund is to be used for capital spending on public projects national in scope. (The rest is allocated to the regions.)

Regional Legislatures
- Decide how much of their portion of the investment fund is to be used for capital spending on public projects regional in scope. (The rest is allocated to their communities.)

Local Legislatures
- Decide how much of their portion of the investment fund is to be used for capital spending on public projects in their communities. (The rest is allocated to their banks.)

Banks
- Decide which loan requests from existing local firms to honor.
- Decide which new enterprise proposals to fund.

---

of the investment fund coming to them is to be set aside for public capital expenditures, then send down the remainder, no strings attached, to the next lower level. Associated with most banks are entrepreneurial divisions, which promote firm expansion and new firm creation. Figures 3.1, 3.2, and 3.3 offer a schematic presentation of this summary.

A final observation: The simplified schema just presented has only local banks making grants to local enterprises. Large enterprises that operate regionally or nationally might need access to additional capital, in which case it would be appropriate for the network of local investment banks to be supplemented by regional and national investment banks. These would also be public institutions that receive their funds from the national investment fund.

3.2 The Viability of Economic Democracy

Worker self-management extends democracy to the workplace. Apart from being good in itself, this extension of democracy aims at enhancing a firm's internal efficiency. The market also aims at efficiency, and acts to counter the bureaucratic overcentralization that plagued earlier forms of socialism. Social control of new investment is the counterfoil to the market, counteracting the instability and other irrational consequences of an overextended market—what Marx calls the "anarchy" of capitalist production.

"Well and good," the skeptic will say, "but will it work? Will an economy structured around workplace democracy and social control of investment be an efficient, dynamic economy, or will it soon fall apart, as did the other socialist experiments of this century—including the Yugoslav experiment in worker self-managed socialism—to which Economic Democracy bears a strong resemblance?"

This is a fair question—even if some of the background assumptions are wrong. Not all the socialist experiments of this century have collapsed. China, Cuba, and Vietnam endure—and will continue to survive (I believe), however problematic the socialist character of their economies becomes. (More on this in chapter 6.) It isn't clear, either, that Soviet-model economies had to collapse. That they were in urgent need of structural reform cannot be doubted, but a case could be made that reforms that moved in the direction of Economic Democracy would have been vastly preferable to the reforms actually undertaken. A decade after the collapse of communism, there were only one or two countries of the region whose income levels had reached those achieved before the collapse, and in all of these postcommunist countries the levels of inequality and poverty were much higher than before. In Russia itself, the human catastrophe that followed capitalist reforms is hard to exaggerate. (Joseph Stiglitz, Nobel laureate economist and former chief economist of the World Bank, reported in 1999 that "for eighteen of the twenty-five countries [of Eastern Europe and the former Soviet Union] poverty on average has increased from 4 percent to 45 percent of the population . . . and life expectancy in these countries on average has fallen even while world life expectancy has risen by two years."[7]) Even now, two decades after the collapse of communism, the per capita income of the Central and Eastern European countries is only a third of the per capita income of the "advanced economies" (G7), essentially what it was in 1989.[8]

We should also be wary of a historical amnesia that blinds us to the actual accomplishments of these first experiments in socialism. Central planning—however badly done and brutally enforced—moved Russia, in less than half a century, from being the most backward country in Europe to the ranks of a global superpower. Chinese socialism, with minimal external assistance, raised more people from abject poverty to relative prosperity in a shorter period of time than any form of capitalism has ever done. (Life expectancy in China was thirty-five in 1949; it is seventy-three today.) The Yugoslav experiment in worker self-management sustained for three decades one of the highest rates of growth in the world, vastly improving the average standard of living, and producing a vibrant intellectual culture. Cuba, on its own today, relentlessly squeezed and blockaded by the United States, continues to record social indicators of health and education of first-world order.

We must be careful in drawing facile lessons from history, negative or positive. Economic Democracy is a different form of socialism from what was initially tried. The first attempt at constructing a socialist economy abolished the market and substituted centralized planning. Economic Democracy is a market economy with workplace democracy and social control of investment. We need to ask what the historical record and empirical data tell us about the viability of these structures.

First, some theoretical considerations. Economic Democracy, like capitalism but unlike Soviet-model socialism, is a competitive economy. Firms compete with one another in selling their products to consumers, so the basic incentive structure is right. An enterprise has a clear incentive to (a) ascertain and produce what consumers want, (b) avoid wasting raw materials, (c) employ the most cost-effective technology, (d) stay abreast of technological change, and (e) be constantly on the lookout for better products, better technologies, and better ways of organizing production. Economic Democracy retains the incentive structure of a market economy, the structure that gives capitalism its efficiency strengths.

"But," it will surely be asked, "will a worker-managed firm respond to these incentives as well as a capitalist firm? Are workers competent enough to make complicated technical and financial decisions? Are they competent enough even to elect representatives who will appoint effective managers?" I can't resist remarking on how curious it is that these questions are so quickly raised (as in my experience they always are) in a society that prides itself on its democratic commitment. We deem ordinary people competent enough to select mayors, governors, even presidents. We regard them as capable of selecting legislators who will decide their taxes, who will make the laws that, if violated, consign them to prison, and who can send them off, the younger ones, to kill and die in war. Should we really ask if ordinary people are competent enough to elect their bosses?

It's a question that has to be asked. The issue is too fundamental to pass over lightly. After all, workers in democratic capitalist societies do not elect their bosses. Perhaps they are not competent enough. Perhaps managers will be reluctant to impose discipline if they are subject to election, or less inclined to exert themselves fully, since they must share profits with workers. Perhaps the time and effort associated with democratic decision making will cut too deeply into productive work time. Perhaps the process will lead to worker frustration, increased alienation, and incoherent policies. Might not economic chaos result, or, if not chaos, at least a precipitous decline in efficiency?

In fact, we can respond to these doubts with empirical findings that are as unambiguous as one would dare hope, given the complexity and significance of the issue. There is overwhelming evidence, based on scores of studies of thousands of examples, that both worker participation in management and profit sharing tend to enhance productivity, and that worker-run enterprises are almost never less productive than their capitalist counterparts. They are often more so.

As to the efficiency effects of greater worker participation, an HEW study in 1973 concludes, "In no instance of which we have evidence has a major effort to increase employee participation resulted in a long-term decline in productivity." Nine years later, surveying their empirical studies, Derek Jones and Jan Svejnar report, "There is apparently consistent support for the view that worker participation in management causes higher productivity. This result is supported by a variety of methodological approaches, using diverse data and for disparate time periods." In 1990, a collection of research papers edited by Princeton economist Alan Blinder extends the data set much further and reaches the same conclusion: worker participation usually enhances productivity in the short run, sometimes in the long run, and rarely has a negative effect. Moreover, participation is most conducive to enhancing productivity when combined with profit sharing, guaranteed long-range employment, relatively narrow wage differentials, and guaranteed worker rights (such as protection from dismissal except for just cause)—precisely the conditions that will prevail under Economic Democracy.[9]

As to the viability of complete workplace democracy, we note that workers in the plywood cooperatives in the Pacific Northwest have been electing their managers since the 1940s, workers in the Mondragon cooperatives in Spain since the 1950s. There are some ten thousand producer-cooperatives in Italy, comprising one of the most vibrant sectors of the economy.[10] Needless to say, not all self-management ventures are successful, but I know of no empirical study that even purports to demonstrate that worker-elected managers are less competent than their capitalist counterparts. Most comparisons suggest the opposite; most find worker self-managed firms more productive than similarly situated capitalist firms. For example, Katrina Berman, on the plywood cooperatives, states:

> The major basis for co-operative success, and for survival of capitalistically unprofitable plants, has been superior labour productivity. Studies comparing square-foot output have repeatedly shown higher physical volume of output per hour, and others . . . show higher quality of product and also economy of material use.[11]

Hendrick Thomas on Mondragon:

> Productivity and profitability are higher for cooperatives than for capitalist firms. It makes little difference whether the Mondragon group is compared with the largest 500 companies, or with small- or medium-scale industries; in both comparisons the Mondragon group is more productive and more profitable.[12]

Will Bartlett, John Cable, Saul Estrin, and Derek Jones on the Italian cooperatives:

> Our matched sample of 85 firms in Tuscany and Emilia-Romagna has provided rich evidence on the comparative behavior, organization and performance of cooperative and private-ownership enterprises. . . . Although the range of observation is restricted to the region of Emiglia-Romagna, there is strong evidence that Italian producer cooperatives achieve higher levels of both labor and capital productivity than comparable private firms.[13]

The negative example of Yugoslavia? Not even Harold Lydall, one of the most severe pro-capitalist critics of the pre-1989 Yugoslav economic system, argues that worker incompetence at selecting managers was the problem. Lydall acknowledges that for most of the period from 1950 to 1979, Yugoslavia not only survived but prospered. Things changed, much for the worse, in the 1980s. How does he account for this precipitous decline?

> It is evident that the principal cause of failure was the unwillingness of the Yugoslav Party and government to implement a policy of macroscopic restriction—especially restriction of the money supply—in combination with a microeconomic policy designed to expand opportunities and incentives for enterprise and efficient work. *What was needed was more freedom for independent decision-making by genuinely self-managed enterprises within a free market,* combined with tight controls on the supply of domestic currency.[14]

The problem in Yugoslavia was not an excess of workplace democracy. In the judgment of one Belgrade newspaper (as summarized by Lydall), "The most convincing explanation for the present social crisis is the *reduction of the self-management rights of workers.*"[15]

It is not really so surprising that worker self-managed enterprises are efficient. Because their incomes are tied directly to the financial health of the enterprise, all workers have an interest in selecting good managers. Since bad management is not hard to detect by those near at hand, who observe at close range the nature of that management and feel its effects rather quickly, incompetence is not usually long tolerated. Moreover, individuals have an interest in seeing to it that coworkers work effectively and in not appearing to be slackers themselves, so less supervision is necessary. As one expert has noted, based on his seven years of field study:

> There exist both personal and collective incentives in cooperatives that are likely to lead to higher productivity. The specific consequences of these incentives are that the workers in cooperatives will tend to work harder and in a more flexible manner than those in capitalist firms; they will have a lower turnover rate and absenteeism; and they will take better care of plant and equipment. In addition, producer cooperatives function with relatively few unskilled workers and middle managers, experience fewer bottlenecks in production and have more efficient training programs than do capitalist firms.[16]

I do not mean to suggest here that workplace democracy is the miracle cure for economic malaise. Efficiency gains are not always dramatic. Not all cooperatives succeed. Failure is often painful—as is the failure of a capitalist firm. Nevertheless, the evidence strongly suggests that worker self-managed firms are at least as internally efficient as capitalist firms. Indeed, all else equal, worker self-managed firms tend to be more efficient than their capitalist counterparts. Of course all else is not always equal. Capitalist firms may have better access to finance than cooperatives, and may employ profit-enhancing strategies that are not available to democratic firms. (They may intensify the pace of work for their employees without raising their pay. They may outsource work to companies that pay their workers much less for doing the same work. These factors do not enhance the technical efficiency of an enterprise, but they give such an enterprise a competitive advantage vis-à-vis a comparable democratic firm.)

Two key elements of Economic Democracy—worker self-management and the market—"work." The evidence leaves little room for doubt.[17] What about social control of investment? Since no such investment mechanism as the one I have described has been put into place anywhere, it is impossible to be as certain about the efficacy of this institution. There are no economic studies to cite. Here we must proceed differently. We must ask about the specific parts of the mechanism.

Is it possible to raise investment funds by taxation rather than by private savings? Of course it is. In all advanced capitalist societies, a large portion is already raised that way. The investments government makes in infrastructure, office buildings, schools, equipment for basic research, to say nothing of the military-industrial complex, come from tax-generated funds.

Could the entire investment fund for a nation be generated by a capital assets tax? Of course it could. The tax is simply a flat-rate property tax applied to businesses. Uniform accounting procedures would have to be adopted, and regular audits undertaken, but these are hardly insurmountable difficulties.

Wouldn't this tax be so high that it would force many businesses into bankruptcy? No—because this is not really an *additional* tax that enterprises have to pay. It is a tax that substitutes for existing "taxes." Since there are no stockholders of the firm, there is no one to whom the enterprise must pay dividends. These dividend payments, which can be thought of as an enterprise "tax" under capitalism, are eliminated under Economic Democracy, as are the interest payments that companies now pay to bondholders and private banks. In essence, that portion of a company's profit that, under capitalism, would be paid out as dividends or interest to private individuals now goes directly into the investment fund, and is then recycled back into the economy—without the mediation of capitalist middlemen. Instead of paying interest and dividends to private individuals, who (we hope) will reinvest most of them, companies make their payments directly to a public institution that injects them (all of them) back into the economy.

I think it fair to conclude that there are no conceptual difficulties or serious practical obstacles that preclude generating society's investment fund by means of a capital assets tax instead of relying on private savings. To be sure, there are powerful, entrenched, special interests that can be counted on to resist any move toward a more rational system, but that is a separate issue, to which we will later attend. (Powerful, entrenched, feudal interests resisted the reforms proposed by the rising capitalist class. Powerful, entrenched interests don't always win.)

Relying on a capital assets tax would be at least as efficient as relying on private savings to generate funds for capital investment. It would probably be more efficient. Not only would the private consumption of the capitalist middlemen be eliminated, but society would now have direct control over the quantity of funds to be invested. If funds are insufficient relative to demand, the tax can be raised. If funds are excessive, the tax can be lowered. Authorities would no longer have to cajole people into saving more, or try to manipulate their behavior by raising or lowering interest rates—indirect procedures of only moderate effectiveness, as central banks are well aware.

The second part of Economic Democracy's investment mechanism is more controversial. Economic Democracy does not rely solely on market criteria to determine capital allocation. Investment funds do not automatically flow to where financial opportunities seem to be the greatest. Instead, an ethical criterion is imposed from the start: each region of the country gets its "fair share" (per capita) of the investment fund.

Neoclassical economists will object: if capital flows are restricted, the outcome cannot be optimally efficient. They will draw the curves to prove it. This objection should not be taken seriously, since it is a disciplinary reflex, not a well-considered judgment. Such economists remember the beautiful theorems proving capitalist efficiency, but they tend to forget how extravagant and un-realistic the assumptions are upon which the efficiency theorems are based: perfect information on the part of producers as to present and future prices and technologies, perfect information on the part of consumers as to current and future tastes and preferences, no externalities of production or consumption, and so forth. The neoclassical faith in the ultimate efficiency of free capital flows is simply that: an act of faith. It has no scientific warrant. As Keynes liked to stress, there is simply too much primary uncertainty involved in making investment decisions to expect optimal efficiency to prevail as the unplanned, uncoordinated outcome of private, self-seeking judgments.

> Enterprise only pretends to itself to be mainly actuated by the statements in its own prospectus, however candid and sincere. Only a little more than an expedition to the South Pole is it based on an exact calculation of benefits to come.[18]

In reality, all capitalist economies interfere to some degree with the free flow of capital, some much more so than others. Japan, particularly during the postwar "miracle years," was quite heavy-handed in directing capital into certain sectors of the economy and into certain industries, while making it harder to get in others. South Korea followed a similar path with equally impressive results. It takes a mighty faith indeed to maintain that Japanese or Korean development would have been more rapid or more equitable or more efficient had market forces been given untrammeled freedom. As Nobel laureate economist Amartya Sen has noted,

> It is remarkable that if we look at the sizable developing countries, the fast growing and otherwise high-performing countries have all had governments that have been directly and actively involved in the planning of economic and social performance. . . . Their respective successes are directly linked to deliberation and design, rather than being just the results of uncoordinated profit seeking or atomistic pursuit of self-interest.[19]

Even if it is conceded (as it must be) that governmental interference with the "natural" flow of capital can sometimes produce better results than the invisible hand, it doesn't follow that the specific mechanisms of Economic Democracy will have such a happy outcome. To make the case that they will, we have to examine such concrete issues as unemployment, inequality, the quality and rate of economic growth, and so forth, and see which system is more likely to deal effectively with these problems. That will occupy us in chapters 4 and 5. For now, let me simply point out that there are no obvious reasons for thinking that Economic Democracy's mechanism for allocating investment funds will not work. In fact, there are at least four consequences of Economic Democracy's allocation procedure that would seem to favor it over the capitalist alternative:

- National development is likely to be more harmonious. If market criteria alone dictate the flow of capital, regional inequalities tend to grow rather than shrink. Capital flows to where the action is. Rich regions tend to get richer, poor regions poorer. Economic Democracy interferes with this "natural" tendency, directing capital to each region in proportion to population.
- Communities are likely to be more stable under Economic Democracy. If markets alone determine capital allocation, people will feel the pressure to move to those parts of the country where job opportunities are greater—those parts, that is, into which capital is flowing. The young, talented, and energetic will be among the first to go—not a good thing for community stability.
- One can expect community life to be richer. If communities are guaranteed an annual influx of capital, to be used for economic development, more people are likely to want to be involved in local politics, since there is more scope now for positive vision.
- Neither communities, regions, nor the nation as whole need worry about capital flight, since the investment capital of the nation, publicly generated, is mandated by law to be returned to the regions and communities that comprise the nation. Vulnerability to the sorts of macroeconomic instability brought about by the rapid flows of finance capital into or out of a region or into or out of the country itself is eliminated completely.

The drawbacks? Perhaps some allocation inefficiencies. Perhaps some bad decisions as to how a community should use the share of capital it receives. Perhaps some corruption—pressure put on bank officials to make inappropriate loans, perhaps some bribery. But there are plenty of allocation inefficiencies, bad investment decisions, and financial corruption under capitalism. It is hard to see why these features would be worse under Economic Democracy, let alone so much worse as to offset the clear advantages.

3.3 The Mondragon Experiment

The case for the viability of Economic Democracy would seem to be strong. We know that workplace democracy works. The evidence is solid. We know that investment funds can be generated by taxation instead of from private savings. This cannot be doubted. And it would seem that allocating these funds in such a way that market criteria are invoked only late in the process, rather than from the beginning, promises egalitarian and stability gains. Of course there will be lingering doubts. We can't point (yet) to the great historical experiment where these institutions have been implemented on a national level. We can, however, point to a smaller scale version of something that looks very much like Economic Democracy. Although little known to the world at large, it is an experiment that, in my view, is of world-historic importance.

Here is the story in a nutshell.[20] In 1943, Don José Maria Arizmendiarrieta, a local priest who had barely escaped execution by Franco's forces during the Spanish Civil War, established a school for working-class boys in a small town in the Basque region of Spain. The "red priest," as he was called in conservative circles, was a man with a large vision. Believing that God gives almost all people equal potential and dismayed that not a single working-class youth from Mondragon had ever attended a university, Fr. Arizmendiarrieta structured his school to promote technical expertise as well as "social and spiritual values." Eleven members of his first class (of twenty) went on to become professional engineers. In 1956, five of these and eighteen other workers set up, at the priest's urging, a cooperative factory to make small cookers and stoves. In 1958, a second cooperative was established, to make machine tools. In 1959, again at Arizmendiarrieta's instigation, a cooperative bank was established. This proved to be a decisive innovation. The bank became the hub of the cooperative sector, providing capital and technical expertise to existing cooperatives wanting to expand and to new cooperatives willing to affiliate with it. It even developed an "entrepreneurial division" that researched new production and marketing possibilities and encouraged the setting up of new cooperatives.

The Mondragon complex spread beyond the town of Mondragon itself. It also developed a host of support structures: a technical university, research institutes, a social security organization, and a network of consumer outlets. The initial experiment, a worker-owned factory making kerosene cookers, has developed since 1956 into a system of more than a hundred enterprises, including eighty industrial cooperatives making home appliances, agricultural equipment, automobile components, machine tools, industrial robots, generators, numerical control systems, thermoplastics, medical equipment, home and office equipment, and much more. In 1991 (fifteen years after Arizmendiarrieta's death), these cooperatives, always linked via the bank, combined formally to form the Mondragon Corporación Cooperativa (MCC). MCC includes not only producer and construction cooperatives, but also a bank (Caja Laboral), two general technology centers (Ikerlan and Ideko), ten corporate R&D centers, an "Innovation Park" specializing in micro- and nanotechnologies (Garaia), a social security service (Lagun Aro), a network of retail "hypermarkets" throughout Spain (Eroski), and several educational institutions (Mondragon University, Politeknika, Otalora, and others).

Today, MCC is the dominant economic power in the Basque region of Spain. MCC's capital goods division is the market leader in metal-cutting tools in all of Spain, as is the division that makes refrigerators, washing machines, and dishwashers. MCC engineers have built "turnkey" factories in China, North Africa, the Middle East, and Latin America. (MCC now has seventy-five production plants abroad, including two in the United States.) The Eroski group is now the third-largest retail food chain in Spain (the only one of the top four controlled by Spanish interests). Caja Laboral has been rated as being among the top 100 most efficient financial institutions in the world in terms of its profit/assets ratio. Ikerlan is the only Spanish research firm to have met the NASA technical specifications and hence permitted a project on the space shuttle *Columbia* in 1993. Mondragon University, enrolling 3,000 students, is considered by many to be the best technical institute in Spain. All in all, MCC now has a workforce of 85,000 (up from 43,000 in 2000), annual sales of $19.4 billion (up from $6.6 billion in 2000), and assets of over $43 billion (up from $13 billion in 2000).[21]

MCC has grown rapidly since its inception, but not for reasons of profit maximization. One of its central missions is job creation, which it takes very seriously. (Hence its setting up of subsidiaries abroad is never at the expense of domestic workers. Setting up such subsidiaries is done with the explicit intent of preserving or enhancing domestic employment.[22])

A principle of solidarity also operates among member coops. When an enterprise has to cut back production, an attempt is made to transfer workers to other cooperatives within the system rather than simply laying them off, and solidarity funds are made available to companies to help them through bad times.

Sometimes, of course, layoffs are unavoidable, particularly during a generalized economic downturn. Here is how one of the Mondragon cooperatives handled layoffs occasioned by the current economic crisis:

> After three days of meetings, the worker/owners agreed that 20 percent of the workforce would leave their jobs for a year, during which they would continue to receive 80 percent of their pay, and, if they wished, free training for other work. This group would be chosen by lottery, and, if the company was still in trouble a year later, the first group would return to work, and the second would take a year off.[23]

MCC has been weathering the global economic storm (which has hit Spain particularly hard) rather well. Profits were up 6 percent in 2008, as was job creation. MCC remained profitable in 2009 ($80 billion), although profits were down (from $94 billion the year before), and, for the first time since

Mondragon's inception, so was total employment. But, overall, the company remains strong, with total employment nearly double what it was a decade ago.

It should also be noted that not all parts of MCC are cooperatives. Most of the businesses set up outside the Basque region and all the enterprises set up abroad are noncooperative subsidiaries of MCC. In January 2009, however, Eroski's General Assembly approved a plan to turn all of its retail stores into cooperatives. (When Spain joined the European Union, MCC, to be able to compete with the European retail giants, bought up supermarkets throughout Spain. It was decided at the time that it would be impractical to turn these all into cooperatives. But now democratic rights are being extended to all Eroski workers, some 45,000 in all.)

In sum: we have here a corporation, comparable in size and technological sophistication to a dynamic capitalist multinational firm, that has an internal structure radically different from a capitalist corporation. This worker-owned, worker-managed "cooperative corporation" is in essence a federation of cooperatives, each of which is wholly owned by its workforce. The workers of each cooperative meet at an annual general assembly to elect a board of directors, which then appoints the cooperative's management and selects delegates to the MCC Congress. These delegates, some 350 in all, then meet to pass judgment on the strategic plan for MCC presented by a congress board, whose twenty-two members include the division heads of MCC (the member cooperatives are grouped into divisions) plus representatives of the special institutions (the bank, the research organizations, and so forth).

All of the cooperatives are bound by the provisions of this plan. Individual cooperatives are free to dissolve their contract of association with MCC if they so desire, and hence opt out of the plan, but only two have ever done so. In general, the benefits of belonging far outweigh the restrictions—wage scales, allowable income differentials, percent of profits to be reinvested in the corporation or in the community—imposed on a cooperative's autonomy.

It is beyond dispute that the Mondragon "experiment" has been *economically* successful, even in the face of the greatly intensified competition to which it has been subjected following Spain's admittance into the European Union. For insight as to *why* Mondragon has done so well, it is worth considering the *values and vision* that animated Arizmendiarrieta and his early disciples.

The Mondragon complex did not develop as a purely pragmatic response to local conditions. Arizmendiarrieta was deeply concerned about social justice and explicitly critical of capitalism, basing his critique on progressive Catholic social doctrine, the socialist tradition, and the philosophy of "personalism" developed by Monier, Maritain, and other French Catholic philosophers. He was likewise critical of Soviet state socialism and of certain elements of the cooperative movement itself. He was particularly sensitive to the danger of a cooperative becoming simply a "collective egoist" concerned only with the well-being of its membership. From the beginning, Arizmendi-arrieta insisted that a cooperative corporation must have a larger goal: "Our goal is more than simple options for individual improvement. It is more. If the cooperative enterprise does not serve for more, the world of work has the right to spit in our faces."[24]

The external goal most explicitly and operationally incorporated by the Mondragon complex has been employment creation. A capitalist firm typically aims at maximizing profits—employment creation is accidental. Indeed, when cutting labor costs becomes a central focus, job creation may conflict with profitability. (To give but one example: General Electric tripled its revenues and profits between 1985 and 2000, while shrinking its employment worldwide from 435,000 to 220,000.) In Mondragon, employment creation has always been a primary goal, with structures put in place to advance that goal. Specifically, the Caja Laboral has not only provided funds for expansion and new cooperative creation but also, for many years, it housed an "entrepreneurial division" to research market opportunities and to provide technical assistance to workers wanting to set up cooperatives. (This entrepreneurial function has since been taken over by a research center [SAIOLAN] specifically devoted to developing both entrepreneurial talent and high-technology new businesses.)

"Community" is also a central value. Businesses have obligations that extend beyond their membership. In Arizmendiarrieta's words,

> Cooperatives have a community dimension, which obliges them not only to give satisfaction to their own membership, but also to fulfill a social function through its structures. We must consider that the enterprise is not only our property, and therefore we have only the use of it. Calculations cannot be thought of as exclusively pleasing the membership, but rather of serving to fulfill more perfectly the mission that society has confided in us.[25]

Does MCC still abide by the ethos of its founder? So as not to paint too rosy a picture of what is, after all, a real-world experiment involving finite and fallible human beings, we should attend to the critics. One such is Sharryn Kasmir, an American anthropologist who spent eighteen months in Mondragon. She entitled her book, based on her field research, *The Myth of Mondragon.*[26]

What myth does Kasmir want to debunk? First, let us be clear as to what is not mythical about Mondragon. Kasmir does not deny that the Mondragon cooperatives have been economically successful. Moreover, the Mondragon cooperatives have succeeded in the face of severe regional economic difficulties. Between 1976 and 1986, for example, the Basque region lost 150,000 jobs, during which time the cooperatives increased employment by 4,200. The early 1990s saw another deep recession, official unemployment reaching 25 percent in the region. This time, the industrial cooperatives were hit, and employment fell from 17,000 in 1991 to less than 15,000 in 2000. Still, overall employment in MCC did not decline. (In 2009 there were 36,500 workers in the industrial sector, more than twice as many as there had been in 2000.) It remains rare for a cooperator in Mondragon to lose work altogether, because cutbacks tend to be effected through reassignment to other cooperatives and nonreplacement of retirees.

Therefore, what is mythical about Mondragon is neither its economic success nor the employment security the cooperatives provide. It is not a myth, either, that Mondragon cooperatives are more egalitarian than their capitalist counterparts, or that Mondragon workers can exert some real control over conditions that affect them. Kasmir notes that the highest-level engineers in Mondragon firms make 30 percent less than comparably skilled engineers employed by capitalist firms in the province. She observes that class differences were not nearly as extreme in the cooperative firm she selected for comparative study as in its capitalist counterpart. She points out that attempts by management to widen the allowable pay differential between the lowest and highest paid (1 to 4.5 in most enterprises) have often been defeated by workers. Workers also voted against (and hence defeated) a management proposal to cut their common four-week August vacation to two weeks with the other two weeks assigned at other times (so as to be able to keep production going fifty weeks per year).

Kasmir acknowledges that Basque labor unions have been reluctant to criticize the cooperatives, since, in the words of one labor leader "the cooperatives [are] valuable national resources, capital that is tied to Euskadi [the Basque region of Spain]. Since the cooperators are owners, they have to vote to approve the movement of capital out of Euskadi. That would be a vote to lose their own jobs, to create unemployment. They wouldn't do it."[27]

On gender issues, there is also a difference between the cooperatives and the capitalist firms in the region. Although not many, there are more women in management positions in cooperative firms than in their capitalist counterparts. Moreover, "in my experience," Kasmir reports, "the issue of gender was debated and taken seriously in the cooperatives in a way that it was not in regular firms."[28]

If Mondragon is as good as Kasmir herself describes, what is wrong with it? What exactly is the myth? The most significant myth Kasmir wants to dispel is the image of a workplace in which everyone regards one another as equals, where workers are happy with their work, and where workers actively participate in daily decision making. Mondragon is often portrayed as an alternative to class struggle and to socialism. Kasmir objects. She notes that one often hears "we're all workers here"—but only when talking to managers. In her comparative survey, in answer to the question, "do you feel you are working as if the firm is yours?" nearly 80 percent of the cooperative manual workers said "no"—a slightly higher percentage than those at the private firm. (Interestingly, managers of cooperative firms identified with their firms far more than did their private-enterprise counterparts. Fully half of the private managers did not feel a part of the firm, whereas only 18 percent of the cooperative managers felt so alienated. Mondragon's success in garnering management loyalty is no small thing; it is doubtless an important factor in explaining the success of the Mondragon cooperatives.)

As Kasmir admits, her sample size was not large, so one must be careful about drawing sweeping conclusions. One should certainly not draw the conclusion that workers are indifferent to the cooperative nature of their firm: only 10 percent of the workers surveyed by Kasmir said they would prefer to work in a privately run enterprise. These results are consistent with a conversation I had with a Mondragon worker when I visited the complex in 1995. The worker had expressed a certain cynicism about the ideals of the Mondragon experiment. "People once took them seriously, but not anymore," she remarked.

"You mean it doesn't matter to you, whether you work here or at a private company?" I asked.

"Of course it matters," she replied. "Here I have job security, and here I can vote."

It must be acknowledged that Mondragon has not wholly resolved the problem of alienated labor. It cannot be expected to do so, so long as it remains a cooperative island in a capitalist sea—an increasingly competitive sea at that. Neither can it be expected to forego completely other mechanisms regularly used by its capitalist competitors: the use of part-time and temporary wage labor, and investing part of its profits in high-return capitalist enterprises, some of them in poor countries. Being more efficient is not always enough because capitalist firms can also avail themselves of other means for enhancing profitability, means that have to do with increasing exploitation rather than technical productivity. (Paying workers less for the same work increases profitability but not productivity.)

The presence of worker alienation and of certain practices that cut against the grain of Arizmendiarrieta's vision should not blind us to two striking lessons that can be drawn from the economic success of Mondragon. First, enterprises, even when highly sophisticated, can be structured democratically without any loss of efficiency. Even a large enterprise, comparable in size to a multinational corporation, can be given a democratic structure.

Second, an efficient and economically dynamic sector can flourish without capitalists. Capitalists do not manage the Mondragon cooperatives. Capitalists do not supply entrepreneurial talent. Capitalists do not supply the capital for the development of new enterprises or the expansion of existing ones. But these three functions—managing enterprises, engaging in entrepreneurial activities, and supplying capital—are the only functions the capitalist class has ever performed. The Mondragon record strongly suggests that we don't need capitalists anymore—which is the central thesis of this book.

3.4 A Note on the Public Sector

This book concentrates on one part of the economic structure of a viable socialism—those institutions that allocate investment funds and those that utilize such funds to produce goods and services for sale in a competitive market. In chapters 4 and 5, I compare them in their consequences to capitalist institutions and defend their superiority. Very little is said during any of these discussions about those goods and services that will be provided to the citizenry outside the market, notably, child care, education, health care, care for the disabled and care for the elderly. Although the socialist tradition has long insisted that such amenities be offered to all citizens on the basis of need, not ability to pay, the provision of such services, free or at nominal charge, no longer serves to distinguish socialism from capitalism, since many, although certainly not all, advanced capitalist societies do just that. (In almost all cases, such services were introduced under pressure from strong labor movements to head off their more radical demands. Social democratic reforms are not "natural" to capitalism. Not surprisingly, now that globalization has substantially weakened organized labor, efforts are underway everywhere to cut back on public social services.)

I will not offer a detailed specification of the public sector institutions that would be present in any real-world instantiation of Economic Democracy. Economic Democracy will have learned from the experiences of those capitalist countries that have been most successful in providing their citizens with universal health care, quality child care, free education, decent retirement benefits, and the like, and will adopt, perhaps with slight modification, their programs.

Since human solidarity is perhaps the most fundamental of socialist principles, we can expect Economic Democracy to embrace the principle of *intergenerational solidarity*. This may be understood as follows: A citizen regards all the children of his society as being, in an important sense, his own children, and all the elderly as being his parents. (Philosophers will hear an echo from Plato's *Republic* here.) It is reasonable to think in such terms, for, in point of fact, each person born into a humane society is cared for and educated by many members of the older generation, not simply her biological parents, and each must be cared for by members of the younger generation when her generation retires from the labor force. To be sure, biological or other legally recognized parents of children have special rights and responsibilities regarding their biological or adopted children, as do children regarding their legal parents, but it remains the responsibility of each citizen to see to it that no child or older person is neglected.

Regarding children, this principle implies, minimally, that:

- Prenatal and child-rearing classes be made available, free of charge, to all parents.
- Quality day care be available, free of charge, to all parents who require such assistance. (For parents who choose to remove themselves from the paid workforce to care for their children at home, a child care tax rebate might be in order. One mechanism that might be employed: all parents of preschool-aged children receive "vouchers"—government-issued certificates denominated in dollars—which can be used to pay for certified day care, or, if not used for that purpose, applied to the family's tax obligations.)
- All children have free access to quality primary and secondary education. (Note: Socialist principles do not preclude providing parents with vouchers to be used at "private" schools. There are two basic rationales for private education. It is sometimes maintained that competition among schools enhances the quality of education. I doubt that this is true, but if a community wishes to try the experiment, it should be free to do so. Market socialism is not opposed to competition. The second rationale concerns religious education. If a society's constitution prohibits the teaching of religion in public schools, it seems not unreasonable to provide those parents who wish to send their children to religious schools with tuition vouchers. There is nothing "antisocialist" about providing free education for all our children.)

Regarding care for the elderly, the principle of intergenerational solidarity points to a "pay as you go" social security system. That is to say, younger people currently working should pay, via their income or consumption taxes, what is required to maintain in dignity those who can no longer work, or who, even if able, have worked long enough and have chosen to retire. That is to say, everyone in society should come under a public pension plan that is funded by general tax revenues.

"Pay as you go" is usually contrasted with systems in which workers, during their productive years, set aside a portion of their paychecks via mandatory social security deductions and/or voluntary contributions to their pension funds so that, when they retire, they can take care of themselves. In a fundamental sense, this distinction is illusory. If we think in terms of material resources, it is clear that *all* social security systems are "pay as you go," because, however pensions and annuities are structured, the material fact is, people who are currently working must produce the goods and services consumed by those who no longer work. It is more honest—and ultimately fairer—for the older generation to acknowledge frankly their dependency on the younger generation than to pretend to be independent—just as that younger generations should acknowledge the fact that their current independence (such as it is) was made possible by an older generation that cared for them for the first two decades or so of their lives.

3.5 Economic Democracy: The Expanded Model

A genuine "right to work" has long been a basic tenet of socialism. Every able-bodied person who wants to work should be able to find decent employment. As we shall see in chapter 4, a capitalist economy cannot, for structural reasons, be a full-employment economy. The basic structures of Economic Democracy do not preclude full employment—but they don't guarantee it either. Hence the need for a supplementary institution that ensures this basic socialist right.

It would be useful to add two more components to the basic, simplified model, components currently existing under capitalism. These institutions may not be necessary to a well-functioning economy, but the citizens of the country might want to retain them anyway, perhaps because they enhance the scope of individual choice and or provide some additional economic benefits. Properly structured, these institutions will not conflict with the basic structure of Economic Democracy or undermine the ethical principles that underlie the system.

Our "expanded model" of Economic Democracy adds three components to the basic model:

- The government as employer-of-last-resort
- Cooperative savings-and-loan associations
- Some private ownership of means of production and some legalized wage labor—that is, some capitalism under socialism

3.5.1 The Government as Employer-of-Last-Resort

Involuntary unemployment is deeply destructive to a person's sense of self-worth and self-respect. If you are alive, other people have worked, and are working, for you. Other people are growing the food you eat, making the clothes you wear, have built the dwelling in which you reside (even if it is only a homeless shelter). Other people are working for you, but you are giving nothing back. If you search for but cannot find employment, society is in effect saying to you, "There is nothing you can do that we want or need. We may, out of compassion, deign to keep you alive, but you are in fact a parasite, living off the labor of others, contributing nothing in return." Is it any wonder that prolonged unemployment breeds social pathologies?

A decent society will see to it that every adult who wants to work can have a job. Citizens will have a genuine "right to work." In Economic Democracy the government will serve as an employer-of-last-resort. It will guarantee a meaningful job to anyone able and willing to work. These jobs will pay an established minimum wage. They will be funded by the central government, but the jobs themselves will be created mostly by regional and local governments in accordance with local needs. Examples of such possible jobs: elder care, child care, playground supervision, caring for parks and other public spaces, nonhazardous environmental cleanup, and low-tech improvement of energy efficiency. On-the-job training will be provided.

3.5.2 Socialist Savings and Loan Associations

In principle, the payment of interest can be abolished under Economic Democracy. Since the economy no longer relies on private savings to generate investment capital, it has no need for the mechanisms that have developed under capitalism to encourage private savings. The economy can function quite well without any private savings at all.

Individuals may still save, but the well-being of the economy as a whole no longer depends on their doing so. Their own individual well-being does not depend on personal savings either. In keeping with the basic principle of intergenerational solidarity, a publicly funded social security system provides all retired persons with decent incomes. People may still want to save, but they don't have to. In any event, they don't need to be paid interest on their savings.

However, instead of eliminating interest altogether, it would not be unreasonable for an Economic Democracy to allow a network of profit-oriented, cooperative savings and loan associations to develop. They would function to provide consumer credit, not business credit. If a person wants to purchase a high-cost item for which she does not have ready cash, she can take out a loan from a cooperative S&L to be repaid over time with interest. Money for this loan would come from private savers who, just as under capitalism, would not only enjoy the convenience of having their savings protected, but would also receive interest on their savings (at a somewhat lower rate than what borrowers pay). Housing loans (mortgages) would likely play the dominant role in this sector—as they did in the savings and loan sector in the United States prior to the disastrous deregulation that ushered in the S&L crisis of the late 1980s.

Such S&Ls do not conflict with the values or institutions of Economic Democracy, nor do they pose a threat to economic stability—as do capitalist financial markets. (More on the stability question in chapter 5.) What should not be done is what capitalism does: merge the institutions that generate and distribute *investment funds* with the institutions that handle *consumer credit*. Business investment, as opposed to consumer credit, is too important to the overall health of the economy to be left to the vagaries of the market.

3.5.3 Capitalists under Socialism

Would capitalist acts among consenting adults be prohibited under Economic Democracy? This taunting question raised by libertarian philosopher Robert Nozick deserves a response.[29] It should be clear from what has been presented thus far that two of the traditional functions of the capitalist can be readily assumed by other institutions. We don't need capitalists to select the management of an enterprise (workers are quite capable of doing that), and we don't need capitalists to provide capital for business investment (such funds can be readily generated by taxation).

There remains the entrepreneurial function. As we observed in chapter 2, the class of entrepreneurs is by no means coextensive with the class of capitalists. Most of the income that flows to holders of stocks, bonds, and other income-entitling securities has no connection whatsoever with productive entrepreneurial activity on the part of the holders of those securities. However, it cannot be denied that some capitalists are entrepreneurs, and that some of the creative innovations such people have produced have been highly beneficial for society. Might it not be desirable to allow a sector of genuinely entrepreneurial capitalism to function under Economic Democracy?

In fact, some capitalism would be permitted in any realistic version of Economic Democracy—or at least some wage labor. The complete abolition of wage labor would require that *all* enterprises be run democratically, one-person, one-vote. In practice, such a rule would be too rigid. Small businesses need not be run democratically. If the owners of these businesses, who in most cases aren't true capitalists (since they also have to work), can persuade people to work for them for a wage, there is no need to prohibit such arrangements. The mere fact that most enterprises in society are democratically run would serve as a check on whatever authoritarian or exploitative tendencies the owner might have. Such small businesses would in no way threaten the basic structure of Economic Democracy. In fact, they would provide added flexibility. Such small businesses can get their start-up capital from the investment banks. These banks, charged with providing investment funds to potentially profitable enterprises that will increase employment, will make funds available to promising small businesses, whatever their internal structure.

But small businesses don't really address the entrepreneurial issue. Certainly, small businesses are often "entrepreneurial" in seizing specific opportunities—a new restaurant here, a new boutique there, a dollar-store on the corner—but such businesses contribute little in the way of technological improvement or new product design. The entrepreneurial talent that creates or exploits large technical or conceptual breakthroughs must be able to mobilize large amounts of both capital and labor. Being able to set up your own small business isn't enough.

The basic model of Economic Democracy encourages communities to set up entrepreneurial agencies—institutions that research investment opportunities and provide technical advice and bank capital to those individuals interested in setting up new worker cooperatives. Society may want additional, complementary institutions to encourage entrepreneurial activity. Business schools, for example, could instruct students in the art of setting up successful cooperative enterprises. Local employment agencies could aid prospective entrepreneurs in recruiting workers. Financial incentives—bonuses and prizes—could be awarded to individuals who set up successful new cooperatives.

Such institutions may well be sufficient to keep the economy dynamic. The record of Mondragon is certainly impressive in this respect. There may well be enough people with entrepreneurial talent willing to exercise those talents in a democratic setting to maintain a healthy flow of new technologies and products. The citizenry of the nation may well be satisfied with the pace of change these "socialist entrepreneurs" would provide. (This pace may not be "maximal"—perhaps not as rapid as under certain periods of capitalism—but new and faster is not always better. Change that is too rapid can be unsettling and sometimes destructive of genuine values. Small is often beautiful. Speed can be an unhealthy addiction.)

An Economic Democracy that chooses a more measured rate of technological innovation than some of its more dynamic neighbors needn't fear that "falling behind" would entail terrible consequences. Economic development need not be viewed as a race, wherein not to win is to lose. We can copy technological developments made elsewhere, if it seems appropriate to do so. We need not fear that our investment capital will flow to greener pastures, or that our workers will emigrate en masse.

However, we might want to encourage more entrepreneurial innovation by supplementing our basic institutions with some large-scale capitalism. If the basic institutions of Economic Democracy provide society with sufficient technological and product innovation, then there is no need for capitalist entrepreneurs. But if society should find the pace of innovation too slow, or if it just fancies the idea of those with entrepreneurial talent being given freer reign, then the prohibition on private ownership of means of production and wage labor could be relaxed. New enterprises could be privately owned. They too could seek funding from our public banks—and would be assured that they would not be discriminated against for being structured as capitalist firms. They could hire whatever workers they could attract. They could grow as large as market conditions permitted, without any legal limitations apart from our basic antitrust statutes. The owners could retain for themselves whatever profits the firm generates.

There is only one restriction. The owners are free at any time to sell their firms—but only to the state. The government will pay them the value of the firm's accumulated assets (upon which it had been paying its capital assets tax), then turn the enterprise over to the employees to be run democratically. (If a firm is not sold, it is turned over to the employees at the death of the founder, the asset value being paid to the estate of the deceased.) In the event of multiple founders, each has the option of selling his share at any time to the state. The state would then receive his share of the firm's profits, until, eventually, the other founders selling out or dying, majority ownership has passed into state hands, at which time the firm is democratized.

These capitalist-entrepreneurs pose no threat to the basic institutions of Economic Democracy. Their ability to treat their workers in an exploitative manner is sharply curtailed by the presence of widely available democratic employment alternatives. Their incomes are tied to their active, entrepreneurial activity, not to their mere ownership of productive assets, and so do not become a source of perpetual reward. Indeed, such capitalists perform two honorable societal functions: serving as sources of innovative ideas, *and* as incubators for additional democratic firms.

As we shall see, the real damage done by capitalists under capitalism is not done by individual entrepreneurs acting creatively but by their collective, nonentrepreneurial control of the investment process. Under Economic Democracy, even with entrepreneurial capitalists, this control remains securely in the hands of the democratically accountable deliberative bodies that oversee the distribution of the tax-generated investment fund.

Capitalist acts among consenting adults need not be prohibited under Economic Democracy.

3.6 Fair Trade, Not Free Trade

The structures of Economic Democracy described thus far pertain to a national economy. But, as everyone knows, we now live in a global economy. How would Economic Democracy fare in this "new world order"? Is Economic Democracy possible in one country or would it have to be implemented on a world scale to be effective? What should be the nature of the economic linkages between an Economic Democracy and other countries?

From an economic point of view, there is no reason to think that Economic Democracy would not be viable in one country. If other countries, however internally structured, do not react with military aggression or an economic blockade, a country structured along the lines of Economic Democracy should thrive. Of course, if the country was poor, it would be difficult to bring the foreign multinationals located in that country under democratic control—but even in such a case, some sort of peaceful accord might be possible. (Much would depend on the state of the counterproject internationally.) It would also be difficult to attract foreign investment, since investment would confer no control over an enterprise—but less reliance on private foreign capital may not be a bad thing, even for a poor country.

In a rich country, Economic Democracy could easily work. Its internal economy would remain efficient and dynamic, and it could continue to trade peacefully with other countries, capitalist or socialist. However, because of the way workplaces and the investment mechanism are structured under Economic Democracy, there would be significant differences in the nature of the economic transactions. Above all, there would be virtually no cross-border capital flows. Since firms are controlled by their own workers, they will not relocate abroad. Since funds for investment are publicly generated and are mandated by law to be reinvested domestically, capital will also stay at home. Capital doesn't flow out of the country—apart from a presumably small flow of private savings looking for higher rates of return abroad. Capital doesn't flow into the country either, for there are no stocks or businesses to buy. The capital assets of the country, apart from those owned by our domestic entrepreneurial capitalists, are collectively owned—and hence not for sale.

The elimination of cross-border capital flows has two exceedingly important positive effects.

- There is no downward pressure on workers' incomes coming from company threats to relocate to low-wage regions abroad.
- Countries cannot cite the need to attract capital as an excuse for lax environmental or labor regulations.

Significant as these effects are, cooperative labor and a publicly generated investment fund do not completely negate international wage competition or the incentives to be soft with environmental regulation. Free trade (i.e., trade regulated only by supply and demand) encourages such behavior. If trade is free, domestic goods produced by high-wage workers will not be as competitive as comparable imported goods produced by low-wage workers. A similar imbalance occurs with respect to environmental or labor restrictions. To insulate itself from such detrimental tendencies, while at the same time contributing toward a reduction in global poverty, Economic Democracy will adopt a policy of "fair trade," not "free trade." Free trade is fine so long as the trading partners are roughly equal in terms of worker incomes and environmental regulations. Such competition is healthy competition. However, when trading with a poorer country or one whose environmental or labor regulations are lax, Economic Democracy will adopt a policy of *socialist protectionism.*

"Protectionism" is, of course, a dirty word in mainstream discourse— despite the fact that virtually every economically successful nation of the capitalist era has been protectionist. We needn't point to Japan. The record goes back much further. Alexander Hamilton, in his 1791 Report on Manufacturers, argued (successfully) that "the United States cannot exchange with Europe on equal terms, and the want of reciprocity would render them the victim of a system of reciprocity which would induce them to confine their views to Agriculture and refrain from Manufactures."

Three-quarters of a century later, President Ulysses S. Grant observed:

> For centuries England has relied on protection, has carried it to extremes and has obtained satisfactory results from it. There is no doubt that it is to this system that it owes its present strength. After two centuries, England had found it convenient to adopt free trade, because it thinks that protection can no longer afford it anything. Very well, Gentlemen, my knowledge of my country leads me to believe that within two hundred years, when America has gotten all it can out of protection, it too will adopt free trade.[30]

In point of fact, a degree of protectionism can be good for a country, not only to allow for the development of local industries (the concern motivating Hamilton and Grant) but to prevent the sort of competition that puts downward pressure on domestic wages and on environmental regulations.

Economic Democracy's fair trade policy is motivated by two distinct considerations. On the one hand, we want to protect our own workers from the sorts of competition that are damaging to everyone in the long run. On the other hand, we want to contribute positively toward alleviating global poverty. Both these goals can be met if trade policy is appropriately designed.

The socialist conviction underlying fair trade is the moral conviction that one should not, in general, profit from, or be hurt by, the cheap labor of others. To the extent that inequalities are necessary to motivate efficient production, they are justifiable. However, consumers should not benefit because workers in other countries work for lower wages than home-country workers, nor should home-country workers be put at risk by these lower wages. This conviction suggests the following two-part trade policy:

- A "social tariff" will be imposed on imported goods, designed to compensate for low wages and/or a lack of commitment to social goals regarding the environment, worker health, safety, or social welfare.[31] (This is the protectionist part.)
- All tariff proceeds are rebated back to the countries of origin of the goods on which the tariffs were placed. (This is the socialist part.)

As a first approximation, the social tariff raises the price of an imported commodity to what it would be if workers in the exporting country were paid wages comparable to those at home and if environmental and other social expenses were the same. This figure would then be adjusted downward to compensate for the fact that poor-country workers may be using less productive technologies. (Unless some such adjustment is made, it will be almost impossible for poor-country manufacturing industries to compete with rich-country industries, since, given the relatively greater degree of labor intensity in most poor-country industries, a tariff that would equalize labor costs would make the poor-country goods much more expensive than that produced by a rich-country competitor.[32])

The point is to allow for competition, but only of a healthy sort. This "protectionist" trade policy derives from the stance Economic Democracy takes with regard to competition in general. Economic Democracy is a competitive market economy, but it discriminates between socially useful kinds of competition— those fostering efficient production and satisfaction of consumer desires—and socially destructive kinds of competition—those depressing wages and other social welfare provisions or encouraging lax environmental controls. Social tariffs are meant to block the latter without interfering with the former.

These social tariffs do more than shield domestic industries from socially undesirable forms of competition, for they are imposed on *all* imports from poor countries—foodstuffs and raw materials, as well as manufactured goods. Consumers will thus pay "fair prices" for goods imported from poor countries as opposed to the lower prices dictated by low wages abroad, whether or not these goods compete with those produced by local industries.

These social tariffs thus embody a socialist commitment to international labor solidarity. Income from these tariffs imposed on imported goods does not go into the general revenue fund of the importing country, but is sent back to the poor countries doing the exporting. Thus, with socialist protectionism, harmful competition is constrained, but the negative effect of the tariffs on poor countries is mitigated. Consumers in rich countries must pay "fair prices" for their imported goods—to protect their own workers from destructive wage competition, *and* to help alleviate global poverty. Because the consumers in Economic Democracy are paying higher prices for consumer goods, in part to help alleviate global poverty, the rebates should be directed to those agencies in the poor country most likely to be effective in addressing the problems of poverty and attendant environmental degradation—state agencies (where effective), labor unions, environmental groups, and other relevant nongovernmental organizations.

To be sure, these higher prices will likely decrease the consumption of imports from poor countries, which will adversely affect certain workers in those countries during the transition period. However, the overall effect of the higher prices accompanied by tariff rebates is to allow poor countries to devote fewer of their resources to producing for rich-country consumption, and thus to have more available for local use. The long-run consequences here are favorable to both rich nations and poor nations alike. (There is something obscene about poor countries using their best land and resources to satisfy the desires of rich-country consumers rather than the needs of their own people—as tends to be the case under capitalist free trade.)

To sum up briefly: Economic Democracy is a competitive market economy, but it is not a free-trade economy. It will engage in free trade with countries of comparable levels of development, but not with poorer countries. With a poor country, fair trade is better than free trade—for both countries.

4

Capitalism or Socialism?

Inequality, Unemployment, Overwork, Poverty

In essence, the grand comparative argument for capitalism (TINA) claims that there is no alternative to capitalism that is

- as efficient in the allocation of existing resources,
- as dynamic in its innovative growth,
- as compatible with liberty and democracy.

Capitalism, so it is said, is optimally efficient, innovative, and free. In the preceding chapter, we saw that Economic Democracy, since it is a market economy, will also be efficient, perhaps even more so than capitalism, because workplace democracy motivates better than does wage labor. We also saw that there are many options open within Economic Democracy to nurture and reward the entrepreneurial spirit. (Whether or not the growth engendered by capitalism is all to the good is a matter to be considered more carefully later. As we shall see, citizens of Economic Democracy may well wish to develop differently.)

Thus far we haven't considered the political framework within which an economy structured as Economic Democracy might be embedded, but there would seem to be no reason to think that Economic Democracy would conflict with liberty or democracy. Economic Democracy is a decentralized market economy. There is no central authority dictating consumption, production, or employment. Economic Democracy would seem to fit well with the structure of basic political liberties now well established in advanced capitalist societies. (This issue will be treated more fully in chapter 5.)

Before defending Economic Democracy, we need to examine some of the issues that TINA glosses over. TINA acknowledges that there are negative features to capitalism, but it avoids looking at them closely. In proclaiming "there is no alternative," TINA cuts short the discussion. Proponents of capitalism may extol its liberty, efficiency, and economic dynamism, but critics of capitalism are silenced.

TINA cannot be taken at face value. It cannot mean, literally, that there are no alternatives to capitalism. Of course there are—some of which have been tried and found wanting. What TINA means to assert is that there are no *preferable* alternatives, none that better accords with our basic values. Is this true? To decide this matter honestly, we have to consider the negatives of capitalism as well as the positives. Seven stand out:

- Inequality
- Unemployment
- Overwork
- Poverty in the midst of plenty
- Economic instability
- Environmental degradation
- The mockery capitalism makes of democracy

I will argue that these difficulties—staggering inequality, systematic unemployment that globalization will almost surely make worse, an unnecessary and undesirable intensification of work, poverty that wrecks minds as well as bodies, an irrational instability, an inherent ecological destructiveness, and a perversion of the democratic process—are causally connected to the structures of capitalism.

But would things be significantly different under Economic Democracy? Is it plausible to think that such deep-seated problems will miraculously disappear if we simply democratize workplaces and socialize investment?

In fact, these problems will not disappear, not all of them, certainly not all at once. Capitalism has imprinted itself everywhere—on our political institutions, our built habitats, our natural environment, our private lives, our souls. It has shaped our desires and expectations. It has broken a lot of people, many of whom will never recover. But it has also opened up possibilities that did not exist before, possibilities for human fulfillment and human happiness on a truly universal scale. Marx's double insight remains valid: capitalism has made a truly human world possible, but we cannot enter that world without transcending capitalism.

How we might accomplish this transcendence will be discussed in chapter 6. In this chapter and the next we examine the claim that certain problems that are irresolvable under capitalism become manageable under Economic Democracy. Economic Democracy will not usher in Utopia, but if we make a few structural changes, a far better world becomes possible than most of us can now imagine.

Before examining the "discontents" of capitalism, we need to consider some of the differences that altering the internal structure of firms (one of the two fundamental changes that Economic Democracy introduces) will make to their individual and collective behavior. Democratizing the workplace can be expected to increase the technical efficiency of a firm, but it will also give the enterprise certain behavioral characteristics that are quite different from those of a comparable capitalist firm. These behavioral differences will in turn give an economy composed largely of such firms different "laws of motion" than we find in a capitalist economy.

4.1 Workplace Democracy: Some Behavioral Consequences of Structural Change

At first glance, it might seem that democratizing enterprises should have little macroeconomic impact. Firms will still seek to make a profit. They will still compete to satisfy consumer demand and to produce efficiently. It might seem reasonable to suppose that an economy of such firms would exhibit pretty much the same characteristics as a capitalist economy. Whatever differences there might be between capitalism and Economic Democracy would be due to the difference in the investment mechanism, not to workplace democracy.

Not so. In fact, democratic firms do not behave like capitalist firms in all respects. For example, since labor is not a cost of production in a democratic firm, such firms have no interest whatsoever in lowering labor costs—since those "costs" are precisely the incomes of the workers. New technology may be introduced to increase productivity or job-satisfaction, but worker-run enterprises, unlike their capitalist counterparts, have no interest in cutting the size of their workforce or in "de-skilling" their workers. Of course, it is theoretically possible for a majority of workers to vote to lay off some of their colleagues or to replace a minority of higher-paid workers with lower-paid ones, but the natural solidarity engendered by democracy sharply mitigates against such behavior. In practice, democratic firms never vote to reduce the incomes of some so that others will have more. They rarely lay off workers at all, apart from circumstances of severe financial exigency, and even in these cases, the tendency is to share the burden as much as possible and to let retirements and voluntary departures bring down the size of the workforce.

There is a second behavioral difference, distinct from a reluctance to reduce labor costs, that has far-reaching consequences: *successful worker-run
firms, unlike their capitalist counterparts, do not possess an inherent tendency
to expand*. There are two distinct reasons for this, each serving to inhibit
expansion. The first has been often noted by economists. Although both capitalist and democratic firms strive to maximize their profits, what exactly is
maximized is different. Roughly speaking, capitalist firms strive to maximize
total profit, whereas democratic firms strive to maximize profit-per-worker.
This difference translates into a different expansionary dynamic.

Consider a simple example. I set up a small business, employing ten workers at $20,000 per year, and I make a profit of $100,000. I sense that demand
for my product is strong, so I hire another ten workers and double production. My company now produces twice what it did before, and, assuming I
was right about demand, my profit doubles to $200,000. If demand remains
strong, the incentive to grow is immediate, palpable, almost irresistible.

Now consider a ten-person worker-run enterprise, producing the same
product in exactly the same environment. Suppose you are one of the workers. You will make more the first year than one of my workers—the $20,000
my worker is being paid, plus another $10,000, your share of the $100,000
profit. You and your fellow workers also sense that demand for your product
is strong. Will you press, as I would, to double production?

Why should you? Assuming no change in technology or work intensity,
this would entail taking on ten more workers. Yes, this would double the
firm's profits—but these profits would have to be shared with twice as many
workers. Each individual worker you included would make exactly what you
made before. So there is no incentive to expand.

The logic of this example does not imply that a democratic firm will never
vote to take on new workers and expand production. So long as there are
sufficient economies of scale involved, the firm will expand, since everyone's
income will increase. It will expand to the point of optimal technical efficiency—but not beyond that. It will not keep expanding when returns to scale
are merely constant, whereas a capitalist firm will keep expanding throughout
that range, continuing until demand is saturated or further expansion drives
down efficiency.

The second reason why a democratic firm lacks the expansionary dynamic
of a capitalist firm has to do with the nature of democracy itself. As a rule,
democratic polities are not expansionary, because increasing the size of the
polity dilutes the political significance of the existing members. Think again
about the above example. Twice as many workers would mean twice as many
participants in the democratic process, hence the weight of your own voice
and vote would be halved. In general, a democratic firm will resist expansion

unless the financial gains are clear and palpable, and when it does expand, it will prefer to expand gradually rather than rapidly, so as not to alter too radically the existing culture of the institution. (This is true of cities, states, even nations, as well as democratic firms. Increased size must promise significant gains to voters if the natural reluctance of a democratic polity to take on more members is to be overcome.)

There are a number of important corollaries to this difference in expansionary dynamic:

- *Firms under Economic Democracy will tend to be smaller than comparable capitalist firms.* Once a firm reaches the optimal size for technical efficiency, it will stop growing. If demand for the product remains strong, new firms will come into being to satisfy this demand, sometimes "hiving off" from parent firms. (This dynamic has been observed among the Mondragon cooperatives.)
- *Firms under Economic Democracy will be less intensely competitive than capitalist firms.* Competition is more defensive than offensive. A firm does not want to lose market share, but it doesn't want to expand rapidly either, not unless a technological development allows for expansion without the employment of more labor. A democratic firm has little interest in driving a competitor out of business, buying it out (which is impossible anyway), or even merging with it (unless the economies of scale are significant).
- *Monopolistic tendencies will be less pronounced under Economic Democracy than under capitalism.* The economy of an Economic Democracy is at once less competitive and more competitive than a capitalist economy. Firms tend to be less cutthroat in competing with one another, while, at the same time, they are less likely to become monopolistic, for monopolies generally arise when successful firms drive their competitors to the wall or buy them out or merge with them, behavior that is rare in Economic Democracy. (Note the paradox of *capitalist* competition: the more intensely competitive the economy, the more likely it is that the big fish will swallow the small fish, with monopoly—the antithesis of competition—the end result.)

Although firms under Economic Democracy will tend to be smaller than their capitalist counterparts, some large firms may be present. Firms will sometimes find it advantageous to combine into a larger entity, as did the Mondragon cooperatives. But these larger entities will likely be structured differently from large capitalist enterprises. Large firms under Economic Democracy will tend to be confederations of smaller firms, each of which preserves a degree of autonomy. As in a political democracy, there will exist a creative tension between centralized authority and local control. It may make economic sense for a number of enterprises to pool their resources so as to fund research and development facilities or marketing departments, but individual units will likely want to maintain some independence. (The Mondragon Cooperative Corporation has such a structure. Individual units sign a contract with the corporation that binds them to certain conditions, but they may withdraw at any time if they so choose.)

With these differences in mind, let us now turn to those deep defects of capitalism that were named at the beginning of this chapter. We will address the first four in this chapter, the remaining three in chapter 5. The "comparative" argument now begins in earnest.

4.2 Inequality

Let us begin with some facts. Everyone knows that capitalism tends to generate large-scale inequalities of income and wealth, but unless you have an acute mathematical sense, the exact contours of these inequalities are hard to grasp. Economists cite Gini coefficients, or they compare the share of income going to the top x percent with the share going to the bottom y percent, but these measures don't do much for the imagination. When I first began researching inequality, I came across a useful devise for visualizing income distribution. I call it, following the economist from whom I borrowed the idea, "a parade of dwarfs and a few giants."[1]

Here's how it works when applied to the United States.[2] As of 2009, there were approximately 120 million households in the United States. The average income of these households was $68,000. Let us imagine a parade involving a representative from each of these households. The parade will last one hour. Representatives will be lined up so that those of the poorest households come first, followed by those with ever higher incomes.

Suppose that, through some feat of biological alchemy, we can make the height of each person proportional to that person's household income. Thus, poor people will be very short, rich people much taller. Let us assume the average height of an American to be six feet (somewhat an exaggeration, but it makes the calculations simpler). This represents a $68,000 annual income. Suppose you are of average height and are positioned along the parade route. What will you see?

As you would expect, the parade begins with a lot of very small people, many just inches off the ground. Indeed, nearly five minutes pass before the participants reach the *one-foot* level—representing an annual income of

$11,300. There are some 10 million households in the United States that make no more than that. After thirteen minutes, the marchers have grown to *two feet*, representing an income of $22,600, slightly over the official poverty line for a family of four. There are 25 million households making less than that— some 45 million people, half of them children.

This parade, you soon realize, is rather boring. There are lots and lots of small people, and they are not growing very fast. Twenty minutes pass, a third of the parade has gone by, and you are still looking way down. The marchers at this point are only *three feet* tall. Their household incomes are $34,000.

Your attention begins to wane. You go off to buy a beer from a street vendor. You return to your spot ten minutes later. The parade is now half over, so you expect to see people your own height. But no, the marchers are still small, less than three-quarters your height, the tops of their heads still lower than your chest.

A statistician, who happens to be standing next to you, notices your puzzlement. He explains to you the difference between "median" and "average" (or "mean"). The median income is that which cuts the population in half. By definition, half the households make less than the median and half make more. In the United States, the median household income is $50,000— making their representatives slightly less than *four and a half feet* tall. You calculate the average income by taking the total income earned by all the households and divide by 120 million. Since the distribution of income is top heavy in the United States, the average income is considerably higher than the median. That is to say (somewhat paradoxically), most people make considerably less than average.

The parade has been going on during this conversation. You look at your watch. Eight more minutes have passed—and so have nearly two-thirds of the marchers. Now, finally, the average incomes, proud *six-footers* making $68,000 walk by, looking you straight in the eye. (These are household incomes; in most cases, that $68,000 is a combined income.)

Heights now begin to increase more rapidly, although not dramatically so. At forty-eight minutes, the marchers have reached *nine feet*—representing incomes of $100,000. We're now at the lower end of the upper quintal (i.e., upper 20 percent). At the fifty-four-minute mark, we reach the lower bound of the top 10 percent. These people, with incomes of $140,000, are *twelve feet* tall—twice your height. Three minutes later, the first members of the upper 5 percent appear, with incomes of $180,000. These people are *sixteen feet* tall, more than two and a half times your (proud?) six feet.

In fact you hardly notice them. For suddenly the giants have come into view. Now the parade gets interesting. People start getting bigger faster. By the time the top 1 percent begin to pass by—thirty-six seconds to go—heights have more than doubled. Incomes are now at $400,000, their bearers *thirty-five* feet tall. (The salary of the president of the United States, the maximal government salary, is $400,000.)

But even at $400,000, a presidential salary is not big money, not in the United States these days. In 2009, 137,000 individuals had incomes of $1.6 million or more, the lower bound of the upper 0.1 percent—four times the president's salary. The smallest of these giants strides by at *140 feet*, the height of a 14-story building.

In the last third of a second, the superrich pass by, the upper 0.01 percent, among them various CEOs of major corporations. The poorest of the super-rich made $9 million, and stand *800 feet* tall. Those in the $15 million range tower above you at *1,300 feet*, their heads reaching the top of the world's tallest office buildings, the 110-story Willis (formerly Sears) Tower in Chicago and the slightly taller Pentronas Towers in Kuala Lumpur. Well over a hundred CEOs made more than $15 million in 2009. The highest paid CEO, Chesapeake Energy's Aubrey McClendon, made $100 million—*1.6 miles*. (You do the math in your head—40 hours per week, 50 weeks a year—he's making $50,000 *per hour*! That is to say, he's making more in an hour than 60 million households—half our population—make in a year.)

The parade isn't quite over. During the last few microseconds the multibillionaires and the hedge fund gurus come flashing by. According to *Forbes*, there were 400 American billionaires in 2009, 204 of which were worth $2 billion or more. We don't know exactly how much income they received, but we can guess. A modest 6 percent return on a $1 billion fortune generates $60 million per year in income—putting a billionaire *a mile* above the earth, taller than all but a couple of CEOs. The multibillionaires, taking in $120 million or more, look down at their fellow marchers from *two miles* up or higher. (Of course they'd need a telescope to see an average six-footer like you. They can barely see McClendon, whose head is 2,000 feet or more below theirs.)

Income of $120 million may seem like really big bucks to a corporate CEO, but not to a successful hedge fund manager. The average income of the top twenty-five hedge fund managers in 2009 was $1 billion. That is to say, the average income of the top twenty-five hedge fund managers was ten times more than our highest paid CEO; their average height is *sixteen miles*. The most successful of them all (in 2009) was David Tepper, founder of Appaloosa Management. He made $4 billion. His head is *sixty-four miles* up. Mount Everest, the tallest mountain on earth, is a little over five miles high. David Tepper is twelve times taller than Mt. Everest. He is 10,000 times taller than someone making the salary of the president. He is (I think) the last person to cross the line.[3] (Figure 4.1 is a graphic summary of the story just told.)

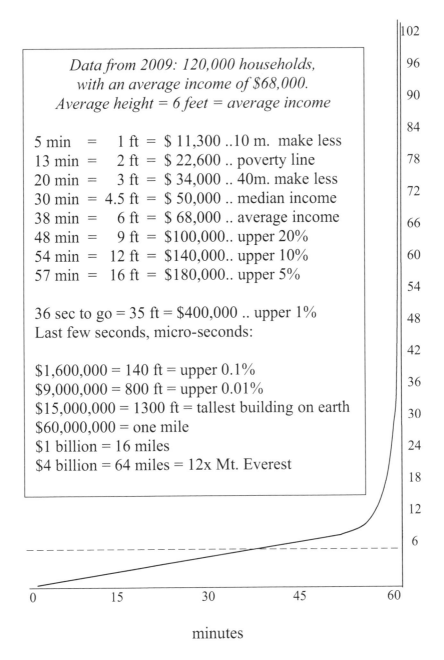

Figure 4.1.   A Parade of Dwarfs and a Few Giants

Such is the distribution of income in the United States. Amazingly enough, this parade actually *understates* the degree of inequality, for it depicts the distribution of income, not wealth. As all economists know, the distribution of wealth is much more unequal than the distribution of income. Income is your cash flow per year. Wealth is the value of what you own—your clothes, furniture, car, home, and all those stocks and bonds. For most people, "wealth" generates minimal income, but for the fortunate few, wealth begets wealth— big time. Dividends and interest flow in, which are compounded into more wealth, which generates more income, and on and on. Men become giants.

The difference in distribution is roughly this: If we divide the *income* of the United States into thirds, we find that the *top 10 percent* of the population gets a third, the *next 30 percent* gets another third, and the bottom *60 percent* gets the last third. If we divide the *wealth* of the United States into thirds, we find that the *top 1 percent* owns a third, the *next 9 percent* owns another third, and the *bottom 90 percent* claims the rest. If we had a Parade of Wealth instead of a Parade of Income, the dwarfs would be more numerous and much smaller, the giants fewer and much, much larger.

Such are the facts. What do we make of them? For some of us, such a distribution appears grotesque and makes us angry. So many millions a few feet from the ground, while the superrich tower above our tallest buildings, some soaring out of sight into the clouds. But for others—well, it's fun to imagine yourself somehow making it to the top, rising miles above the earth, too high up even to see those tens of millions of envious, silly dwarfs. Who's right? We can't just rely on feelings here. We have to ask the basic ethical question: What's wrong with inequality? As it turns out, this is not so easy to answer. Moreover, the correct answer has implications for the transition from capitalism to Economic Democracy. (The giants need not be lined up against the wall and shot, or even compelled to live like dwarfs. They will have to come down from the clouds, however.)

To get at this question, we must distinguish the issue of poverty from the issue of inequality per se. Would we be concerned about inequality if everyone in our society had *enough*? If the dwarfs at the beginning of our parade weren't so small, would we worry about the giants? Wouldn't our objection to those giants be simply a matter of envy?

Plato voiced the two most common objections to inequality long ago. First of all, excess, he said, is corrupting. Excessive poverty corrupts, but so too does excessive wealth. (We don't have to look far these days for evidence backing him up on this one.) Secondly, inequality is said to undermine the unity of society, the "community" of people.[4]

Recent empirical research suggests a third objection. Stark inequality, even apart from poverty, is bad for the physical and mental health of the citizenry.

Two British researchers, Richard Wilkinson and Kate Pickett, surveyed scores of studies, looking for correlations between levels of inequality and various medical and social indicators: levels of trust, mental health, drug abuse, physical health, life expectancy, infant mortality, obesity, educational performance, teenage pregnancies, violence, rates of imprisonment, and social mobility. They found them—across the board.

They looked at twenty-three rich countries. (Japan and the Scandinavian countries are the most equal, the United States, Portugal, and Great Britain the most unequal.) They then looked at the fifty states of the United States. (Alaska, Utah, Wisconsin, and New Hampshire are the most equal, New York, Louisiana, Mississippi, and Connecticut the most unequal.) In every case they found statistically significant correlations: the greater the inequality, the more pronounced the pathology. They venture a causal hypothesis: stress levels are, in general, higher in more unequal societies—and stress is bad for personal and societal health.[5] It is not simply that more unequal societies have more poor people, and hence higher rates of pathologies. In *all strata* the pathologies tend to be more pronounced in the more unequal societies than in the more egalitarian ones (i.e., even the rich die younger in more unequal societies), which suggests that it is inequality per se, and not merely poverty, that is the problem.

Of course none of the surveyed studies offers an indictment of capitalism per se, since all the societies studied are capitalist. It is noteworthy, however, that in a section of their concluding chapter, "What Can Be Done," Wilkinson and Pickett write: "An approach which would solve some of the problems is democratic employee-ownership."[6]

There will still be inequality under Economic Democracy. There will be inequalities within firms, since enterprises employ financial incentives to acquire and hold qualified workers. Workers may also find it desirable to insist on seniority differentials, to give tangible credit to loyalty and service over time. The workplace will not be a site of strict equality unless the workers in a particular firm choose to make it so.

There will also be inequalities among firms. Economic Democracy is a competitive market economy. Some firms will do better than others. Skill and hard work will account for some of these differences; luck will also be a factor—being at the right place at the right time when demand shifts in your direction or guessing right as to what new products people will want. Luck will always play a significant role in a market economy; hence, certain inequalities will always be "undeserved."

It does not follow that the structure of inequalities within Economic Democracy will be the same as under capitalism. Workplace democracy tends to keep intrafirm inequalities in check. In Mondragon, for example, the differential between the highest-paid worker in a firm and the lowest was for many years held at 3 to 1. More recently, as competition with capitalist firms, particularly the European multinationals, has intensified, the allowable spread has been raised to 4.5 to 1 and in some cases even more. Nevertheless, even though MCC is now a multinational corporation in its own right, it has nothing like the 400 to 1 or more differential common in large capitalist firms.

It is to be expected that democratic firms will be more egalitarian than capitalist firms. Democracy is always a check to inequality. (Even in the United States, where ideological justifications of inequality are largely unquestioned, the highest salary of a government official is only $400,000—a fraction of top private-sector salaries.) When managerial incomes have to be justified to the workers themselves, they will tend to be less than when CEOs and other upper administrators are free to determine their own salaries (perhaps in consultation with major stockholders, who are themselves very rich and not averse to being generous to those whose duty it is to keep them that way).

How much inequality can be expected *between* firms? Given the variables involved, no hard-and-fast answer to this question is possible, but structural differences point to far less inequality than under capitalism. In Economic Democracy successful firms do not expand rapidly and drive their competitors out of business. Hence, successful innovations in product design or production techniques will diffuse to competitors over time, and reestablish intra-industry equality. To the extent that certain industries themselves are more profitable than others, market forces will encourage a shift of resources from less profitable sectors to more profitable. Investment banks can be expected to assist this transition. Since firms are smaller and competition less intense under Economic Democracy than under capitalism, it will be easier for a new start-up firm—or a retooled existing firm—to enter the more lucrative industry.

If we make the rough estimate that in Economic Democracy workers in the strongest firms make three times what those in the weakest firms make, and if we assume that without the pressure of capitalist firms trying to lure away top personnel, income differentials within a firm will also be about three to one, we can say that in Economic Democracy the overall spread between top incomes and bottom incomes will be about ten to one. If we further assume that under Economic Democracy, the minimum wage is high enough to keep you out of poverty (say, in the United States, $15/hour), this would put the range between $30,000 and $300,000. This is the difference between someone in the United States now making twice the minimum wage and what would put a household today in the upper 2 percent. This is far from total equality, but it is nothing like the inequality under capitalism. In terms of our parade, we are looking at dwarfs a little over two and a half feet tall and giants of twenty-six feet. We don't see dwarfs just inches from the ground or giants with their heads in the clouds. (There might be a few soaring figures, those entrepreneurial capitalists that our system might allow. But the egalitarian character of our society would likely induce self-restraint, that is, higher pay for their workers, less profit for themselves. A few might make a million, that is, grow to ninety feet or so, three times taller than anyone in the cooperative sector, but they would never soar above the Willis Tower or Mt. Everest. Moreover, since these individuals would be few and highly visible, their wealth would not easily translate into political power, nor could their investment decisions put the economy at risk.)

Under Economic Democracy, greater equality is a by-product of structures introduced for other purposes rather than a matter of direct design. What we want (we who want Economic Democracy) is not equality per se, but a genuinely democratic, fully employed, stable, ecologically sustainable society without overwork or poverty. If we get in the process a degree of equality that reduces the health and social pathologies, that is a welcome bonus. If there are still a few giants among us, that is no cause for concern, for their existence is consistent with our fundamental values and poses no threat to our basic institutions.

4.3 Unemployment

In Chicago we have a free weekly newspaper, the *Reader*, which used to run, along with a great number of ads for movies, music, theater, and phone sex, a syndicated weekly compilation, "News of the Weird," by Chuck Shepherd. Here's a telling entry from 1994: "In November the city of Bombay, India, announced it had 70 job openings for rat catchers; it received 40,000 applicants—half from college graduates."[7]

Things have not improved. In January 2010 the International Labour Organization reported that global unemployment has reached 212 million, an all-time high, up an unprecedented 34 million since 2007. Unemployed and underemployed together total about a billion people.[8]

Not so many years ago, reports such as these might have been greeted with indifference by most Americans—"Yes, yes, things are terrible in those poor countries, but there's not much we can do about it, is there?" Today the response is different. Far more Americans than ever before are troubled by such news—for that bad news now impacts us directly. That vast pool of unemployed labor keeps wages very low in those countries, and those low-wage workers now represent job competition.

We often hear it said that "Communism is dead! Socialism is dead!" but it is not often observed that the political-economic structures of Eastern Europe and the Soviet Union were undermined by the very developments that now make American workers tremble. Those same technological advances that allowed the dazzling images of Western consumer society to penetrate the Iron Curtain and generate widespread discontent have rendered *all* national boundaries porous. Innovations in communications and transport have given fierce new meaning to the concept "global competition."

In a sense, there's nothing new in any of this. As Marx and Engels pointed out over 150 years ago:

> The bourgeoisie has through its exploitation of the world market given a cosmopolitan character to production and consumption in every country. . . . All old-established national industries have been destroyed or are daily being destroyed. They are dislodged by new industries, whose introduction becomes a life and death question for all civilized nations, by industries that no longer work up indigenous raw material, but raw material drawn from the remotest zones, industries whose products are consumed, not only at home, but in every quarter of the globe.[9]

It is true that the dislocations we are suffering, others before us have suffered as well. However, for most Americans, what we are experiencing is new *for us*. For most of our lives, we have benefited from low labor costs abroad, which translated into low-cost raw materials and mass-affordable coffee, tea, chocolate, and bananas. The workers in poor countries worked for us, not in competition with us. Now the game has changed. As consumers, we still benefit; as workers, we are threatened.

Why has the game changed? The driving force behind the dislocation so many of us now experience or fear is the current *hypermobility* of capital. Recent technological developments now make it possible not only for "money capital" (i.e., investment funds) to flash almost instantaneously from one capital market to another, but also for up-to-date "real capital" (i.e., buildings and machinery) to set up almost anywhere. Factories now "move." Shops "run away."

How are we to think about this hypermobility of capital? Is it ethical? The usual procedure in ethics is to consider the matter from two perspectives: from the point of view of rights (the "deontological" approach) and from the point of view of human happiness (the "utilitarian" approach). Are rights being violated? Is the principle of "the greatest happiness for the greatest number" being transgressed?

Well—it is hard to see any rights being violated if I decided to invest in the Singapore stock market, or even if I decide to move my toy factory from Chicago to Juarez. Workers might claim that they have developed certain employment rights with respect to the company that employs them, but it is hard to see how I can give these rights much credence, when honoring them might drive me out of business and leave them jobless anyway.

Things don't look much different from a utilitarian perspective. Surely unemployment hurts more in poor Mexico than in rich United States. It is hard to see how I can be faulted on utilitarian grounds if I provide employment to 300 Mexicans who would otherwise live in squalor, even if this comes at the expense of 300 Americans, who can collect unemployment compensation and enroll in job-retraining programs.

The fly in the ointment of such ethical reasoning becomes visible only through the lens of economic theory—theory that many economists who should know better have, for several decades now, scornfully ignored. The theory is basic Keynesian macroeconomics. (The neoclassical counterattack against Keynesianism began in the 1970s. Among those leading the charge was the University of Chicago's Robert Lucas—later to receive a Nobel Prize for his efforts. As he remarked so triumphantly in 1980, "One cannot find good under-forty economists who identify themselves or their work as 'Keynesian.' At research seminars, people don't take Keynesian theorizing seriously anymore; the audience starts to whisper and giggle to one another."[10])

Let us draw out the implications of Keynesian theory, about which—in light of the Great Global Recession that none of the neoclassical economists saw coming—people are no longer giggling.

Nobody disputes the fact that capitalism is immensely effective at producing goods. Indeed, it is capable of producing far more goods than it is presently producing. Most plants have excess capacity, and many workers are out of work. Excess capacity and unemployment are basic features of real-world capitalism. Full employment of workers and resources (except during wartime) is a textbook fantasy.

As Keynes pointed out, the key to capitalist production is *effective demand*—needs or desires backed up by purchasing power. If the demand is there, goods will be produced. Rarely are there production shortages, and when there are, they are temporary. But if demand is not there, the economy slumps. Effective demand comes from three sources: private consumers, private investment (real investment—building new factories, installing new technologies, and so on—not "investment" in the stock market, which is saving, not investing), and government expenditures.

The variable upon which Keynes focused his attention was private investment. The health of a capitalist economy depends on "investor confidence," on the "animal spirits" (as Keynes liked to say) of the investors. Thus we get his famous policy prescription: When investor confidence flags, the government should step in and make up the difference. The government should spend more than it takes in, in order to provide the requisite stimulus to the economy. If necessary, pay people to bury cash in bottles and let others dig them up. Not productive, but better that than just praying to the market gods. "It would, indeed, be more sensible to build houses and the like; but if there are political and practical difficulties in the way of this, the above would be better than nothing."[11]

Keynes is certainly right that flagging investor confidence can throw an economy into recession. But why do investors lose confidence? Sometimes there are good reasons for this loss. Suppose consumers simply can't buy all the goods being produced. Then it makes no sense to keep investing. We are staring here at one of capitalism's central contradictions. Wages are both a cost of production *and* an essential source of effective demand. Capitalist firms are always interested in cutting costs, expanding markets, and developing new products. But to the extent that the first of these goals, namely cost cutting, grows in importance relative to the other two, effective consumer demand will tend to be depressed—and hence also those "animal spirits" of investors. This can mean a stagnating economy and rising unemployment, perhaps on a global scale.

The logic is straightforward. If aggregate demand declines, which it will if average wages decline, which they will if the search for low wages dominates the movement of capital, then production—and hence employment—will also decline. That is to say, if the search for lower wages comes to dominate the movement of capital, the result may be not only a lowering of worldwide wage disparities as poor-country workers gain at the expense of rich-country workers (the good to which some economists point) but also a lowering of total global income (a straight-out utilitarian bad).

Keynes's fundamental point is clearly valid. A laissez-faire capitalist economy has no tendency whatsoever toward full employment. Equilibrium can occur at any level of unemployment. Hence it is quite possible for a capitalist economy to marginalize large numbers of people, who, in the absence of governmental intervention, will remain permanently unemployed. In a globalized capitalism, large sections of the world can be so marginalized. In fact, they have been. And it looks like ever more will be—even in the developed parts of the world, particularly in the United States. As Paul Krugman has observed, there is "growing evidence that our governing elite just doesn't care—that a once-unthinkable level of economic distress is in the process of becoming the new normal."[12]

If this "new normal" is allowed to stand, the effects will likely be brutal—for millions of individuals and for society at large. Don Peck, drawing on research into the long-term effects of the Great Depression, paints a grim picture:

The Great Recession may be over, but the era of high joblessness is probably just beginning. Before it ends, it will likely change the life course and character of a generation of young adults. It will leave an indelible imprint on many blue-collar men. It could cripple marriage as an institution in many communities. It may already be plunging many inner cities into a despair not seen for decades. Ultimately, it is likely to warp our politics, our culture, and the character of our society for years to come.[13]

To counteract unemployment, Keynes urged governmental action. Governments should aim at full employment. His prescriptions were widely adopted after the Second World War, and for a while they worked. But then things got complicated. We can now see the problem. To the extent that a government engages in deficit spending to boost aggregate demand, and thereby succeeds in reducing the unemployment rate, the economy tends to "overheat." For when labor markets become tight, workers demand higher wages. These extra costs are then passed onto consumers, and *inflation* ensues. Workers, feeling cheated, demand still more, and so inflation accelerates—until the capitalist class decides enough is enough and slams on the brakes. (The "stagflation" of the 1970s set the stage for the conservative revival that brought Ronald Reagan to the presidency. The worst recession since the Great Depression, deliberately engineered by Federal Reserve chief Paul Volcker, quickly followed.).

Liberal confidence in Keynesian full employment is not much in evidence these days. Economists have stopped speaking of full employment For a while they invoked the term, "natural rate of unemployment," defined as that below which inflationary pressures set in. This, of course, is an utterly ideological manner of speaking, since there is nothing "natural" about unemployment. Perhaps because the term was so transparently ideological, a couple of innocuous acronyms have been substituted: "NAIRU" (nonaccelerating inflation rate of unemployment) and LSUR (pronounced "lee-sur," lowest sustainable unemployment rate).

But whatever its name, the concept points to something real, something emphasized long ago by Marx but overlooked by Keynes: a healthy capitalism *requires* unemployment. It is precisely this "reserve army of the unemployed" that serves to discipline the workforce. If unemployment is too low, workers get uppity and make wage demands that either cut into profits to the degree that future investment is jeopardized or are passed on to consumers, thus generating inflationary instability.

We need to be clear on this point. Unemployment is not an aberration of capitalism, indicating that it is somehow not working as it should. Unemployment is a necessary structural feature. Capitalism cannot be a full-employment economy, except in the very short term. Unemployment is the invisible hand—carrying a stick—that keeps the workforce in line.

There is another problem with the Keynesian solution, which is more acute now than it used to be. The effectiveness of Keynesian deficit spending depends on a "multiplier effect." The government spends x dollars more than it has, putting y unemployed people to work. These people now have money, so demand for goods goes up, which generates more employment, which generates more demand, and so on—a virtuous *upward* spiral. A deficit of x dollars generates many times x dollars of new effective demand. Hence, the deficit does not have to be excessive.

However, if an economy is wide open to imports, which contemporary capitalist economies increasingly are, then the multiplier effect is attenuated. A significant portion of the government stimulus will be used to buy imported goods—which may increase employment abroad, but not at home. This is especially true when so many imported goods are the *low cost* goods particularly attractive to insecure consumers threatened by hard times. (Think Wal-Mart.) Hence, to reinflate the economy, a government must go much deeper into debt than was necessary before.

This is a serious problem. The costs of the debt are borne by the nation's taxpayers, while the good effects spread globally. So governments become reluctant to apply the Keynesian remedy too forcefully, and when they do, it doesn't work so well. Hence, the specter of a "new normal"—permanently high unemployment.

What about Economic Democracy? Does it possess an automatic tendency toward full employment, or will it be caught up in precisely the same set of difficulties? At first glance, the prospect does not look promising. An economy of worker self-managed enterprises has no stronger tendency toward full employment than does a capitalist economy. If anything, the tendency is weaker, for, as we have noted, worker-run firms are actually less inclined to take on new workers than comparable capitalist firms. Insofar as firms aim at maximizing profit per worker rather than total profits, they will not increase employment under conditions of constant returns to scale, whereas capitalist firms will. Moreover, since workers once hired are rarely let go, there is a reluctance to take on new workers, even when there would be gain all around by doing so, if this gain might be only temporary. In this respect, an economy of worker cooperatives would be similar to many Western European economies today, where work rules (strongly fought for by labor movements) make it difficult to lay off workers. Such countries tend to have higher rates of unemployment than do countries with "more flexible" work rules.

An economy of worker self-managed enterprises will not, in and of itself, tend naturally to full employment. All else being equal, it will fare worse than unfettered capitalism at job creation. However, all else is not equal. The other structural feature distinguishing Economic Democracy from capitalism, namely social control of investment, serves to mitigate this defect. Investment banks under Economic Democracy are public institutions, specifically charged with expanding employment whenever possible. These banks are not unconcerned about the profitability of the projects they fund—projects that appear economically unfeasible will not be funded. However, the *degree* of profitability is not the decisive criterion. Funds will be more readily granted to firms willing to expand production by taking on more workers, to groups of workers with a promising idea wanting to start a business, or to an entrepreneurial capitalist start-up than to existing firms wanting to keep their workforce constant. (These latter firms are not denied all access to investment funding. They have their depreciation funds at their disposal, and they may seek additional funding from the investment banks, but their requests will be given lower priority than those of firms wanting to increase employment.) Economic Democracy recognizes that, like capitalism, it does not naturally gravitate toward full employment. Unlike capitalism, its banking system is specifically designed to counter this defect.

These factors point to lower unemployment under Economic Democracy than under capitalism, but they do not guarantee full employment. Full employment can be assured in a market economy only by having the government function as the employer-of-last-resort. In Economic Democracy, the government assumes this role. A universal "right to work" has long been a socialist demand. This demand is honored in Economic Democracy. Work is crucial to a person's sense of self-respect. All but the most severely disabled should have the opportunity to engage in productive labor. If the market sector of the economy does not provide sufficient employment, the public sector will fill the gap. Even if it would be cheaper simply to provide people with welfare checks (capitalism's "solution" to the unemployment problem), our sense of social solidarity demands more than that. Economic Democracy is committed to providing decent work for all who want to work—which means the government will provide jobs for people who cannot find work elsewhere.

As noted earlier, Economic Democracy embraces the principle of intergenerational solidarity: citizens regard care for children and the elderly as a public responsibility, not a wholly private matter. Our children are a *collective* responsibility, to be cared for by us when they are young. They in turn will care for us when we are old. Since the caring professions—child care and care for the elderly as well as health care—are labor intensive, the commitment to intergenerational solidarity dovetails nicely with the commitment to full employment. Economic Democracy will make quality day care available to all who need it. Unemployment is thereby reduced and the national quality of life enhanced. (Day-care providers can be public institutions, like public schools, or they can be cooperatives or small private businesses financed by vouchers, or perhaps a mix of both. Economic Democracy does not automatically favor one system over the other. It does, however, insist that care for all who need it is a public responsibility, and so care-giving institutions will be subsidized.)

Care for our planet is also a collective responsibility. Otherwise-unemployed people can be put to work caring for our public spaces, helping with environmental cleanup and engaging in low-skilled ecological projects. There is much work to be done in this sector.[14]

Full employment is not an impossible dream, as the past century's socialist experiments, for all their faults, have shown. There were times when governments of capitalist countries, forced to compete ideologically with socialist societies, also aspired to full employment. In the United States, for example, the Humphrey-Hawkins Act of 1978 committed the federal government to a full-employment policy. The original formulation of the proposal went so far as to include the provision we have incorporated into Economic Democracy—that the government serve as employer-of-last-resort. That provision, however, proved to be too much for Congress, which dropped it, thus turning the act into an empty platitude, soon forgotten.

It is hard to fault Congress for excising the key provision, for, as we have seen, capitalism is fundamentally incompatible with full employment. The threat of job loss remains the basic disciplinary mechanism of the system. Under capitalism, workers do not see their own interests as being in fundamental alignment with the interests of their enterprises because, objectively, they aren't. A capitalist enterprise is structured to serve the interests of the owners, not the workers. Lowering skill requirements, reducing wages, intensifying the pace of work—none of these familiar capitalist strategies benefits the workforce, so worker allegiance to company interests is not sufficient to maintain work discipline. Fear of unemployment is essential.

Not so with Economic Democracy. Unemployment is not required to maintain work discipline. The fundamental incentive is positive. You work hard because your income, and that of your fellow workers, is tied directly to your company's profits. You also know that incompetent or irresponsible behavior on your part affects the well-being of your coworkers and will not be suffered by them lightly. The large, crude stick, fear of unemployment, is replaced by the carrot of profit sharing and the more subtle stick of social disapproval.

Since unemployment is not necessary to Economic Democracy as it is to capitalism, full employment is possible under the former, but not the latter.

4.3.1 A Note on Inflation

The importance of unemployment in keeping capitalism healthy is well known to the capitalist class and to the business press that articulates their concerns, although unemployment is never stated to be a matter of worker discipline. Instead, concern about too-low unemployment is phrased as concern about inflation. When labor markets are tight, workers push for higher wages. They have more bargaining power when unemployment is low, and they use it. So wage concessions are granted, which are then passed on to consumers in the form of higher prices.

Inflation is widely viewed to be a menace. Newscasters signal red alert when the Consumer Price Index goes up. This is curious since, from a societal point of view, it is not so obvious that inflation is a terrible thing. If prices are going up, but wages are going up also, not much is lost. Yes, there is some "noise" introduced into the price mechanism, making long-range planning more difficult, but this isn't usually substantial. Most economists concede this fact privately, although they rarely say so in public. Paul Krugman is an exception: "It is one of the dirty little secrets of economic analysis that, even though inflation is universally regarded as a terrible scourge, most efforts to measure its costs come up with embarrassingly small numbers."[15]

Krugman understates the issue. Inflation has often accompanied quite positive economic performance. In Japan, for example, consumer prices increased twenty-five-fold from 1946 to 1976, a huge rate of inflation, but its real economy grew an astonishing fifty-five-fold during this same period.[16]

Of course, working people don't like inflation; they feel robbed of their wage gains. But there are other things that hurt working people more—high unemployment, work speed-ups, cuts in benefits—none of which are viewed with comparable alarm by politicians or the media. In point of fact, working people tend to come out ahead during periods of relatively high inflation and often lose ground during periods of low inflation.

Why then so much fear of inflation? The answer is simple enough, although rarely discussed. The people who really don't like inflation are capitalists in the financial sector. To be sure, people on fixed incomes are squeezed by inflation, as are those working people whose wage gains do not keep pace with rising prices, but the people who take the biggest hit are the moneylenders. The logic is straightforward. Suppose I borrow $1,000 during a period of time when the annual inflation rate is 10 percent. At the end of the year, I repay the loan. But the $1,000 I repay will buy 10 percent *less* now than it did when I took out the loan. Of course I must also pay interest on my loan, but if the rate of interest lags behind the rate of inflation, I *gain* by borrowing—and the moneylender *loses*. He can buy less now with his $1,000-plus-interest than I did a year ago with the $1,000 he lent me. Since people with money to lend tend to have more of it than people who borrow, inflation tends to redistribute income downward—not a welcome prospect for the upper classes, or one they will accept without resistance.

Once again, we must be impressed by how well capitalism works for capitalists. Since everyone feels the adverse effects of inflation, it is not hard to convince the general public that inflation is a terrible thing. People didn't laugh when President Ford proclaimed, "Our inflation, our public enemy number one, will, unless whipped, destroy our homes, our liberties, our property, and finally our national pride, as surely as any well-armed enemy."[17] Instead, they nodded their approval. What most of those nodding didn't realize—since "responsible" opinion makers weren't telling—is that the capitalist solution to inflation is unemployment. So, in 1979 Jimmy Carter appointed Paul Volcker to head the Federal Reserve, who quickly engineered the worst recession since the 1930s—to discipline labor, bring inflation down, and allow real interest rates to rise. (This recession cost Carter his second term, bringing to power Ronald Reagan, who continued the Carter policy of deregulation, gave the green light to corporations to go on the offensive against labor unions, cut taxes for the wealthy, and stopped enforcing antitrust laws.)

To say that inflation is not a great evil is not to say that it is good. Innocent people do get hurt. Savings are eroded. People on fixed incomes suffer. Although inflation is good for borrowers, bad for lenders, and thus tends to reduce the gap between the rich and the rest, those who benefit the most are not the worst-off members of society but the more privileged sectors, those with access to credit and those with the strength to negotiate wage increases that keep up with inflation. It is preferable to live in a world of price stability—if the price for such a world is not too steep. Unfortunately, under capitalism, the price is often steep indeed: serious unemployment and rising inequality—not a bargain.

Can we expect price stability under Economic Democracy? To the extent that the economy is competitive, inflation shouldn't be a problem. Workers can't simply press for higher wages—since workers don't receive wages but a share of the profits instead. Workers could insist on raising the prices of the goods they are producing, but if they do so and their competitors don't, they stand to lose, not gain. Of course, democratic competitors will be tempted to collude so as to set prices, just as capitalist firms do, so antitrust laws prohibiting such behavior must be kept on the books. Since firms tend to be smaller in Economic Democracy and, therefore, in a given industry, more numerous, collusion is more difficult and should be easier to detect. If antitrust laws prove ineffective, some price controls might be in order.

4.4 Overwork

If unemployment is a structural feature of capitalism that seems destined to become ever more severe, so too is its accompaniment, overwork. We have here another paradox. A visitor from another planet would be perplexed to discover that in a purportedly free and rational society there are millions of people who want to work more, living with millions who want to work less. The visitor would be even more perplexed to learn that new technologies allow us to produce ever more goods with ever less labor, and yet the intensity of work—for those who have work—has increased.

Of course, this paradox is no mystery to those of us who live here. The more precarious your job is, the more you must do everything possible to keep it. The more competitive the economy becomes, the more managers insist that they—and everyone under them—work harder. It's the treadmill effect: all must intensify their efforts just to remain in place.

The threat of job loss is real. Once-secure jobs in major corporations are now vulnerable. "Downsizing" is hardly a myth. In the United States, for example, the 800 largest firms, whose assets comprise half of all corporate assets, employed a million and half fewer people in 1993 than they did twenty years before. The global recession that began in 2007 has further exacerbated this trend—while allowing profits to soar.[18] Clearly, not only is income distributed in a vastly unequal manner under capitalism; so too is leisure. Millions have more leisure than they want—the underemployed and unemployed. Millions more would love to slow down, work less, but can't—most of the rest of us, I suspect.

Neoclassical economists like to deny that such "Pareto-non-optimality" (i.e., inefficiency) can exist in a competitive economy. They like to say that those who are working long hours have chosen to do so. They have chosen consumption over leisure. For some, this is doubtless the case. There are people who get into debt, then work a second job to get out. There are people who, given the option of overtime, leap at the chance. There are people who, given the choice between taking their "raise" in the form of fewer working hours or taking home a larger pay check, would opt for the money.

But "some of us" is not "all of us." (A 2004 study found that 44 percent of the respondents reported that they were often or very often overworked.[19]) It is quite false to conclude that, by and large, capitalism has given us the consumption-leisure combination we really want. Two considerations call such a conclusion into question.

The first is obvious. For the vast majority of jobholders, the hours of work are fixed. Once hired, you do not have the choice of trading a bit of income for a bit more leisure. You can quit your job and try to find less demanding work that pays somewhat less, but you have virtually no chance of negotiating a consumption-leisure tradeoff with your current employer. (There are exceptions, but these are rare.)

The second consideration is more subtle. Because leisure is not a real option, people adjust their consumption accordingly. You spend most of what you make, since there is not much else to do with your money. Indeed, you often spend more than you make, for, in an overworked, insecure society, buying things confers status and is a source of quick—if ephemeral—pleasure. Of course, you can always substitute a large increase in leisure for a large decrease in consumption by quitting your job, but that is a choice that few of us would want to make, and one altogether different from the marginal option—to substitute somewhat more leisure for somewhat less consumption. In the absence of the marginal option, you orient your life toward consumption; you search for happiness in things; you even go into debt in search of that fulfillment that consumption alone (you know in your heart) can never bring.

Economist/sociologist Juliet Schor has calculated just how much leisure our increased productivity could in fact support. Suppose, in 1948, we in the United States, happy with our standard of living (which was the envy of the world), had opted to take our productivity gains in leisure instead of increased consumption:

> We could now produce our 1948 standard of living (measured in terms of marketed goods and services) in less than half the time it took that year. We actually could have chosen the four-hour day. Or a working year of six months. Or, every worker in the United States could now be taking every other year off from work—with pay.[20]

Let us think about this for a moment. The year 1948 was not a bad time to be alive in America. People had washing machines, refrigerators, cars (not as many as today, but more buses and trams), telephones, record players, TVs (admittedly black and white and not big-screen), typewriters, lots of movie theaters. True, they didn't have smart phones, CDs, PCs, or DVD players, but life was hardly uncomfortable. (I'm thinking here of middle-class life. Life for poor people was miserable—as it still is.) Suppose we (current voters) were given a choice: either our current standard of living or a 1948 standard with a full-pay sabbatical every other year. Or perhaps a third option: a consumption midpoint between 1948 and now, say 1980, and a six-hour work day, or three-month vacation every year? If we were given the choice, is it so obvious that we would choose the present consumption-leisure tradeoff? But of course we are given no such choice.

Although our technologies might have given us more leisure, in fact, as Schor's research shows, the hours of work (for those who have work) have been steadily *increasing*:

> The average employee now spends 200 more hours per year on the job, or five extra weeks of work, than he or she did thirty years ago. Fifty years ago, American work hours were substantially lower than those in Western Europe; they now exceed them by more than 300 a year (or about eight weeks). Even Japan,

the world's workaholic when I began my research in the 1980s, now has shorter annual hours of work than does the United States.[21]

It is possible that we as a society prefer it that way, but the fact is, no choice was ever offered. This is not an accidental feature easily remedied. A bias for consumption is built into the structure of capitalism. Even though workers in an enterprise might prefer to take a part of their productivity increase in leisure rather than income, the owner of an enterprise has nothing whatsoever to gain from such a tradeoff. A capitalist wants to get as much work from his workforce as possible. Unless it can be demonstrated that there would be a significant gain in worker productivity, the capitalist has no reason to consider such a proposal. The fact that workers might be happier is irrelevant.

From the perspective of the capitalist class as a whole, the undesirability of allowing leisure to substitute for consumption is even more striking. Capitalist firms make a profit only from selling things. If profit rates are to remain high, then goods and services must be consumed in ever increasing quantities. Any kind of cultural shift that emphasizes leisure over consumption bodes ill for business. To be sure, individual businesses catering to the increase in leisure that people would have might profit, but if this leisure comes at the expense of income, overall aggregate demand will fall, profits will decline, and the economy will stagnate or slip into recession. Consumption is good for business. Leisure—if not oriented toward consumption—is not.

It is true that the length of the working day has declined since the mid-nineteenth century (having massively increased during the early phases of capitalism). But this decline, effected in steps, is anything but natural to capitalism. The reductions have always been the result of class struggle. Workers in the mid-nineteenth century fought for a ten-hour day. The first working-class May Day demonstration (Chicago, May 1, 1886) pressed further, for an eight-hour day—a demand not granted in the United States until half a century later. (The forty-hour week was signed into law in 1933, but then was promptly thrown out by the Supreme Court, not to be reinstituted until 1938. It is not easy to pry more leisure out of capitalism.)

There has been no reduction since in the United States. Indeed, in recent years, working hours have increased. Overtime work in manufacturing, for example, has increased from 2.2 hours per week in 1982 to 3.0 today. Overall, nearly three-quarters of the American workforce now puts in more than forty hours a week.[22] (European workers, more highly organized than their American counterparts, have been more successful at continuing the fight for work time reduction. Most get four to six weeks of paid vacation. In 1998 French workers succeeded in gaining a thirty-five-hour workweek—although they had to grant capitalists considerable flexibility in work scheduling to get it.)

In principle, a labor-saving technological improvement introduced into the workplace can be used to increase either production or leisure. Do we want more goods with the same labor or the same goods with less labor? Or perhaps something in between: a bit more goods and a bit more leisure. Tradeoffs are, in principle, possible. In a worker-managed firm, all these options are on the table. There would seem to be no systemic bias to the choice. Making more money is always attractive, but so too is working less. It is generally easier to increase production than to rearrange work. However, increasing production means more things have to be sold, so it is safer to produce the same amount as before and take more leisure. (Productivity gains can also be used to enhance the quality of the working environment. Since the logic in this case is identical to that of opting for more leisure, I will only discuss the former. Like leisure, meaningful work is a good that workers might want, even if profits aren't increased—which means it is a real option under Economic Democracy, but not under capitalism.)

Under capitalism, labor-saving technology does not provide workers with a choice between increased consumption and more leisure. The capitalist option for "leisure" means workers are laid off. The capitalist option for consumption is the decision to increase production so as to increase profits—for the owners. Over time, this increased production may result in lower prices and hence more worker consumption, but there is nothing in this process that resembles a conscious choice.

Since choices between consumption and leisure can be freely made under Economic Democracy, we would expect to see, over time, various patterns develop, some firms opting for more leisure, some for higher incomes. Indeed, workers within a given firm could opt for different leisure-income packages, so long as overall production can be effectively coordinated. Raises and bonuses might be formulated in terms of choices between more income and more leisure. Reduced-time work, earning the same hourly rate as full-time work, could be readily offered.

We, as a society, might want to press enterprises to choose leisure over consumption rather than stay politically neutral and see what develops. There are at least two good reasons for opting for shorter working hours over increased personal income. First, there is the problem of unemployment, which, as we have seen, does not disappear under Economic Democracy. In theory at least, cutting the workweek by x percent could increase employment by x percent while maintaining output at the same level. The work is spread around. Leisure is redistributed—from the unemployed, who had too much, to the employed, who could now work less. Second, substituting leisure for consumption makes sense from an ecological point of view. The capitalist drive to keep consumption ever expanding is putting severe, perhaps unbearable, strain on our natural environment. Rich-country consumption needs to be restrained. Choosing leisure over consumption is a step in that direction.

Is it plausible that a democratic citizenry will choose to trade consumption for leisure in order to expand employment opportunities for their fellow citizens and to live more harmoniously with their environment? I think so, although it will be incumbent on environmentalists and other citizens concerned with the common good to persuade their fellow citizens to make such a choice. There are several reasons for being optimistic that such efforts at persuasion would bear fruit.

- We know that increasing consumption does not, as a general rule, make people happier. Poverty is painful and degrading, but once you have reached a certain level of material comfort and security, consuming more does little for your overall sense of well-being. In fact, it may contribute to the opposite.
- We know that large numbers of people, perhaps most of us, feel squeezed for time. To do the things that give a human life texture, meaning, and real pleasure, apart from work itself, requires real leisure: to cultivate friendships, to sustain intergenerational family ties, to engage in community service, to develop our artistic or musical or literary or dramatic abilities, to devote ourselves to a hobby or a sport, to read, to go to movies or concerts or dances, to listen to all the music we've purchased, to play with our computers, to meditate. Time has become a highly precious commodity.
- Finally, there is the ethical appeal of living a life more consonant with the demands of planetary fairness and ecological justice. It is not right to use far more than our share of the Earth's scarce resources or to contribute far more than our share of sustainable pollution. We do, after all, have certain obligations to other members of our species and to future generations. Deep down we know this, most of us do, however much capitalism tries to blind us to this basic ethical imperative.

It may not be obvious to everyone in the advanced industrial parts of the world that we need to slow down, consume less, and opt for more leisure or meaningful work as the fruits of our technology, but it is obvious to many people, and it would be more obvious still if meaningful choices between consumption and leisure were widely available. So long as capitalism remains dominant, such choices won't be on offer.

4.5 Poverty

The link between unemployment and poverty is more obvious than the link between unemployment and overwork. The vast majority of poor adults in advanced capitalist countries are able-bodied people who are unemployed or who work at minimum-wage jobs. (Working full-time at minimum wage garners $14,500 a year; the poverty line for a family of four is $22,000.) But the connection goes deeper than this straightforward observation, because poverty is not simply a matter of material deprivation. An old radical song makes the point: "Hearts starve as well as bodies; give us bread but give us roses."

It is important to distinguish "living in poverty" from "being poor." The people of Cuba, for example, are poor. The per capita income of Cuba is but a fraction of that of the United States (one-fifth, according to the CIA's *World Fact Book*[23]), yet there is little malnourishment or homelessness in Cuba, and everyone has access to basic health care. The striking result: infant mortality and life expectancy in Cuba are nearly identical to what they are in the United States. The people of Cuba are poor, but they do not live in poverty.

Grinding material poverty is a terrible thing: hunger and malnourishment, homelessness, pain, and sickness—bloated stomachs, teeth that ache and rot and go untreated, diseases that prey on weakened bodies. But poverty is not only a material phenomenon. Poverty can destroy the spirit as well as the body. What is it like to be evicted from your apartment because you can't pay the rent? What do your children think of you? What is it like to watch your child cry from hunger or a toothache or a sickness you know can be cured, but you can't afford the treatment?

4.5.1 Poverty in Rich Countries

Damage to the human spirit is particularly acute in a rich society that has removed the legal barriers to equality. The message in such societies: If you don't make it, it's your own fault. Poverty becomes unbearable. It destroys self-respect. Is it any wonder that if you are poor and without prospects, you join a gang and wreak havoc? Is it any wonder that you seek relief in alcohol, crack, meth, or some other chemical that gives a thrill and dulls the pain? Is it any wonder that you are tempted to deal the poison—your only chance, however slim, at the (false) happiness of big money? Sure, you'll likely go to prison, but so what? Inside is not so very different from outside. (The United States, during the past four decades, has seen its prison population nearly quintuple. With less than 5 percent of the world's population, the United States now contains an astonishing 25 percent of the world's prisoners, some 2.3 million adults—with another 7.3 million on probation.[24])

The only real cure for the material and spiritual ravages of poverty is decent work. We all know that. Liberal and social-democratic welfare measures can never really solve the problem, and they sometimes make it worse—as conservatives delight in pointing out. Human beings need to work. Work—good work—gives structure and meaning to your life. As a living human being, you consume, or else you would cease to be a living being. But if you consume, other people have worked for you. Self-respect demands that you contribute something in return.

But a normal psyche can bear only so much shame and guilt, so defensive mechanisms kick in: self-deception, cynicism, a hardening of the heart, a brazen disregard for basic principles of human decency. Without the pride and self-discipline that good work instills, the human spirit shrivels.[25]

Capitalism cannot provide work for all—work, period, let alone good work. Unemployment is essential to a healthy capitalism. A healthy capitalism requires not only poor people but poverty, a painful, degrading, shameful condition that people will strive mightily to avoid. How else can employers keep those workers in line? You can beat slaves or serfs but not "free" men and women. (There was a time when we dreamed of eliminating poverty in the United States. Back in the heyday of Keynesian liberalism, when "full employment" was taken seriously as an achievable goal, President Johnson declared a "War on Poverty," in his words, "a total commitment by this President, this Congress and this nation to pursue victory over the most ancient of mankind's enemies."[26] No mainstream thinker or politician would propose such a thing today. All know it is impossible—though none will point to *capitalism* as the insurmountable obstacle.)

A full-employment policy, which would eliminate domestic poverty, *can* be implemented under Economic Democracy, and will be. It doesn't follow that such a policy will be easy to design and carry out, particularly during the transition. Capitalism will have left a lot of human wreckage in its wake. Whole regions of the country (I'm thinking here of the United States, but the same is true of most rich countries) and large sections of most cities have suffered long-term impoverishment. Various "cultures of poverty" have emerged that have left many inhabitants bereft of the skills, habits, and attitudes necessary for productive work. It will doubtless take a societal commitment that calls on the resources of many dedicated people to undo the damage that has been done. We should have no illusions about the magnitude of the problem, but it is a worthy task, one that can be accomplished under Economic Democracy but not under capitalism.

4.5.2 Poverty in Poor Countries

We have been considering poor people in rich countries—and there are many. But as we all know, the situation globally is far worse: nearly half the world's population live below the World Bank's $2.50/day poverty line; 880 million people live on less than $1/day.

Poverty statistics can be presented more dramatically. Peter Singer, a philosopher long concerned with the issue of global poverty, notes that on September 11, 2001, 3,000 people died in the World Trade Center attack; on September 13, 2001, two days later, UNICEF released its report indicating that 30,000 children under five had died that day of preventable diseases—and 30,000 *every other day* during the past year, some 10 million in all.[27]

Thomas Pogge, another philosopher who has turned his attention to global poverty, observed (in 2005):

> [In the fifteen years since the end of the Cold War] some 18 million human beings have died prematurely each year from poverty-related causes, accounting for fully one-third of all human deaths. This fifteen-year death toll of 270 million is considerably larger than the 200-million death toll from all the wars, civil wars, genocides and other government repressions of the entire 20th century combined.[28]

For those who find this assertion incredible—as I did, initially—Pogge supplies a breakdown, adding up the figures for some 284 "mega-death events of violence and repression" that occurred during the century just passed, among them World War I, World War II, the atrocities of Stalin and Mao, and some 280 other calamities. The total for the *century* is a quarter less than the poverty deaths since the end of the Cold War.

Proponents of globalized capitalism like to point out that the percentage of desperately poor people has declined in recent years. They fail to note that this is largely due to the success of well-protected, market-socialist China in lifting hundreds of millions out of poverty. On the other hand, the most precipitous drop in living standards ever witnessed in peacetime occurred in the ex-Soviet Union, following its renunciation of socialism.[29]

What is so galling, tragic, heartbreaking, hideous (choose your adjective) about global poverty is how little it would take, in material terms, to eliminate it. So many human beings dying so young, so many people too famished or disease ridden to function normally, so many members of our species without a chance at human happiness: how much would it cost to end this nightmare? Oxford economist Partha Dasgupta sums up his calculations thus:

> Resources required for eliminating poverty amount to approximately ten percent of their national income in sub-Sahara Africa and the Indian subcontinent. . . . Assuming a growth rate of income per head of one percent per year [a growth rate routinely exceeded in India and Pakistan], poverty in these parts could in principle be eradicated in ten years.[30]

Peter Singer has offered some calculations of this own. He took a look at the UN Millennium Development Goals, which were set in 2000 by the largest gathering of world leaders in history. Among the goals, endorsed by these 189 dignitaries, to be accomplished by 2015:

- To reduce by half the proportion of people who suffer from hunger
- To ensure that children everywhere can take a full course of primary schooling
- To reduce by two-thirds the under-five infant mortality rate
- To reduce by half the number of people without access to safe drinking water
- To halt, then begin to reverse the spread of HIV/AIDS, malaria, and other major diseases

Singer looked at the cost estimate for meeting these goals, as calculated by the special U.N. task force charged with making such an estimate. He then looked at the incomes of the *top tenth of 1 percent of the U.S. taxpayers.* His conclusion was startling, even to himself: if the top 0.01 percent (the top one one-hundredth of 1 percent) contributed a third of their annual income (leaving each household with an average $8 million to spend as they please) and the rest of the top 0.1 percent contributed a quarter (leaving them with an average of $1.5 million with which to play)—we would have $126 billion to $5 billion *more* than was needed that year (2006) to meet those goals. That is to say, without any additional contributions from *any* government (including our own), *any* non-U.S. citizen, or *any* U.S. citizen from the bottom 99.9 percent of our population, we could meet the Millennium Goals.

Global poverty could be eliminated. Unfortunately, it won't be—not so long as global capitalism prevails, not in ten or fifteen years, not ever. The link between capitalism and the poverty of poor countries is more complex than the link between capitalism and the domestic poverty in rich countries, but is no less sure. Domestic unemployment—and dispiriting poverty—is necessary for a healthy capitalist economy. Labor must be disciplined. Poor-country poverty is more a by-product of global capitalism than a structural necessity. To be sure, poor-country capitalists need their workforces disciplined, but the extent of poverty in their countries far exceeds this structural requirement. Capitalism requires some poverty, but not an impoverished majority.

Historically, most currently poor regions of the world were plundered by capitalist colonial empires and had their autonomous development blocked.[31] The centers of capital wanted access to cheap raw materials and outlets for their surplus production. Force was employed to secure these ends. Exploitation enriched the powerful and impoverished the weak. As Marx observed,

> The discovery of gold and silver in America, the extirpation, enslavement and entombment in mines of the aboriginal population, the beginning of the con-

quest and looting of the East Indies, the turning of Africa into a warren for the commercial hunting of black skins, signalized the rosy dawn of the era of capitalist production.[32]

That was then. What about now? The centers of capital still want access to cheap raw materials and outlets for their surplus production, but force is not so necessary any more. Nor do rich-country capitalists stand to gain from an increase in global poverty. To the contrary—poor people buy less than rich people. Capitalists like low wages, but they also like healthy workers and good consumers. Stark poverty is unattractive, even to capitalists. Nevertheless, the unintended effect of rational capitalist action is to increase global poverty rather than ameliorate it.

How capitalism can increase poverty is no mystery. In *Capital*, Marx notes the horrendous consequences to Indian textile workers that the opening of Indian markets to British textiles brought about. Their hand-looms couldn't compete with British power-looms. He quotes from the governor-general's report of 1834–1835: "The misery hardly finds parallel in the history of commerce. The bones of the cotton weavers are bleaching the plains of India."[33]

This scenario has been repeated countless times in poor countries: local agriculture and local industry wrecked by cheap imports. The technological advances nourished by capitalism, which could, in theory, better the conditions of everyone without making anyone worse off, have, in practice, destroyed the livelihoods of millions and torn apart the social fabric of vast regions.

God forbid that poor countries try to protect themselves! The British used their gunboats to bring China into line—in the name of free trade—when the Chinese tried to block the importation of opium into their country. (It might be noted that capitalism's first "drug war," the Opium War of 1839–1842, was a war *in favor of* drugs.) Subsequently, the mechanisms became more subtle, but the goal has remained constant: keep all countries "open"—not necessarily to liberty or democracy, but to Western capital and commodities.

Poor countries, most now firmly in the hands of pro-Western elites, go along, although now, with the income gap ever widening, the smaller countries have become less important to global capitalism's health and well-being. They continue to serve as minor markets for rich-country production and as a source of cheap raw materials, but unemployed people in poor regions generate little effective demand, and so, apart from being a source of cheap labor (which now exists in near infinite abundance), most are of little interest to global capital. In the coming decades, if the structures of global capitalism continue to dominate, a few poor countries might make it into the ranks of the middle-income countries, but most will not. For all the fine talk of "emerging markets" (a current euphemism for what used to be called the

"Third World"), very few countries will "emerge" from poverty. Most will sink ever deeper, as cheap imports and new technologies render more and more workers superfluous. The younger workers, particularly the men, will be ever more drawn into crime and internecine warfare, killing for crumbs and the brief thrill of violence. A few may decide to wreak a little havoc in rich countries—especially in the one that dominates all others.

Some of the world's superfluous poor will migrate to the advanced capitalist countries. From the point of view of the capitalist class, this is a good thing: low-cost nannies and housekeepers, workers willing to work harder and for less than domestic workers, and a source of potent racial resentment to keep the working class confused and divided. (Small wonder that capitalists love the invisible hand. It acts so shrewdly on their behalf, while absolving them of all personal responsibility.)

The people left behind must go begging to international agencies that insist that their countries be made attractive to foreign capital. Their ruling elites comply, despite the fact that there will be few, if any, winners among these countries and lots of losers in this beggar-thy-neighbor game of fools. The elites know this, but, so they say, "it's the only game in town." The watchword becomes *sauve qui peut*—every man for himself. The luckiest (and/or most corrupt) among the elite will make it. There are enclaves now in all of the world's major cities where the poor-country rich can live a lifestyle not much different from their rich-country counterparts—and ignore the megaslums outside their walled and guarded compounds and the even more wretched countryside beyond. At least for now.

How do things look from the point of view of Economic Democracy? If all or a large part of the world were structured along the lines of Economic Democracy, what could be done?

The analysis developed so far points to some basic prescriptions. Let us consider the question from two points of view. What should rich countries do to help poor countries? What should poor countries do to help themselves?

Suppose a rich country were restructured as an Economic Democracy. If this transformation came about as a result of a social movement inspired by deep humanistic ideals (which is the only way it will ever come about), it would want to do something to alleviate the global poverty that capitalism both profited from and exacerbated. The first order of business would thus be to stop the exploitation. Three steps would take us a long way toward that end.

- Forgive all poor-country debts owed its banks. It is criminal for poor countries to be drained of scarce resources to pay interest on loans that can never be repaid, loans, moreover, the proceeds from which were usually squandered in graft or used for projects (often recommended by rich-country advisors) that made lives worse for the majority of the citizenry.[34] Individuals and businesses in advanced capitalist countries are allowed to declare bankruptcy when things get too bad and start over with a clean slate. The same privilege should be extended to poor countries. Since banks under Economic Democracy are public, not private, and get their funds from the capital assets tax, debt forgiveness will have little or no negative impact on the forgiving country's economy.

- Reconstitute the subdivisions of the multinationals that are located in poor countries as worker self-managed enterprises. If the multinational has been nationalized under Economic Democracy and turned over to its workers, formal ownership remains with the government. (Remember, workers *lease* their enterprises from society, paying the capital-assets tax as a leasing fee.) Subsidiaries in foreign countries can be deeded to the workers there, or turned over to their government, on condition that the enterprise be managed democratically. The newly constituted company will enter into a contractual agreement with the parent company to continue to supply whatever goods or services it currently supplies as a subsidiary, so as to minimize economic disruption.

- Phase in a policy of socialist fair trade. Fair trade works to the benefit of poor countries by assuring them higher prices for their exports. As a result, fewer local resources need be devoted to export production; more will be available for local use. Fair trade should be phased in gradually, to give rich countries time to adjust their consumption patterns in response to higher-priced poor-country imports, and poor countries time to adjust their own productive capabilities in accordance with the resulting altered demand.

Apart from ending the mechanisms of exploitation inherent in capitalist financial, production, and trade relationships, what else might a rich Economic Democracy do that would be helpful to poor countries? Such countries would doubtless welcome free technology transfer—an exemption from the patent restrictions, for example. All "intellectual property" should be free to poor countries. Poor countries would also benefit if rich countries would redirect a meaningful portion of their research and development budgets toward dealing with poor-country problems, and would incorporate poor-country researchers into the process. (Malaria kills nearly a million people each year and debilitates millions more, and yet only $1.8 billion is spent each year, worldwide, on malaria control—less than half of David Tepper's income in 2009, and less than one-quarter of 1 percent of the $700 billion the United States spent on the military that year.[35])

These steps should be taken, regardless of the internal structure of the poor countries themselves. Suppose the poor country is itself an Economic Democracy. What should it do to address the issue of poverty? Clearly, the government should make basic education and basic health care a top priority. Both of these areas are labor intensive and not terribly expensive. We know from the experience of Cuba, the Indian state of Kerala (which elected a communist government in 1957 and has since returned the party to power many times), and elsewhere that large gains can be made at a modest cost if the right sorts of institutions are put in place.[36] A poor country could use some aid from rich countries to help with this process and to develop its economic infrastructure, but it should view this aid as temporary. It would want to avoid relationships of economic dependency that could impede its own autonomous development—whether that dependency is called "foreign aid," "foreign direct investment," or "reparations." Its leaders know that large infusions of cash and credit can be corrupting and can often make bad problems worse. Moreover, such money transfers feed the illusion that rich-country models of development and patterns of consumption are optimal, which they most surely are not.[37]

Well-governed poor countries, individually or in confederation with countries at similar levels of development, should aim at basic sustainable self-sufficiency. Some international division of labor may be in order, but since new technologies have tended to make possible the production of almost anything almost anywhere, countries and regions can aim at "import substitution," using resources locally available and technologies appropriate to their specific environments. These countries know that they will need to develop their own models of development and their own patterns of consumption. In doing so, they may well teach rich countries some important lessons. (For an inspiring account of what local scientists, engineers, and artisans working together with peasants, urban street kids, and indigenous peoples can accomplish even under extremely adverse conditions, see Alan Weisman's report on Gaviotas, an experimental, sustainable, beautiful community in the harsh savannas of eastern Colombia. To see what progressive city planning can do when conditions are right, consider the imaginative innovations that have made Curitaba in Brazil a model city.[38])

4.5.3 A Note on Racism

In ethnically mixed rich countries, poverty tends to fall disproportionately on minorities. This is vividly true in the United States. In 2009, the median income for black families was $32,500, that of non-Hispanic white families $54,000—a ratio that has remained essentially unchanged over the last forty years.[39]

But why should poverty be concentrated among minorities? As we have seen, capitalism needs unemployment, and it needs that unemployment to be unpleasant, but these requirements would seem to have nothing to do with race. To be sure, capitalism is historically linked to racism. Racism provided the ideological justification for the European colonization of the nonwhite world and for the immensely lucrative commercialization of slavery, factors that gave vital impetus to capitalism's takeoff. But that was long ago. We are speaking here of mature capitalism. Might it not be one of the progressive features of capitalism that it should, over time, eliminate racism—just as it eliminated feudal serfdom and (eventually) the very slavery that had initially proved to be so valuable to it?

Free-marketeers are fond of claiming that capitalism is inherently antiracist. Capitalists, they say, want the best workers they can get; hence, anything that artificially restricts the labor pool runs contrary to their interests. To the extent that racism persists under capitalism, it is white workers, not capitalists, who are to blame, since these workers have an interest in restricting competition for better paying jobs.[40]

This argument is not wholly specious. It is true that workers want to keep job competition to a minimum. When jobs are in short supply—as they almost always are under capitalism—an objective basis for working-class racism exists. It is also true that certain interests of the capitalist class are ill served by racism. Capital wants its various labor pools to be large and well qualified. Racial barriers to employment restrict these pools. Capital wants its reserve army to be well equipped to work. Racially concentrated poverty does not serve this end.

However, against these disadvantages to capital occasioned by racism, we must set a huge advantage. Racism keeps the working class divided. In the United States, from post–Civil War reconstruction onward, southern business interests fought hard—by any means necessary—to prevent transracial class alliances from forming. Meanwhile, northern industrialists imported black strikebreakers from the South to foil early attempts at labor organizing, thus exacerbating racial animosities. Methods are more subtle now, but it is no accident that the political party most closely identified with business interests (i.e., the Republican Party) is the one that plays the "race card" most often. Working people do not spontaneously identify with the interests of business—for good reason. Hence, those politicians representing business interests most blatantly must make their appeal to voters on other grounds. No better ground exists than racism. (The racist undercurrent in the Tea Party movement has been widely noted.[41])

Here the racialization of poverty works to their advantage. Politicians need not appeal to race directly, which would now alienate many voters, but can take their stand against "crime" and against "welfare." Their policies, when implemented, make matters worse, but no matter. This merely gives their next round of appeals for "law and order" all the more force—so much so that the opposition Democratic Party must distance itself from its "liberal" past and also promise more toughness on crime and "an end to welfare as we know it."

Since racism is so effective at short-circuiting class solidarity, you will never find the capitalist class (i.e., the ruling class) exerting themselves collectively to eliminate racism. Certain segments of that class will be concerned with ameliorating the uglier aspects of racism—particularly those that interfere with workplace efficiency or adversely affect the business climate of a community, region, or the nation, but the wealthy can shield themselves from most of the social consequences of racial stratification. And they know that should a class-based political movement emerge that seriously calls corporate (capitalist) interests into question, they will need to galvanize voters into opposition. The politically active elements know from long experience how useful racism can be in this regard.

If it is unreasonable to expect racism to be eliminated under capitalism, can we be any more optimistic about Economic Democracy? The answer is yes, for two reasons:

- Job competition will not be so fierce under Economic Democracy, so the objective basis for racism among workers is weakened. Economic Democracy will be a full-employment economy. Capitalism cannot be.
- There will not exist a politically powerful class with a vested interest in keeping the working class divided; hence, a political commitment to end racism faces fewer obstacles.

It does not follow that racism will disappear automatically with the advent of Economic Democracy. Neither of its two basic institutions, workplace democracy and social control of investment, guarantees that minority interests will not be sacrificed to majority interests. The elimination of racism becomes objectively possible under Economic Democracy, but it will take conscientious effort to make that possibility a reality.

Thus, it is important for anyone hoping for a future beyond capitalism to confront the problem of racism now. The struggle against racial injustice cannot be postponed until "after the revolution" (nor the struggle against sexism and homophobia either, to which at least some of the above analysis also applies).

4.5.4 A Note on Immigration

We should be careful not to confuse the issue of racism per se with issues surrounding the large-scale immigration of people from poor countries to rich countries, which is now fanning the fires of racism in many parts of the world. Obviously, the rights of people who enter a country legally should be fully respected. Under present conditions, the rights of "illegal" immigrants must also be protected. But we shouldn't lose sight of three important points.

First, there is nothing inherently wrong or inherently racist about a country's wanting to restrict the flow of immigration. A sense of common identity and common culture is vital to a healthy society. Taken to excess—with no allowance for diversity within a shared framework—this sense can become ugly and chauvinistic, but the radical individualism that constitutes the other pole of the community-individual dialectic is also problematic. Controlled immigration can contribute to invigorating a society, but uncontrolled immigration has negative consequences that are by no means equally shared. Such immigration is good for the capitalist class and others in the upper-income brackets, who reap the benefits but bear little of the costs. The costs, however, are real—and are borne largely by the lower classes: downward pressure on wages, upward pressure on rents, and an additional burdening of already meager social services. (It is often said that immigrants are willing to do the work that local workers won't do. This is a half-truth. Local workers may not be willing to work for the same low wage as immigrant workers, but if labor is in short supply, wages will rise or the jobs will be redesigned. That is the way a market economy works.)

Second, large-scale emigration impacts negatively on poor countries. The term "brain drain" has gone out of fashion, but the reality remains. Poor countries lose large numbers of their best and brightest—not only their educated "best," but young people generally who have the most courage and initiative. After all, it is not easy when you are poor to make your way to a foreign land, nor is it easy for you when you get there—a land where the customs, laws, and language are different from your own, and where many people are hostile to your presence. Typically, these emigrants remit large amounts of their earnings home, which cushions the loss, but the fact remains that they are no longer on hand to contribute their energy, intelligence, and skills to resolving the problems of their own country.

Third, so long as the heavy weight of globalized capitalism presses down on poor countries, the pressure to emigrate will intensify. Few poor people undertake the arduous trek from their home country simply because rich countries are rich. Usually they are driven by desperation. More often than not, conditions have become desperate because of the dynamics of global capitalism, which we have analyzed. The free flow of goods and capital, so beloved by global corporations and their allies in government, academia, and the media, exacts a terrible price. Small businesses are destroyed. Labor-intensive subsistence agriculture is replaced by more capital-intensive cash-crop farming. We are told that these "disruptions" will only be temporary, but not even those doing the telling really believe that line any more. No one really expects those mysterious flows of capital, guided by the invisible hand, to revitalize south Asia, sub-Sahara Africa, or Latin America. A few lucky countries might make it—although the dearth of good examples, despite decades of trying, does not inspire much hope. If capitalism continues, our children and grand-children will almost surely live in a world where millions of desperate people, fleeing from poverty, disease, and social disintegration, will be trying to find a saving niche in a rich country—where they will not be met with open arms.

5

Capitalism or Socialism?

Economic Instability, Environmental Degradation, Democracy

The preceding chapter examined four fundamental problems with capitalism: staggering inequality, widespread unemployment, the intensification of work for those who remain employed, and intractable poverty, both domestic and global. There it was argued that these problems are causally connected to the deep structures of capitalism, and hence are not amenable to simple reform. It was also argued that these problems would be either nonexistent or at least far less serious under Economic Democracy. This chapter takes on three more such issues: economic instability, environmental degradation, and the absence of genuine democracy. Here too we will see the connections between fundamental problems and the deep structures of capitalism and how different things might be in an Economic Democracy.

5.1 Economic Instability

In 2003 Robert Lucas, Nobel laureate in economics, during his presidential address to the American Economics Association, declared that "the central problem of depression prevention has, for all practical purposes, been solved, and has, in fact, been solved for many decades." It was time, he declared, for the profession to move on. As Paul Krugman has remarked, "Looking back from only a few years later, with much of the world in the throes of a financial and economic crisis all too reminiscent of the 1930s, these optimistic pronouncements sound almost incredibly smug."[1]

Capitalism, throughout its history, has been prone to crises, crises of a sort different from those to which any previous economic system ever experienced, crises due not to some external event—drought, flood, plague, war—but to some internal feature of the system itself. As Marx and Engels noted, "In these crises there breaks out an epidemic that, in all earlier epochs, would have seemed an absurdity—the epidemic of overproduction."[2]

But how are crises of overproduction possible? If the weather is good, and I get an exceptional harvest of zucchinis from my vegetable garden, that is not a problem. I can always give away the excess. Of course, if I am producing for a farmers market, and all the other zucchini growers also bring in more zucchinis than usual, competition may drive down the price for all of us. That would be a problem for us, the zucchini growers, but not for the community at large. We would have less money in our pockets, and so we wouldn't be able to buy as much from others—but our happy customers would have more money in their pockets, so they could pick up the slack.

It is only when wage labor becomes predominant in the economy that generalized overproduction becomes a major threat. For when there is too much produced in a given industry, causing prices to fall, *production will be cut back*. That is to say, *workers will be laid off*. But these workers are also consumers. If they are laid off, they can't buy what they did before, hence demand drops for the goods they would have bought. So there is now "overproduction" in those other areas as well, causing layoffs in those industries too, further decreasing demand, which affects more and more industries, and so on.

We have encountered this contradiction before: On the one hand, wages are a cost of production, and hence capitalists (owners of means of production) are motivated to keep wages down. On the other hand, capitalists must sell their products in order to realize a profit. If wages are too low, workers can't buy all the goods produced.

"But workers aren't the only consumers," you say. "So are capitalists." True, but the trouble is, there are too few of them to consume all the surplus. Anyway, that's not how capitalism works. That's the way feudalism worked. Those feudal lords consumed the surplus produced by their peasants, living high and making war on each other. It is a fundamental feature of capitalism that the capitalist class, unlike its feudal counterpart, does not consume all the surplus, but *invests* a significant portion, thus giving capitalism its extraordinary economic dynamism. ("The bourgeoisie, during its rule of scarce one hundred years, has created more massive and more colossal productive forces than have all preceding generations altogether." That's Marx and Engels, not Milton Friedman.[3])

But what does "investment" mean in real, material terms? It means putting a portion of the labor force to work creating more factories and other means of production, so that the scale of an enterprise or industry can expand. It means developing new technologies so as to enhance productivity. This enhanced productivity makes possible a better life for all.

This possibility remains only that—a possibility. If the fruits of the productivity gain remain only with the capitalist class (which is what Marx thought would happen), society as a whole does not benefit. Indeed, when wages fail to keep pace with increased production gains, the threat of overproduction—and ensuing crisis—increases.

But there have been many periods when the fruits of the new technologies *have* been widely distributed. The postwar "Golden Age" (1945–1975) in the United States was one such happy time: real wages rose steadily, and most Americans saw their living standards improve dramatically. It became a cliché of the time: "We live better than our parents; our children will live better than us. That's how capitalism works." Only it doesn't. Not always.

"Golden-age growth," that is, steady growth that enhances the standard of living for most people in society, is possible under capitalism, but for the possibility to become a reality, at least five conditions must be met:

1. Capitalists must invest in the real economy.
2. The investments must enhance productivity.
3. Overall production must increase.
4. Workers must have enough money to buy the increased production.
5. Workers must want to buy the increased production.

Let us consider these factors more carefully.

1. Capitalists must invest in the real economy. A healthy capitalism requires steady investment in the real economy to compensate for the facts that (a) workers themselves do not have sufficient funds to purchase all of the goods and services produced and (b) personal consumption by the capitalist class is insufficient to make up the difference. Investment, which also involves buying things (not consumer goods, but "capital goods"—the machinery, raw materials, and other intermediate goods that will be used to produce more goods during the next production period than were produced during the present period), must fill the gap. If investment falls off, workers in the industries supplying capital goods are laid off, demand drops throughout the economy, more workers are laid off, and so on.

Thus we see that a healthy, stable capitalism requires *investor confidence*. If capitalists simply save their profits, savings will outstrip investment, goods will remain unsold, workers will be let go: recession. (This was Keynes's essential diagnosis: recessions occur when savings exceed investment.)

2. The investments must enhance productivity. For investor confidence to be maintained, investments must pay off. Not all of them, of course, but most of them. That is to say, the anticipated productivity gains must materialize. If they don't, investors lose confidence in the economy and hold on to their money—or send it abroad in search of greener pastures.

Will investment always lead to productivity gains sufficient to keep investors happy? There is an act of faith operating here, faith that human ingenuity will always come up with ways of producing more products that people can be enticed to buy, *and* that these investment opportunities will be sufficiently numerous to absorb the funds the capitalists have on hand to invest.

(The possibility of declining opportunities for profitable investment was a serious concern among first-generation Keynesians. The American Keynesian Alvin Hansen, for example, formulated his "stagnation thesis" in the late 1930s. The Keynesian-Marxist economists Paul Sweezy and Paul Baran made this thesis the focus of their influential critique. But, "military Keynesianism" saved the day. World War II broke out shortly after Hansen's *Full Recovery or Stagnation?* was published. The Vietnam War escalated shortly after Baran and Sweezy's *Monopoly Capital* appeared.[4] The "military-industrial complex" seemed to provide endless opportunity for technological innovation that could be translated into private-sector, highly profitable output, thus keeping workers employed and the economy growing. With the Cold War raging and the "arms race" in full swing, investment opportunities were abundant. Economists stopped worrying.)

3. Overall production must increase. A necessary condition for stable capitalist growth is ever-rising productivity, but this is not a sufficient condition—for higher productivity need not translate into more production. An increase in productivity means that more goods *can be* produced. It doesn't follow that more goods *will* be produced. When businesses are concerned about being able to sell all they can produce, they can (and often do) use their productivity gains not to increase production but to decrease their costs, that is, *to cut back their workforces*—which decreases overall worker consumption, which decreases effective demand, which leads to trouble.

4. Workers must have enough money to buy the increased production. Stable capitalist growth requires that effective demand remain high. In particular, workers must have *enough money* to keep increasing their consumption. When worker consumption drops off, capitalists can increase their own consumption to pick up some of the slack, but there are simply too few of them to offset lagging worker consumption. (In recent years, the wealthy have increased their own consumption dramatically, purchasing private jets, ever larger yachts, ever more spectacular villas, etc., creating what *Wall Street Journal* reporter Robert Frank has labeled "Richistan," a separate country within

our country. Three unnamed members of this country provided Frank with their annual expense statements. To cite but one: yachts—$20 million; air-charters/private jets—$3 million; house staff—$2.2 million; personal beauty/salon/spa—$200,000, including $80,000 for massages.[5])

One way of keeping up effective demand is for the capitalists to pay their workers ever higher wages. This is the "Golden Age" solution. It is, in fact, the only long-run solution. There is, however, another way of increasing worker consumption. Rather than pay higher wages, give workers access to *credit*. "You don't have enough money now to buy what we need to sell you?" asks the capitalist. "That's okay. We will *loan* you the money. You can keep consuming more and more, even if your wages don't go up." For the capitalists, this solution looks better than paying higher wages. Not only do their products get sold, but they also collect interest on those loans. The best of all possible worlds.

Or so it might seem until you do the math. If your wages are stagnant, but you keep consuming more and more, you have to borrow more and more—to pay for your ever-rising consumption *and* the interest on your ever-mounting debt. (Anyone who has seen his credit card debt explode as a result of making only minimum payments will recognize this phenomenon.)

Needless to say, this can't go on. You no longer look to be a good credit risk. Your sources of credit dry up. Your consumption declines precipitously. Those from whom you used to buy can no longer sell you as much . . . the downward spiral.

5. Workers must want to buy the increased production. One might wonder: why do people keep consuming more and more, even when they don't have the money to do so? Or even if they do. Common sense, reinforced by all the major religious traditions, tells us that money doesn't buy happiness. Science tells us the same thing. Happiness has been much studied of late. Bill McKibben cites some of the findings:

> Compared to 1950, the average American family now owns twice as many cars, uses 21 times as much plastic, and travels 25 times farther by air. Gross Domestic Product has tripled since 1950 in the U.S. We obviously eat more calories. And yet—the satisfaction meter seems not to have budged. More Americans say their marriages are unhappy, their jobs are hideous, and they don't like the place where they live. The number who, all things considered, say they are "very happy" with their lives has slid steadily over that period. . . . In the United Kingdom per capita gross domestic product grew 66 per cent between 1973 and 2001, and yet people's satisfaction with their lives changed not a whit. Nor did it budge in Japan, despite a fivefold increase in income in the postwar years.[6]

But if our common/religious/scientific sense were to be translated into widespread behavior, capitalism would be in trouble. If people don't want ever more goods and services, how can investors continue to make money with their money? What could capitalists do with all the money they rake in each year, far in excess of that they can spend on personal consumption? What would happen to "investor confidence," that psychological state that holds a capitalist economy hostage?

There is only one solution within the framework of capitalism. Common sense must be overridden. People must be *persuaded* to buy. In the United States $300 billion was spent in 2007 on advertising (about half of what was spent on national defense or on *all* primary and secondary education), and advertising is but one aspect of the "sales effort." Advertising comprises about 30 percent of "marketing," the latter totaling $1 trillion.[7] This effort has been remarkably successful. As Juliet Schor has noted,

> From the perspective of fifty years earlier, when the nation was already very pros- perous, the expansion of consumption is striking. In 1960 the average person con- sumed just a third of what he or she did in late 2008. Since 1990, inflation-adjusted per-person expenditures have risen 300 percent for furniture and household goods, 80 percent for apparel, and 15–20 percent for vehicles, housing and food. Overall, average real per-person spending has increased 42 percent.[8]

Schor also points out that consumption in wealthy countries is now driven less and less by need or even convenience, more and more by its role in symbolic communication: "Brands, styles, and exclusivity are used to convey social status, construct identity and differentiate or join with others. These symbolic aspects of consumption have become more valued."[9] Needless to say, so many goods have taken on significant symbolic value only because of successful marketing campaigns.

Economists are well aware of the necessity of this irrationality, although few ever say so openly. Paul Krugman is (once again) an exception:

> There is one very powerful argument that can be made on behalf of recent American consumerism; not that it's good for consumers, but that it has been good for producers. You see, spending may not produce happiness, but it does create jobs, and unemployment is very effective at creating misery. Better to have manic consumers American style, than the depressive consumers of Japan. . . . There is a strong element of rat race in America's consumer-led boom, but those rats racing in their cages are what have kept the wheels of commerce turning. And while it will be a shame if Americans continue to compete over who can own the most toys, the worst thing of all would be if the competition comes to a sudden halt.[10]

The advertising and related marketing techniques that encourage consumers to compete over who can *own the most toys* help maintain effective demand,

and hence employment, but there is another kind of marketing that can have the opposite effect—marketing that stresses *lower prices*. To the extent that enterprises emphasize ever-lower prices, they must exert ever more effort at keeping the wages of their own workers down and must also keep the pressure on their suppliers to keep *their* costs of production down, thus putting downward pressure on the wages of the supplying industries also. If consumers begin to shift from buying ever more toys to buying ever-cheaper toys, the prospect of steady, stable growth diminishes and the specter of rising unemployment increases, not only because overall aggregate demand does not increase, but also, and more immediately, because more and more small businesses go under.

To summarize: we see that although relatively steady, stable, golden-age capitalist growth is possible, there are obstacles to achieving this happy state. Among the most serious:

- Insufficient investment in the real economy.
- Hoped-for productivity increases don't emerge.
- Productivity gains translate into laying people off rather than producing more goods.
- Increasing indebtedness substitutes for increasing wages to keep up effective demand.
- Marketing efforts shift toward emphasizing lower costs rather than superior quality.
- Consumers become more resistant to marketing efforts.

We have focused thus far on recessionary instability, but there's also the flip side: surging optimism out of all proportion to underlying economic reality—soaring stock markets, rising home prices, that is, the good-time "bubbles" that so often precede recessions. Just as investor pessimism can become a self-fulfilling prophecy, so too can investor optimism: when asset prices are rising, more and more money flows into those asset markets, pushing prices ever higher. (Notice how different financial markets are from ordinary markets: When the prices of goods or services rise, people tend to cut back on their purchases—as Adam Smith's invisible hand encourages them to do. But when asset prices are rising, people do just the opposite; they buy more and more. Such behavior should cast doubt on the invisible-hand "efficiency" of financial markets.[11])

When an asset bubble is inflating, people feel richer, spend more, the economy appears strong. But as we all now know, stock bubbles, tech bubbles, real estate bubbles: they all burst. What goes up can come crashing down—and inevitably does so when asset values diverge too far from their underlying real-economy values. Just as people rush to buy when others are buying, because market values are going up, the same people rush to sell when others are selling, because market values are dropping fast.

Although linked, there is a large, fundamental asymmetry between the bubble and the bust: *bubbles always burst—but recessions need not end.* As stock prices diverge further and further from the real value of the assets that the stock shares represent, the cleverer shareholders begin to watch closely. (Since a share of stock is an ownership stake in a real company that owns real property, real equipment, and real inventory, one can calculate, at least approximately, the real value of the firm's real assets.) When should they bail out? Their paper wealth has increased dramatically as their shares have gone up in price. But they know their paper wealth can deflate just as fast or faster, so, at a certain point they must sell, so as to convert that paper wealth into cash—and they must do so before others rush to sell. Hence, inevitably, there comes a point when the clever ones begin to sell. Stock prices stop rising, begin to decline, then comes the stampede. This always happens.

But when a bubble bursts and a recession ensues, we now know what to do, don't we? Remember Lucas's confident assertion: "The central problem of depression prevention has, for all practical purposes, been solved, and has, in fact, been solved for many decades." How has it been solved? Well, *the government* is supposed to step in. Laissez-faire capitalism may sink into permanent depression, but we need not stand idly by. This was Keynes's fundamental point.

The government has four tools in its economic recovery tool kit, two constituting *monetary policy* (under control of the government's central bank) and two constituting *fiscal policy* (under the control of the legislature). Tool 1 involves reducing interest rates to encourage borrowing and spending. Tool 2 involves printing money (or the keystroke equivalent) and injecting it into the economy—which is done by using newly created money to redeem government bonds, or by adding it directly to the accounts of troubled banks.

It is crucial for the banking system to remain viable. If this means bailing out the banks from time to time, so be it. For when banks get into trouble, they stop making loans. These loans are needed by businesses in the real economy, since, typically, these businesses must pay for their raw materials and their workers' wages *before* they sell their products. If they can't borrow funds to do this, they cut back production, lay off workers, and so on. The downturn intensifies.

But simply saving the banks doesn't insure an economic recovery. Consumers must spend more so that investors will invest more. Investor confidence, remember, is the key to economic growth. Unless investor confidence is restored, the bad times continue.

If monetary policy proves insufficient, fiscal policy must be used. In essence, fiscal policy involves deliberately running a deficit. The government, during a recession, must spend more than it takes in, so as to stimulate the economy. Tool 3 is cutting taxes. This is a popular option. It adds to the deficit, but it does so by putting money into consumers' pockets directly, which, even more than reducing interest rates, encourages them to spend.

But if consumers save this money instead of spending it, or use it to pay down their debts, this element of the Keynesian stimulus also fails. There remains one final programmatic option, tool 4: create or expand government programs. The government can create jobs directly, paying for them by borrowing or by printing the money. (Remember Keynes: put banknotes in bottles, pay people to bury them, and let others dig them up. Better than doing nothing—though there are doubtless more useful things that these workers might do.)

And if this doesn't work? Well, so far it always has. "The central problem of depression prevention has been solved," Lucas assures us. "Cross your fingers," says Krugman.

Things would be very different in a democratic economy. Social control of investment counters capitalism's constant vulnerability to both "irrational exuberance" and recession. The former occurs, as we have seen, when speculators begin pouring money into assets expected to go up in value, that is, into land and housing or into pieces of paper—stocks, bonds, commodity futures, and assorted other financial "derivatives." The latter occurs when investors lose confidence that investments in the real economy will pay off. They don't invest, workers are laid off, demand decreases—the downward spiral.

Speculative bubbles are impossible in Economic Democracy for a very simple reason. Apart from community-based savings and loan associations, *there are no financial markets* in Economic Democracy: no stock markets, bond markets, futures markets, currency markets, markets for "mortgage-backed securities" or for any other financial "derivative." The institutions that generate and allocate funds for investment are simple and transparent. They present no opportunity for speculation (i.e., financial gambling), and little room for gaming the system. (In 2009 more than a quarter of *all* profits in the United States were made by financial firms, "an industry that doesn't design, build or sell a single tangible thing."[12])

Economic Democracy is not vulnerable to the recessionary dynamic either, for three reasons:

- Most importantly, Economic Democracy does not depend on private investors. There is no class of people who can "lose confidence" in the economy and either park their funds in a savings institution or send them abroad. If demand for new business investments slackens under Economic Democracy, the excess accumulating in the investment fund will be returned to the firms as a tax rebate, to be refunded immediately to their workers, who now have more money to spend. There need be no reduction at all in overall effective demand.

- The policy of socialist protectionism also keeps recessionary tendencies at bay. Not only does capital not flee the country when investment opportunities decline, but socialist protectionism blocks the downward pressure on wages that imports from low-wage countries exert under free-trade capitalism. Jobs are more secure. Effective demand remains high.
- Finally, there is the positive flip side of a democratic firm's reluctance to take on new workers. It is also reluctant to let workers go when times turn bad. All may see their incomes reduced, but there are no sudden, dramatic layoffs. This reluctance puts a brake to the downward spiral.

Would a stable economy be too boring? You can still get rich in an Economic Democracy. You can start up a business, which might succeed big time. Such thrills remain available. But the thrill of seeing your stock portfolio soar in value, the agony of watching it tumble—alas: no more.

5.1.1 A Note on the Current Crisis

Let us consider the current economic crisis, which began in the United States in late 2007, in light of the preceding analysis. Why did it happen? What is to be done?

Let us set aside the immorality and illegality that have garnered so much attention:

- Unscrupulous real estate brokers enticing people to sign contracts they didn't understand
- Corrupt rating agencies giving triple-A ratings to high-risk securities
- Lax regulators
- Investment banks concocting securities they knew were rotten, then buying "credit default swaps" so as to bet against them

Let us begin with the standard account: The current crisis was caused by the bursting of the housing bubble, which led to those "mortgaged-backed securities"—securities created by bundling hundreds of mortgages, then slicing and dicing the pile into parts of varying risk, then selling the parts to investors—becoming "toxic," that is, unsellable, thus causing the credit markets to freeze up. Without access to credit, businesses had to cut back, lay off workers, which decreased consumer demand, which caused more layoffs, which decreased demand further, and so on.

Well and good, but this story doesn't address the more basic question: Why did we get a housing bubble in the first place? Why did we have a concurrent stock market bubble? (The U.S. stock market soared in tandem with housing prices, the Dow surpassing 14,000 in 2007.)

Let us think about the basic Marxian-Keynesian analysis discussed in the previous section. As Marx pointed out, capitalism is prone to crises that would have been incomprehensible to early forms of society—crises of *over*production. In all previous epochs, economic crises were due to scarcity—not enough stuff. But under capitalism we get crises because of *too much* stuff—not too much relative to human needs or wants, but too much relative to consumer purchasing power. Marx located the source of the crisis in the defining institution of capitalism: wage labor, which is both a cost of production and a source of effective demand. Capitalists strive to keep wages down—and yet workers' wages need to keep going up for them to buy all the stuff being produced.

Keynes agreed with Marx that a free-market, capitalist economy is crisis-prone. In particular, it has no built-in tendency toward full employment. Indeed, it can stabilize at *any* level of unemployment. However, Keynes argued, although the *invisible hand* of the free market may not pull us out of a recession, the *visible hand* of the government can intervene. If worse comes to worst, government can put people to work, people who will spend their wages, thus creating more demand for goods, which will put more people back to work, thus generating an economic recovery.

Keynesian economics was born during the Great Depression, at a time when Marx's prediction that capitalism would not only face recurring crises but that these crises would become ever more severe seemed to be coming true with a vengeance. Keynes appeared to have saved capitalism. For three decades following World War II, productivity increased steadily, incomes kept pace, life got better and better for more and more.

But then, suddenly, trouble in paradise. The picture in figure 5.1 tells the story.

Wages went flat. Household incomes have increased slightly, up only 16 percent since 1973, and this increase is due almost exclusively to the influx of women into the workforce. As Krugman notes, "For men ages 35–44— men who would a generation ago have been supporting stay-at-home wives—we find that inflation adjusted wages were 12 percent *higher* in 1973 than they are now, . . . [whereas] the value of the output an average worker produces in an hour, even after you adjust for inflation, has risen almost 50 percent since 1973."[13]

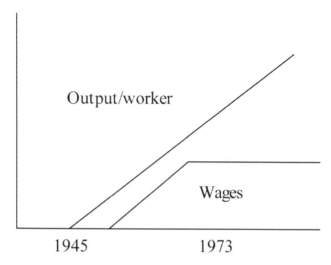

Figure 5.1   Trouble in Paradise

The above picture raises a question. If wages haven't kept pace with production, who has been buying all that extra stuff? Why hasn't the economy been in recession for the last quarter century or so—as the Marxian analysis would lead us to expect?

I think we know the answer. Recall the analysis of the last section. Instead of being paid higher wages, workers can be given access to *credit*. Consider two statistics:[14]

1. In 1975 outstanding household debt in the U.S. stood at 47 percent of GDP. It currently stands at 100 percent. That is to say, the amount of debt people hold, adjusted for inflation, is twice what it was thirty years ago.
2. Personal outlays as a share of disposable income was 88 percent in 1981—that is, the average household saved 12 percent of its income. Today it is 100 percent—meaning zero net savings. (This doesn't mean that nobody saves. It means that large amounts of the social surplus have been loaned out to finance consumer spending.)

Over the last several decades there has been a massive increase in home-equity loans, credit-card debt, student loans, and automobile loans. Never before have so many borrowed so much. In effect, our capitalist class has opted for the second method described in the previous section for keeping up effective demand. Instead of raising wages, they have lent out a large piece of their profits to the working class, to be repaid with interest. Pretty clever. Except for that inconvenient truth: what can't go on, won't. Debt levels cannot keep increasing indefinitely when incomes are stationary. Soon enough, borrowers can't even pay the interest charges on their debt, let alone repay the principal. Lenders get nervous. Credit dries up. Defaults and bankruptcies proliferate.

Why then did we get those asset bubbles? With wages flat, but sales up, the capitalist class was making a lot of money during this period. What to do with it? Some is spent on (often lavish) personal consumption, some is invested in the real economy (hence productivity keeps going up), but a large portion is "invested" in real estate or in the stock market. (Remember, "investing" in a fixed asset because it is expected to go up in value is not *investing* in the real sense of putting people to work creating new means of production, but is instead a form of saving.) With all this money flowing in, asset prices shot upward—until the bubble burst.

Might we be able to reform the system so as to return to a high-wage, social democratic, post-WWII-type economy? Can we get back to the Golden Age? This possibility would seem to be out of reach. We are now living in a global economy. High wages drive businesses abroad. Indeed, this need to stay globally competitive was a key factor in ending the social democratic "class compromise" in the first place. (Recall Bruce Springsteen's "My Home Town," recorded in 1983: "Foreman says these jobs are going, boys, and they ain't coming back." Well, they haven't come back, nor have they been replaced by other, better jobs.)

What is to be done? It is sobering to realize that Keynesian stimulations of the standard sort, the kinds undertaken by the Roosevelt administration, did *not* bring an end to the Great Depression. Although the recovery officially began in March of 1933 as the economy began to expand again, the unemployment rate, which had dropped from 25 percent in 1933 to 14 percent in 1937, shot up again to 19 percent the following year. (It had been 3.2 percent in 1929.)

It wasn't Roosevelt's welfare and employment provisions that ended the Great Depression. As Krugman reminds us, "it took the giant public works project known as World War II—a project that finally silenced the penny pinchers—to bring the Depression to an end."[15]

But for us, there isn't going to be a World War III. Nuclear war is too destructive for even our most jingoistic neoconservatives to contemplate seriously, and our embarrassing, tragic debacles in Iraq and Afghanistan have demonstrated unequivocally the limits of conventional warfare. This is not bad news—for us as human beings, that is—but it does close off an important Keynesian route out of the current crisis. Moreover, even as a Keynesian stimulus, modern warfare has lost much of its punch, since modern warfare is far more capital-intensive, far less labor-intensive, than the warfare of the Vietnam era and before. And with the United States now spending more on its military than all the rest of the world combined, there is no political-ideological case to be made, even on the Right, for a massive increase in military spending, the "military Keynesianism" that did so much to sustain the Golden Age.

Then there's the globalization problem (discussed earlier in Section 4.3). The effectiveness of Keynesian deficit spending depends on its "multiplier effect"—putting some people to work gives them more money to spend, which puts more people to work, and so on—the reverse of the recessionary downward spiral. But globalization has cut into this multiplier. When newly employed people spend their money, which they tend to do frugally, they buy those cheap imported goods at Wal-Mart—which may put more Chinese workers to work, but not their compatriots.

In the previous section we uncovered six obstacles to healthy capitalist stability. The analysis of this section has focused on one of them: *increasing indebtedness substitutes for increasing wages to keep up effective demand*. But there are two other contemporary developments that also stand in the way of recovery.

The major technological developments of the early and mid-twentieth century that transformed everyday life created large industries and massive numbers of jobs, far more than they displaced. The automobile industry employed vast numbers of people, and led to highway construction and suburban home building that employed many, many more. Electrification led to the mass production of not only radios and television, but washers, dryers, and countless other home and office appliances. But the great technological developments of the current period—the information technologies that have given us PCs, the Internet, smart phones, e-books, GPS systems, and such, have *not* been, on balance, job creators.[16] That is to say: *productivity gains have translated into laying people off rather than producing more goods*.

Then there is the problem of the "new monopolies," which have focused ever more insistently on lower prices, driving down wages and forcing their smaller competitors to the wall. A major shift has occurred in the American economy in recent years, taking us from a General Motors (high-wage) economy to a Wal-Mart (low-price) economy, and this shift is having ugly consequences.[17] That is to say, *marketing efforts have shifted toward emphasizing lower costs rather than superior quality*.

So—if traditional Keynesian monetary and fiscal policies can't end this recession, if there's not going to be another major war to pull us out, if new technologies are destroying more jobs than they create, and if the "new monopolies" are intent on keeping wages low, what *are* we going to do? Frankly,

I don't think that there is *anything* we can do to get us out of the economic mess we are in—short of a restructuring of our basic economic institutions in a way that goes well beyond anything currently contemplated by even the most radical elements of respectable opinion.

I could be wrong. Perhaps a combination of judicious policies and good luck will pull us out of this recession. But even if this should turn out to be the case, we are far from home free, for there is another crisis waiting in the wings.

5.2 Environmental Degradation

Marx has remarked that humanity never sets itself problems until the material conditions are at hand for their resolution.[18] Could this strikingly optimistic assertion be true? We *have* pulled back from the brink of nuclear holocaust. At the point when it became possible for us to put a quick end to our species, we grabbed the emergency brake, proving false (at least for now) the adage that new weapons are always used.[19]

We have pulled back from nuclear destruction, but there is another time bomb ticking. Concern for our natural environment has developed rapidly over the past several decades. We are now, more than ever, conscious of the threats posed to the natural infrastructure of the planet by our current ways of living. This concern has mobilized millions of people around the globe and has freed up funds for large-scale scientific investigations of almost all aspects of the various dangers we now face.

Marx may again be proven right. These researches have borne fruit—at least at the level of knowledge. The fact of the matter is, we know enough now to deal with the problems that are upon us. We know both the proximate behaviors and deep structures that are intensifying ecological stress, and we can see what changes need to be made if we are going to preserve our planet in its basic integrity. This is the good news. The bad news is, our knowledge will not be put into effective practice so long as capitalism remains dominant.

Let's first look at the good news: our basic problems have solutions.

5.2.1 Overpopulation

The world had 1.6 billion human inhabitants when the twentieth century began. It has 6.8 billion today. Most of the increase, 3.5 of the 4.4 billion, has occurred since 1950. If present trends continue, there will be 12 billion humans on earth by 2050 and 24 billion by the end of twenty-first century. Of course, present trends *will not* continue, because they *cannot* continue.

The question is, how will these trends be reversed—by warfare, famine, and disease, or by our acting reasonably and humanely?

Clearly, population growth is not an uncheckable biological phenomenon. The populations of the industrialized nations of the world, apart from immigration, are flat or declining. We have the technical means to limit population increase. Why are these means ineffective in large parts of the world? Why do people living in poverty produce so many children? The answer is straightforward: among the poor, especially in poor countries, children constitute an economic resource for their parents. They are an important source of income even when they are young, and they provide a measure of social security for their parents when the parents get old. Moreover, given the high infant mortality rates in most poor countries, a woman must have many children to ensure that enough survive. Other factors interact with these purely economic considerations—lack of education, lack of access to means of family planning, and above all, male dominance. (Men and women both share in the economic gains from having children, but men tend to gain disproportionately, whereas the costs are borne overwhelmingly by women.) Poverty exacerbates all these conditions. It can be safely said that poverty is the root cause of the population problem.

The distinction drawn in chapter 4 between being poor and living in poverty is relevant here. A country does not have to be rich to satisfy the conditions for population stability, at least not "rich" as measured by GDP per capita. To cite the best-known example: China has a per capita GDP of about one-seventh that of the United States, yet its fertility rate has dropped below that of the United States. Or to cite two cases that haven't involved coercive measures: Cuba's rate of population increase is identical to that of the United States, although its per capita income is one-fifth the U.S. figure. Social programs in Kerala, and the far greater degree of gender equality there than in the rest of India, have given the citizens of one of the poorest states of India near first-world rates of literacy, infant mortality, and life expectancy, and a rate of population increase only slightly above that of the United States (and falling faster). A country can be *poor* and have population stability—but not if the majority of its people *live in poverty*.

Poverty need not persist. As we have seen, it wouldn't take much in terms of basic resources to eliminate it. The fact is—and this is an important fact— the steps that need to be taken to enable all the citizens of a country, men and women alike, to have an education, basic health care, and significant economic security are not particularly expensive. Both education and public health, for example, are labor-intensive services—and there is no shortage of labor in poor countries. As China, Cuba, and Kerala have all demonstrated, the population problem is not intractable.

5.2.2 Food Scarcity

If people aren't the problem, perhaps resource shortages are. The most serious potential resource shortage is the most basic: Although agricultural productivity has increased greatly since the 1950s, faster than population growth, these gains have slowed considerably during the last decade. Moreover, large amounts of cropland are giving way to urban development, and even more is being degraded by overuse. Water, too, is becoming scarce. Seventy percent of the water used by human beings goes to irrigate crops; water demand has tripled over the past century; aquifers around the globe are being dangerously depleted. It would seem that global food production is approaching capacity. Indeed, if major changes are not forthcoming, food production may well decline, for the "green revolution" that has produced so much food is heavily dependent not only on water for irrigation, but on oil—to run all the big farm machinery and the trucks, trains, and planes that now transport food across and among continents. As Bill McKibben notes, "The numbers are astounding: the average bite of American food has traveled more than 1,500 miles before it reaches your lips."[20]

It is an important and hopeful fact that at present, on the supply side, there is no food problem at all—if we eat right. Lester Brown, president of the Earth Policy Institute and one of the leading environmental thinkers/writers of our time, offers some numbers:

> I am often asked, "How many people can the earth support? I answer with another question. "At what level of food consumption?" Using round numbers, at the U.S. level of 800 kilograms of grain per person annually for food and feed, the 2-billion-ton annual world harvest would support 2.5 billion. At the Italian level of consumption of close to 400 kilograms, the current harvest would support 5 billion people At the 200 kilograms of grain consumed by the average Indian, it would support 10 billion.[21]

The current population of the world is 6.8 billion. If everyone were to consume at slightly less than Italians currently consume, there would be enough for all of us. Moreover, if we moved from industrial farming/food factories to a smaller scale, more humane, more locally oriented, more labor-intensive agriculture—capable of providing good, meaningful work—we could produce more and better food. As McKibben, observes, "Smaller farms produce far more food per acre, whether you measure in tons, calories or dollars. They use land, water and oil much more efficiently; if they have animals, the manure is a gift, not a threat to public health," as it is in many of the mega-meat hog and chicken factories today. Small farms may well be central to sustainable food production.[22]

The malnourished need not be always with us. Current resources exist to feed everyone at a decent level. But only if current production, consumption, and distribution patterns are radically altered, and population growth is checked. Once again, we see what needs to be done. We needn't pin our hopes on new technologies (although some of these might help, particularly when oriented to enhancing small-scale, sustainable production). There is enough to go around—but we have to make it go around.

5.2.3 Pollution/Climate Change

It might well be argued that the most serious environmental threat to our future comes not from what we consume, but from what we don't consume—the effluents we discharge daily into our rivers, seas, ground waters, and atmosphere, especially those greenhouse gases implicated in global warming. Is the regenerative capacity of our planet sufficient to handle the unwanted by-products of our overall production and consumption?

Let us consider two specific cases involving atmospheric pollution. The general lesson to be drawn will apply to other forms of pollution as well.

First, a success story: In 1987, the Montreal Protocol on Substances That Deplete the Ozone Layer went into effect, having been negotiated by representatives of countries rich and poor, East and West. It was signed on the spot by twenty-four countries and the European Community. It has since been ratified by some 150 nations. The protocol calls for strict restrictions on the production and use of chemicals that damage the ozone layer, principally chlorofluorocarbons. These restrictions have been mostly obeyed, and the results have been impressive. By 1995, production of ozone-depleting chemicals was down 76 percent from its 1988 peak. Recent scientific estimates suggest that the ozone layer has stabilized, and that, if all countries continue to comply with the Montreal Protocol, it may begin to recover in the coming decades.[23]

Given the complexities of the factors involved, we cannot be certain that the ozone layer problem has been definitively solved, but the success of the Montreal Protocol is surely a life-affirming event. At least with respect to one ecological disaster, our species seems to have again confirmed Marx's optimistic assessment.

Can such a success be repeated with respect to the other major global atmospheric problem, the carbon dioxide emissions that are causing the "greenhouse effect," and hence global warming? In 1992, a Framework Convention on Climate Change was established at the Earth Summit in Rio de Janeiro (and signed there by, among others, then president George H. W. Bush). In 1997, the United States and 100 other countries signed the Kyoto Protocol, requiring the industrialized nations—which are overwhelmingly responsible for existing carbon dioxide levels—to reduce their emissions of greenhouse gases 5 to 7 percent below 1990 levels by 2012.

This was to be done in two ways—by increasing energy efficiency so that less overall energy is required, and by shifting from high-carbon energy sources to low-carbon or no-carbon sources. How do we motivate producers and consumers to make these changes? The basic, multipart answer is clear enough:

- Stop subsidizing coal and oil production. (Globally, fossil fuel subsidies currently run to more than $550 billion a year—as compared to $43 to $46 billion for renewable energy.[24])
- Set strict emission limits for automobiles, power plants, and other heavy polluters.
- Impose a stiff carbon tax on all fossil fuels or a comparable cep-and-trade system.
- Underwrite the research and development of cleaner technologies.

Will the Kyoto targets be met? Unfortunately, no. George W. Bush, son of the president who signed the Rio Convention, withdrew the U.S. commitment to the protocol. A 2010 World Bank report noted that the Kyoto Protocol has had only a slight effect on curbing global emissions growth. By 2005, eight years after the protocol pledging reductions was negotiated, energy-related emissions had grown 24 percent.[25] The Kyoto target for 2012 will not come close to being met—and this target is now considered by most experts to be far more modest than is required.

Why did we not take at least a small step forward? A sustainable world economy based solely on renewable, non-carbon-based energy would seem not beyond our reach. Bent Sørensen, at the University of Roskilde, has put together scenarios for achieving this happy state by 2050. As Seth Dunn of the Worldwatch Institute reports,

> The Roskilde study concludes that a combination of dispersed and more centralized applications—placing solar PVs and fuel cells in buildings and vehicles, and wind turbines adjacent to buildings and on farmland, plus a number of larger solar arrays, offshore wind parks, hydro installations—would create a "robust" system capable of meeting the world's entire energy demand.[26]

The Montreal Protocol should not lull us into thinking that capitalism can readily accommodate all sensible environmental solutions. The phasing out of chlorofluorocarbons has been relatively costless to the companies that produced them. The major chemical companies did not oppose the treaty, since chemical substitutes were available or at least on their drawing boards. In 1988, DuPont Chemicals announced that it was phasing out its $600 million chlorofluorocarbon business altogether to concentrate on developing and marketing alternatives, which it has successfully done.

Unfortunately, the obstacles to a global-warming agreement are vastly more formidable than those to an ozone treaty. Some of the world's most powerful industries, oil and automobile among them, are massively implicated in the problem, and they are prepared to fight. (In 1998, under the headline, "Industrial Group Plans to Battle Climate Treaty," the *New York Times* reported on the multimillion-dollar effort then underway.[27] The effort was successful.) There are cleaner ways of generating energy than burning oil, and cleaner ways of transporting people than relying on private automobiles, but it is hard to envisage a transition to these cleaner modes that preserves the status and incomes of these giant industries.

The problem goes deeper than just corporate resistance. While the phasing out of chlorofluorocarbons had no direct impact on consumption habits, a transition away from carbon-based energy most certainly would. Whatever good things might be said about bicycles, buses, trams, and trains, it is more convenient to have your own car—particularly on a rainy day, particularly if you have children, particularly if the nearest bus stop is a long walk away.

An additional complication: not only must people in rich countries cut their oil-based energy consumption drastically, but people of poor countries must be induced not to imitate the consumption habits of rich countries—no easy task, particularly since so many in poor countries are being encouraged to do just that. Given the titillating images of rich-country life and the relentless propagandizing on behalf of consumption that now constitute the essence of mass media everywhere, Austrian journalists Hans-Peter Martin and Harald Schumann are probably not wrong when they write:

> If the nearly six billion inhabitants of the planet could really decide by referendum how they want to live, there would be an overwhelming majority for the kind of middle-class existence lived in a suburb of San Francisco. A qualified, informed minority would opt in addition for the social standards of the Federal Republic of Germany before the Wall came down. The luxury combination of a Caribbean villa with Swedish welfare protection would be the dream to end all dreams.[28]

This is an impossible dream—and a dangerous one. In Martin and Schumann's apt phrase, "everything is everywhere"—but most of "everything" is tantalizingly, maddeningly out of reach of most members of our species, and must forever remain so. Our planet cannot sustain universal consumption at that level.

Can we really imagine solving all or even most of our environmental problems? Although we may know how to solve environmental problems taken one at a time, it might seem that we cannot possibly solve them altogether, for they are interrelated in contradictory ways. To solve the population problem, we must eliminate global poverty. But if we eliminate global poverty, then people will consume even more than they do now, thus intensifying both the food problem and the carbon emission problem. If we try to reduce energy consumption by imposing energy taxes, then higher food and energy prices will make the problems of poverty worse. If we try to redistribute food and energy by means of some sort of rationing scheme . . . well, who would (or could) draw up a coherent plan? How would it be administered? How would it be enforced?

As a matter of fact, it *is* possible to envisage feasible comprehensive solutions to global ecological problems. Many ecological theorists have been doing just that. Most think we can solve our problems within a capitalist framework—although all serious thinkers recognize that the structures of existing capitalism must be substantially modified.

Consider *Natural Capitalism*, published more than a decade ago, by Paul Hawken, Amory Lovins, and Hunter Lovins. The authors agree that we need a revolution—although not one against capitalism. Their book is subtitled "Creating the Next *Industrial* Revolution"[29] (emphasis mine). Then president Clinton is reported to have called it one of the five most important books in the world today.

Hawken and the Lovinses acknowledge that "capitalism, as practiced, is a financially profitable, nonsustainable aberration in human development," but they do not see the problem as residing in capitalism itself. The problem with the current form of capitalism, they argue, is its radical mispricing of "natural capital." Current market prices woefully undervalue—and often do not value at all—the natural resources and ecological systems "that make life possible and worth living on this planet."[30]

All economists, no matter whether conservative, liberal, or Left, recognize that market transactions can involve "externalities"—costs (or benefits) that are not paid for by the transacting parties. All agree that there is a role for governments to play in rectifying these defects. The standard remedies tend to be taxation (for negative externalities) and subsidies (for positive externalities). More recently, "cap and trade" schemes for carbon emissions have been added to the list.

Hawken and the Lovinses argue that a correct mix of taxation and subsidies can put our economy on a path to sustainability. The first step, they say, is to eliminate the *perverse* incentives now in place. They document the massive subsidies that governments currently provide for ecologically destructive behavior, for example, highway construction and repair, which encourages suburban sprawl and the shift away from more efficient modes of transportation, agricultural subsidies that encourage soil degradation and wasteful use of water, as well as subsidies to mining, oil, fishing, and forest industries.

Second step: impose resource and pollution taxes so as to reflect the true costs of "natural capital." Sweeten the pie by phasing out all taxes on labor (which should increase employment) and income taxes as well. The point is to level the playing field so that more sustainable energy technologies and more energy-efficient processes can compete fairly with the destructive practices of "industrial capitalism."

Natural Capitalism is full of examples of the stupendous waste inherent in our current modes of production and consumption and of the existing technologies and procedures that could reduce our impact on the environment to a small fraction of what it is now. Many of these changes are already underway. Many more will follow, the authors argue, if appropriate government policies are adopted. Hawken and the Lovinses envisage a bright future:

> Imagine for a moment a world where cities have become peaceful and serene because cars and buses are whisper quiet, vehicles exhaust only water vapor, and parks and greenways have replaced unneeded urban freeways. OPEC has ceased to function because the price of oil has fallen to five dollars a barrel, but there are few buyers for it because cheaper and better ways now exist to get the services people once turned to oil to provide. Living standards for all people have dramatically improved, particularly for the poor and those in developing countries. Involuntary unemployment no longer exists, and income taxes have been largely eliminated. Houses, even low-income housing units, can pay part of their mortgage costs by the energy they *produce*.[31]

Such a future will come about, they argue, if we harness the creative energy of capitalism and let the markets work their magic.

James Gustave Speth, dean of the School of Forestry and Environmental Studies at Yale University, makes a similar argument in his more recent *The Bridge at the Edge of the World: Capitalism, the Environment, and Crossing from Crisis to Sustainability* (2008).[32] He too acknowledges that "modern capitalism is destructive of the environment, and not in a minor way but in a way that profoundly threatens the planet." But he thinks that "a large array of initiatives has been identified to transform the market and consumerism, redesign corporations, and focus growth on high-priority human and environmental needs" within the framework of a "reinvented capitalism."[33]

Perhaps the most comprehensive plan has been put forth by Lester Brown. His *Plan B 4.0: Mobilizing to Save Civilization* ("The best book on the environment I've ever read," says Chris Swann of the *Financial Times*) is a comprehensive, global plan to address *all* the issues and contradictions raised above. Plan B 4.0 is an action plan for stabilizing climate, stabilizing populations, eradicating poverty, and restoring the earth's natural support system. Brown notes that these four goals are interdependent, and that all are "essential to restoring food security. It's doubtful that we can reach one without reaching the others."[34]

If we know how to solve our basic environmental problems, why don't we set about seriously to do so? The answer is straightforward. The fundamental environmental problems (contrary to what advocates of "green" capitalism believe) cannot be resolved under global capitalism.

At first glance, this claim may seem implausible. After all, thanks to the efforts of determined environmental activists, air quality is better now than it was three decades ago in virtually every advanced capitalist country, and rivers and lakes are cleaner. Environmental protection laws have been passed and "green" taxes imposed in many countries—so that, for example, the per capita carbon emissions in Germany and Japan are only half those of the United States. Is it really so unreasonable to imagine a future in which similar restrictions and taxes are applied the world over, thus stimulating the introduction of ecology-friendly technologies worldwide? If such taxes and restrictions are compatible with capitalism in Western Europe or Japan, why shouldn't they be compatible with global capitalism?

It won't do to say that the fundamental problem is the market. To be sure, unregulated market prices do not reflect true costs, but green taxes can be imposed on commodities and production processes that have negative environmental effects. These taxes, which can be varied to account for differential impact, discourage the production and consumption of ecologically damaging products and, at the same time, generate funds for health compensation and clean up. They also motivate the development of cleaner technologies and more ecologically friendly consumption substitutes. Such price regulation is fully compatible with capitalism.

To concentrate on market failure is to miss the real story. There are three features of capitalism that, taken together, give the system its ecologically destructive dynamic. It is not the market *per se* that is problematic, but

- capitalism's expansionary dynamic,
- its peculiar crisis tendency deriving from its basis in wage labor,
- the unrestrained mobility of its defining element, "capital."

These elements interact as follows: Capitalism is enormously productive. Every year, enormous quantities of commodities are produced that, when sold at anticipated prices, generate enormous profits, a large fraction of which are reinvested back into the economy in anticipation of still greater production and still more profits. Every enterprise within a capitalist system is under competitive pressure to behave in exactly this fashion: to produce, make a profit, reinvest, and grow.

The ever-present danger to system stability is deficient demand. When supply outstrips demand, the economy falters. If goods can't be sold, production is cut back, workers are laid off, and demand declines further. A contracting economy, as we know, is bad all around. Businesses go bankrupt, unemployment rises, and tax revenues fall off. Under capitalism economic growth is in the immediate interest of virtually every sector of society—growth in the straightforward sense as measured by GDP. Whether or not such growth makes people happier or enhances the overall quality of life is beside the point.

Under capitalism, you get either growth or recession, and nobody wants a recession. Two parallel growth strategies are employed: on the one hand, the stimulation of domestic demand via easy credit and an ever more sophisticated sales effort; and, on the other hand, an ever-increasing orientation toward production for export. The strategies soon come together, since exports must be sold. Where demand does not exist, it must be created. So the sales apparatus of modern capitalism, honed to near perfection in the domestic market, is unleashed abroad. The culture of consumption spreads throughout the world.

But enterprises in the core capitalist countries are not content to merely sell abroad; they also want to produce abroad. New opportunities thus arise for capitalists and entrepreneurs in poor countries to join forces with the transnational elites of the advanced capitalist countries. Barriers to capital flows are removed. Labor-intensive manufacturing blossoms in (some) poor countries, with production aimed at rich-country markets.

The race is now on. Every poor country now strives to become rich, rich through the mechanism of export-led growth, rich in precisely the same sense that the advanced countries are rich. They are encouraged in this pursuit by the business press, by most respectable economists, by the governments of the rich countries, by international lending agencies, and by their own (usually Western-trained) technocrats. Whatever doubts might arise are quickly swept aside. It's a globalized economy. Not to grow is to stagnate, regress, slide into chaos. TINA.

From an ecological point of view, this is madness. Environmental sanity requires that rich countries cut back on consumption and poor countries target their resources to eliminating poverty—the exact opposite of what globalized capitalism demands. From the perspective of globalized capitalism, rich countries must consume ever more, because they are the key markets for the "lesser-developed" ones, whereas poor countries must cut back on public spending, keep wages low, open up their economies, look the other way when ecological issues surface, because they must, above all else, attract foreign investment.

So long as the structures of global capitalism remain in place, there is no alternative to this madness. If rich countries continue to grow, poor-country elites will emulate the consumption patterns of their rich-country counterparts, and will target their countries' resources to rich-country markets—putting ever more pressure on our planet's limited supplies of food and natural resources, and subjecting the environment to ever-increasing quantities of toxic wastes. If rich countries cease to grow, their own economies will stagnate or implode—and so will the economies of poor countries, increasing the level of poverty, increasing the level of environmental degradation that poverty entails, and decreasing the amount of funds available for environmental damage control.

(It should be noted that a healthy capitalism depends not simply on ever-increasing consumption, but on a steady *rate* of growth. When the growth *rate* declines, investors pull back. But a steady rate of growth implies *exponential* growth, and exponential growth, to anyone with mathematical sensibilities, is deeply disturbing. If an economy grows 3 percent per year—the U. S. average during the 20th century—consumption doubles every twenty-four years—which translates into a *sixteenfold* increase in consumption over the course of a century. That is to say, if it can sustain this modest 3 percent growth rate, the U.S. GDP, which was $10 trillion in 2000, will be $160 trillion in 2100. To recall Kenneth Boulding's remark, quoted in the early pages of this book: "Only a madman or an economist thinks exponential growth can go on forever in a finite world."[35])

How might things be different in a world where Economic Democracy predominates?

To think clearly about our environmental predicament, we need to consider "overdevelopment" as well as underdevelopment. Herman Daly offers a concise definition of the former: "An overdeveloped country is one whose level of per capita resource consumption is such that if generalized to all countries could not be sustained indefinitely." (If we consider carbon emissions as a measure of development, the United States is overdeveloped by a factor of four.[36])

Both overdevelopment and underdevelopment are undermining our environmental security. Some countries are consuming more than their sustainable share of the world's nonrenewable resources and are contributing more than their sustainable share of greenhouse gases and other forms of pollution. Such economies need to contract, not expand. Others are mired in poverty, which often leads their inhabitants to engage in ecologically destructive practices—for example, overgrazing, overplowing, deforestation. These economies need to expand.

We have already addressed underdevelopment—the problem of poverty. In a world of Economic Democracies, poor countries will have the autonomy to develop in accordance with their own priorities. They will work to develop appropriate technologies. They will devote resources to undoing the damage done to their societies by globalized capitalism. They will employ their creative energies to invent ways of living that are healthy and humane, but do not put the unbearable stress on the local and global environment that overdevelopment does. Rich countries can help in this process by making available their scientific and technical resources, and some material aid, but poor countries, in federation with similarly situated countries, will likely employ mostly their own human and material resources to restructure their societies. There is no reason to think that this cannot be done. The constraints to eliminating poverty in poor countries are for the most part social and institutional, not material or technological.

Redressing underdevelopment will not be easy, but this task may be less daunting than that of weaning overdeveloped countries away from their consumption addictions. This is not to say that the consumption changes necessary for sustainability must bring down the quality of life in overdeveloped countries. Indeed, if the transition is properly managed, the quality of life—and the level of human happiness in such societies—can be markedly improved.[37] Addiction does not, in general, contribute to overall well-being, however difficult it is to break.

It must be said that the structures of Economic Democracy do not guarantee success here. Economic Democracy is a market economy. Hence, stimulating consumer demand is in the immediate interest of every enterprise—just as it is under capitalism. No firm, worker-run or capitalist, wants its customers to consume less of its product. All firms want to keep demand strong.

However, several features of Economic Democracy make ecological sustainability vastly more feasible than under capitalism. The most important difference is that capitalism requires economic growth for stability, whereas Economic Democracy does not. The primary motivation of a healthy worker-run firm is to avoid losing market share. It is less concerned with expansion. A worker self-managed firm (where gains are shared among the workers) can be quite content with zero growth, particularly if it is utilizing new technologies to increase leisure and make work itself more interesting. What is true of the parts is true of the whole. A steady-state economy, with consumption patterns that are stable over time, is perfectly compatible with a healthy Economic Democracy.

Economic Democracy does not have the same underlying growth imperative as does capitalism, but ecological sustainability would seem to call for more than that, at least on the part of rich countries, namely a scaling back of material consumption. It is here that social control of investment becomes crucial. The scaling back of consumption is not something that can be done quickly—at least, not without severe social disruption. Consumption habits, and the production facilities that satisfy these habits, must be given time to adjust. Moreover, much of our excessive consumption has become "necessary," given the structure of our built environment. It will take investment to alter these various patterns and structures.

For example: every environmentalist knows that the private automobile is one of the prime culprits in atmospheric pollution. But we have designed our communities so that many people must use cars to carry out the functions of daily living. Communities needn't be designed that way. We could have better public transportation, more bicycle paths, more small markets near our residences, and more decent, affordable housing close to our work sites. But to redesign and reconstruct our communities, we must have the investment funds to do so.

Under Economic Democracy, such funds would be available. Each year, the national, regional, and community legislatures decide as to investment fund priorities—how to allocate investment funds between the public sector and the market sector, and what public sector projects to undertake. These decisions can be taken without worrying about how the "financial markets" will react, or whether businesses will flee. To the extent that local industries will be adversely affected by certain sustainability-motivated decisions, investment funds can be made available to help them retool or otherwise adjust. The process of redesigning our communities to bring them into compliance with rational standards of ecological sustainability may not always run smoothly, but serious attempts can be made, the more successful serving as examples to be emulated.

Of course, it cannot be said with certainty that a serious attempt at ecological sanity will even be made. Economic Democracy is, after all, a democracy—and hence the quality of its "general will" is dependent on the particular wills of the individual citizens. But I don't think it overly optimistic to suppose that the vast majority of our planet's inhabitants would agree to adopt ecologically sustainable practices—if they are secure in their basic necessities and if they can look forward to a future of increased leisure and more meaningful work. Neither condition is plausible under capitalism. Both can be realized under Economic Democracy.

5.3 Democracy (Lack Thereof)

The coexistence of political equality with material inequality has long been a conundrum of democratic theory. Plato thought, not unreasonably, that democracy would always degenerate, precisely because the demos (the people) would insist on redistributing the wealth, thus provoking a backlash, which would ultimately lead to tyranny.[38] All classical liberal philosophers during the rise of capitalism worried about the threat to property that an extension of democracy to the propertyless masses would entail. (Even so decent and progressive a thinker as John Stuart Mill, who favored universal suffrage, proposed giving multiple votes to bankers, merchants, manufacturers, and other employers to counterbalance the excessive influence of the laboring classes.[39])

Why has this threat not materialized? How has it come to pass that political democracy now seems to be the natural concomitant of capitalism rather than its antithesis? How is it possible, in a democratic society such as ours, where 1 percent of the population owns a third or more of the wealth, that no serious attempt is made at redistribution?

In its starkest form, the answer is simple. We do not live in a democracy. Capitalism is not compatible with democracy. What passes for democracy in advanced industrial societies is something else.

Yale political scientists Robert Dahl and Charles Lindblom have long argued that we should distinguish between democracy and polyarchy. A *polyarchy* is a system in which a broad-based electorate selects political leaders from competing candidates in elections that are reasonably honest. In Dahl's words, a polyarchy is a political order in which "citizenship is extended to a relatively high proportion of adults, and the rights of citizenship include the opportunity to oppose and vote out the highest officials of government."[40]

All the advanced industrial societies of the world are now polyarchies, as are most other countries. Polyarchy (if not democracy) has spread rapidly throughout the world during the last several decades. Not only have the communist regimes of Eastern Europe and the Soviet Union crumbled, but so have the military dictatorships of Latin America and racist rule in southern Africa.

Polyarchy is not a bad thing. It is better than tyranny. But polyarchy is not democracy. Following Dahl and Lindblom, let us keep "democracy" close to its etymological meaning, "rule by the people." Let us define *democracy* to be a system in which

- suffrage is universal among adults, and
- the electorate is "sovereign."

An electorate is "sovereign" if

- its members are reasonably well informed about the issues to be decided by the political process and reasonably active in contributing to their resolution, and

- there exists no stable minority class that is "privileged."

A class is "privileged" (this is the key concept) if

- it possesses political power at least equal to that of elected officials and unmatched by any other stable grouping.

In short, *democracy is a system in which a universal electorate is reasonably well informed, active, and unobstructed by a privileged minority class.*

But the capitalist class in a capitalist society *is* a privileged minority class. It is a "stable minority class that possesses political power at least equal to that of elected officials and unmatched by any other stable grouping." Thus we do not live in a democracy.

It is not fashionable to talk about class these days, certainly not about a "capitalist class," but such a class exists. Author Gore Vidal, born into this class and thus well positioned to know, puts it this way:

> That is the genius of our ruling class. They're so brilliant that no one knows they even exist. The political science professors, perfectly sane men, look at me with wonder when I talk about the ruling class in America. They say, "You are one of those conspiracy theorists. You think there's a headquarters and they get together at the Bohemian Grove and run the United States." Well, they do get together at the Bohemian Grove and they do a lot of picking of Secretaries of State. But they don't have to conspire. They all think alike. It goes back to the way we're raised, the schools we went to. You don't have to give orders to the editor of *The New York Times*. He is in place because he will respond to a crisis the way you want him to, as will the President, as will the head of Chase Manhattan Bank.[41]

Vidal marks out the "ruling class" as the top 1 percent of society. This upper 1 percent comprises what we have defined as the "capitalist class"—namely, people who own enough productive assets that they can live comfortably on the income generated from these assets.

Is this class truly "privileged," in the technical sense of possessing power at least equal to that of all elected officials? If the capitalist class is a ruling class, how does this ruling class rule? Vidal says they all think alike. This may be too simple, and in any event, we need to know more. How are capitalist attitudes translated into public policy? What are the mechanisms that enable a small and nearly invisible class in a "democratic" society to exercise decisive power?

Some of these mechanisms are obvious, some less so. The most obvious, at least in the United States, is campaign financing. Election campaigns have become exceedingly sophisticated in their techniques, utilizing focus groups and polling data to see what hot-button issues to push, selective mailings combined with television saturation to get one's carefully tailored "message" across. These campaigns are enormously expensive. (In 2010 Russ Feingold spent $13 million, losing his Senate race to an opponent who spent even more. Meg Whitman spent ten times that much—$130 million—in losing the California governor's race to Jerry Brown. Even local races require an astonishing amount of fundraising. In 2010, the race of the governorship of Illinois cost candidates $33 million. Fifteen races for seats in the Illinois legislature cost $1 million or more. Illinois Supreme Court chief justice Thomas Kilbane spent $3.2 million to retain his position.[42]) Hence, wealthy "contributors" must be courted and wooed. That is to say, they must be assured that their interests will be looked after. Of course, it is theoretically possible to raise large sums from small contributions, but consider: to raise $1 million, you would have to persuade *50,000* fellow citizens to give you $20—or just 50 wealthy contributors to give you $20,000. Given that that upper 1 percent consists of 1.2 million households for whom $20,000 is small change, it is hardly surprising that rational politicians fish mostly in the pond with the big fish. (The recent Supreme Court ruling, *Citizens United*, has added multinational corporations to the pond. Corporations as well as individuals may now spend freely. Of course corporations, via the bundled contributions of top management and their army of lobbyists, have long been dominant players on Capitol Hill, but now the meager restrictions that were in place—including disclosure requirements—have been set aside.)

Certain members of the capitalist class pour staggering sums of money into politics. To give but one example: David and Charles Koch, having inherited their father's oil and energy business, now have a combined fortune exceeded only by the fortunes of Bill Gates and Warren Buffett. As Jane Mayer, staff writer for the *New Yorker*, reports:

> Only the Kochs know precisely how much they have spent on politics. Public tax records show that between 1998 and 2008 the Charles G. Koch Charitable Foundation spent more than forty-eight million dollars. The Claude R. Lambe Charitable Foundation, which is controlled by Charles Koch and his wife, along with two company employees and an accountant, spent more than twenty-eight million. The David H. Koch Charitable Foundation spent more than a hundred and twenty million. Meanwhile, since 1998 Koch Industries has spent more than fifty million dollars on lobbying. Separately, the company's political-action committee, KochPAC, has donated some eight million dollars to political campaigns, more than eighty per cent of it to Republicans. So far in 2010, Koch Industries leads all other energy companies in political contributions, as it has since 2006. . . . In the second quarter of 2010, David Koch was the biggest individual contributor to the Republican Governors Association, with a million-

dollar donation. Other gifts by the Kochs may be untraceable; federal tax law permits anonymous personal donations to politically active nonprofit groups.[43]

Adding up the numbers, we get $255 million, contributed by just two guys— and that's just the money that can be traced via public records.[44]

I hardly need to belabor the point that big money influences politics, since the evidence is all around us. Here's a typical example, cited in the 2002 edition of *After Capitalism*, but perhaps even more relevant now, given the "maverick" protagonist's subsequent career trajectory:

> In February [1999], with customer complaints about air travel at an all-time high, the Senate Commerce Committee chairman John McCain, Republican of Arizona, took off on a passenger rights crusade. He filed an Airlines Passenger Fairness Act to force airlines to clean up their acts, then held dramatic hearings to spotlight tales of marooned, bumped and otherwise mistreated travelers. . . . In June, though, after the airline industry announced a voluntary plan to im- prove customer service—and directed a hasty infusion of "soft money" dona- tions to both parties—the issue seemed to disappear. Mr. McCain replaced his bill with a much weaker version that simply encourages the airlines to follow their own plans, and his committee overwhelmingly approved the substitute.
>   "We were stunned," said Peter Hudson, director of the Aviation Consumer Action Project. "This wasn't just a sweetheart deal; it was a giveaway." The week before the committee vote, the airline industry shelled out $226,000 in soft money. . . . In the first six months of 1999, the airlines spent more than $1.3 million on political donations.[45]

Effective control of campaign financing is not in itself sufficient to maintain class rule. In a capitalist polyarchy, where it is theoretically possible for a political party to challenge the basic institutions of the system, it is important that the interests of the capitalist class be well formulated and buttressed by argument and data that will make it appear that these interests coincide with the general interest. Among the most important means to this end are the large numbers of "private" (i.e., capitalist-funded) foundations, ranging from "liberal," that is, moderately conservative (e.g., Ford, Rockefeller, Carnegie) to rabidly right wing (e.g., Bradley, Schiafe, Olin). These foundations, in turn, fund various think tanks and roundtables, ranging from the moderately con- servative Brookings Institute, Rand Corporation, and the Council on Foreign Relations to such right-wing bastions as the Hoover Institute, Cato Institute, and American Enterprise Institute. These institutes undertake policy re- search, draw up model legislation, bring together representatives from the business community, government officials, respectable (i.e., nonradical) aca- demics, and members of influential media to debate, discuss, and refine such proposals. These institutes also provide a steady supply of reliable "experts" to testify before Congress and to appear on mass media news programs.

The major foundations have enormous quantities of assets under their control. To point to just the tip of the iceberg: the National Committee for Responsible Philanthropy reported that between 1992 and 1994, twelve major right-wing foundations, with assets totaling $1.1 billion, gave some $210 million to promote conservative policy groups and educational efforts.[46] By way of contrast, during that period the one national weekly news magazine still identifying itself as socialist, the highly respected *In These Times*, nearly went bankrupt, due to an outstanding debt of $100,000—less than half of one-tenth of 1 percent of what the top right-wing foundations were devoting to their causes each year. (*In These Times* did in fact survive, but it no longer calls itself socialist.)

The Koch brothers have been particularly effective at setting in up "think tanks," among them the oft-cited Cato Institute as well as the Mercatus Center, the latter housed at George Mason University and called by the *Wall Street Journal* "the most important think tank you've never heard of." They have also funded The Institute for Justice (which files lawsuits to oppose state and federal regulations), the Institute for Humane Studies (which underwrites libertarian academics), and the Bill of Rights Institute (which promotes a conservative slant on the Constitution). In addition, they have set up and/or funded a vast array of "citizens' groups": "Americans for Prosperity," "Citizens for a Sound Economy," "Citizens for the Environment," and "Parents United Now." Not surprisingly, they have been a major force behind the Tea Party movement.[47] (The Kochs have friends in very high places. Supreme Court justices Antonin Scalia and Clarence Thomas, whose votes secured the *Citizens United* ruling, have attended at least one of Charles Koch's political retreats in Palm Springs.[48])

Not only must class interests be well formulated but they must also be disseminated to the general public. Hence the importance of the major media—virtually all of which are privately owned, that is to say, controlled by the class that controls most the other productive assets of society. These media, moreover, depend for their own economic survival on advertising revenues, hence, on the good will of their corporate sponsors. In the United States, even "public" radio and "public" television are heavily dependent on corporate sponsorship, for which the producers "publicly" (i.e., during every broadcast) express their gratitude. Moreover, various key programs in public television, for example, *The PBS NewsHour* and *The Nightly Business Report* are purchased from private owners.[49]

It should come as no surprise that not a single major newspaper or television station in the United States, public or private, features a regular commentator who articulates principled, consistent anticapitalist arguments.

Although money dominates our politics, it should not be supposed that individual contributors of large sums always get their way. All wealthy contributors want their interests protected, but these interests are not always harmonious. Wealthy contributors will have divergent feelings about many of the issues that come within the purview of elected officials, issues specific to narrow economic interest, but also issues of broad social significance. (They don't all think exactly alike.) So there is room within capitalism for genuine electoral competition—hence, polyarchy. Nevertheless, none of these big contributors (surprise, surprise) favors policies that might erode the basic structures by which they maintain their wealth, namely, the basic institutions of capitalism itself.

Apart from these mechanisms—which ensure that the interests of capital will be well protected by elected officials—the capitalist class possesses another powerful weapon, perhaps the most powerful in its impressive arsenal, that can be brought into play should a government be elected that proposes policies deemed inimical to their interests. Capitalists can engage in an "investment strike." This is a particularly formidable weapon, since it requires no planning or coordination to implement. Indeed, it will come into play automatically if a government deemed unfriendly to "business interests" should come to power.

The mechanism is simple enough. As we know, capitalism relies on the savings of the upper classes for a large portion of its investment. Since these funds are private funds, they may be disposed of in any manner their owners see fit. Now more than ever, investors have many options. They can invest in their own country, or they can invest elsewhere. They can play the Nikkei Stock Exchange or speculate in Latin American currencies. They can do whatever they want with their funds in this "free and open" world, for these funds are *their* money. Hence, if significant numbers of investors lose confidence in a government, they, not unreasonably, will stop investing in the country. This lack of confidence thus becomes, for the usual Keynesian reasons, a self-fulfilling prophecy. When investors fail to invest, effective demand falls, layoffs ensue, demand declines further, triggering further cutbacks—the familiar downward spiral that constitutes a recession.

We know what happens next. In a polyarchic government, leaders are held responsible for the economic well-being of the nation. During bad times, every oppositional candidate proclaims some form of the same slogan, "It's the economy, stupid!" Since the point of polyarchy is to allow the electorate to remove officials who are not thought to be performing appropriately, governing politicians unloved by the business community will be removed—and those problematic programs will be reversed.

Clearly, as long as investment decisions remain in private hands, governments that want to survive—which is to say, all governments—have little choice but to cater to the sensibilities of the capitalist class.

The problem goes even deeper. It is not only elected officials whose self-interest is structurally bound to the interests of this class. So too are the interests of almost everyone else. When an economy slumps, private sector workers are laid off. Tax revenues decline, so public sector workers are also squeezed, as are people on welfare, whose benefits now seem too expensive. So we see, a capitalist economy is ingeniously structured. Almost everyone has an interest in maintaining the animal spirits of its ruling class. This is one of the features that give capitalism its remarkable resiliency. So long as the basic institutions of capitalism remain in place, it is in the rational self-interest of almost everyone to keep the capitalists happy.

In a true democracy, the electorate could alter these basic institutions. Since the ways in which the interests of capital diverge from those of the great majority are not so hard to grasp, a sovereign electorate probably *would* want to try something else—which is why capitalism will tolerate polyarchy but *not* democracy. (Capitalist societies tend to be "tolerant" societies—unless the basic institutions of capitalism are threatened. Then the gloves come off, and we get death squads, military coups, and fascism. At least, that has been the historical record to date.)

Economic Democracy, as its name suggests, greatly expands the role of democratic institutions in society.

- The most obvious and dramatic extension of democracy is to the workplace. The cornerstone authoritarian institution of capitalism is replaced by one-person, one-vote democracy. This is small-scale democracy, comparable in scale to that of the ancient Greek city-states. (Even large companies are small in comparison to most towns and cities.) Although most enterprises will have representative worker councils, this form of democracy is not far removed from the ancient ideal of direct democracy.
- "Market democracy" (that is, the ability of individuals, by their purchases, to "vote" for what they want the economy to produce) is preserved under Economic Democracy, but in such a way that the most objectionable feature of market democracy is removed. Market democracy is one dollar, one vote, not one person, one vote. It remains so in Economic Democracy, but since the degree of income inequality is vastly reduced under Economic Democracy, this feature is now relatively harmless. Indeed, if the inequalities in society are to serve their motivational purposes, we want our productive output to be determined by monetary demand. (There is no point in allowing some people to make more money than others if there is nothing worth buying with the extra money.)

- Representative political democracy of the familiar sort is also extended under Economic Democracy in that matters of common concern that do not come up for a vote under capitalism would be regularly considered by the national and regional legislatures. How much economic investment should the nation undertake this year? How much of this investment should be for projects of national and regional scope? How should investment be allocated between public capital expenditures and the market sector within our community? These decisions, which strongly affect our economic future, will be made by accountable elected representatives, and not by the invisible hand of the market.
- By law, every community receives its per capita share of the national investment fund. Local politics suddenly becomes more interesting. Citizens have a chance to shape the general structure of their community without having to worry that their decisions may inhibit fresh capital from coming in or cause local businesses to flee. We can anticipate a higher degree of participation by the citizenry in public matters under Economic Democracy than is typical under capitalism.

These are the pluses. Economic Democracy also avoids or greatly reduces the negatives associated with capitalist polyarchy. The much greater degree of economic equality lessens distorting effects of money on the electoral process. Control of the media will no longer be in the hands of the economic elite. Most important of all, there no longer exists a small class of people who, when displeased with government policy, can throw the economy into recession by staging an investment strike. If we recall our original definition of democracy—universal suffrage, a reasonably active and well-informed citizenry, no privileged class—we see that Economic Democracy is, in fact, a democracy and not merely a polyarchy.

5.3.1 A Note on Anticommunism

Looking back over the twentieth century, one cannot fail to notice how deeply the ideology of anticommunism has shaped Western foreign policy. From the beginning, communism has triggered hostile passions among the upper classes. Long before the Russian Revolution, long before the Soviet Union had any sort of serious military capability, fear of communism was promoted by the dominant political, educational, and economic institutions of society. Communism came to be hated with far greater intensity than fascism or Nazism or any other sort of nondemocratic rule. Indeed, the polyarchical Western powers did not intervene when democratic institutions disappeared in Italy, Germany, and Spain during the interwar years and were quite "tolerant" of the new governments. After all, Mussolini's Italy, Hitler's Germany, and Franco's Spain were all vehemently and murderously anticommunist.

But why has capitalism been so profoundly opposed to communism while tolerating all other kinds of repressive antidemocratic regimes? At first sight, the answer would seem to be straightforwardly economic: capitalism needs access to cheap raw materials, foreign markets, and cheap labor; communist countries would deny them all this.

The problem with this answer, plausible on the surface, is that the existing communist states did *not* deny capitalist corporations these things. Communist regimes have always wanted to trade with the West and have often been eager for foreign investment. It is the West, led by the United States, that imposes trade sanctions, embargoes, and blockades. To be sure, capitalist enterprises, when allowed to operate in communist countries, have been more closely regulated than they would doubtless have preferred to be, but foreign corporations have been tightly regulated in other capitalist countries as well (in Japan, for example) without provoking a hostile response, let alone a "cold" war that a slight miscalculation could have turned catastrophically hot.

The real motivation behind anticommunism runs much deeper than concern about access to raw materials and markets. It is the profound worry on the part of the capitalist class that the communists might in fact be right: that capitalism is not the end of history, that there is a brighter future beyond capitalism, and that sooner or later workers in capitalist countries (i.e., the vast majority of the citizenry) will come to realize this and take appropriate action. Recall the dominant metaphor: communism is a "disease." Infected countries must be quarantined. No country is safe from the deadly germ, no matter how healthy and prosperous. It must be mercilessly fought at home and abroad. "No, of course tiny little Vietnam is not in itself a threat to our national security, but the *spread of communism* must be checked—no matter how many people have to die."

To grasp the magnitude of our relentless war against communism, try to imagine what the history of the twentieth century might have been like had Western foreign policy been guided by the ideals of democracy instead of anticommunism. To confine ourselves only to the most important player, let us suppose that the United States had been truly committed to democracy. Then:

- It would not have sent troops into Russia in 1918 to oppose that revolution.
- It would not have looked so kindly on Mussolini's seizure of power in Italy, or supported so readily an "appeasement" policy toward Hitler.
- It would not have endorsed the coming to power in the 1930s of the patriarchal dictatorships in Central America and the Caribbean (Her-

nandez Martinez in El Salvador, Somoza in Nicaragua, Ubico in Guatemala, Carias in Honduras, Trujillo in the Dominican Republic, Batista in Cuba).

- It might have aided Republican Spain in its fight against Franco's anti-democratic revolt—which was supported materially and with personnel by both Hitler and Mussolini.
- It would not have supported the corrupt and brutal rule of Chiang Kai-shek in China, supplying his government with some $6 billion in aid during its civil war with a vastly more popular Communist insurgency that eventually triumphed.
- It would not have supported the efforts of the French to regain control over Indochina after World War II.
- It would not have insisted on partitioning Korea after World War II, or supported the installation of a vicious right-wing dictatorship in the South (and hence would have avoided the Korean War).
- It would not have engineered the overthrow of the democratically elected Iranian government and the installation of the Shah in 1953 (and hence would not have been regarded as the Great Satan by the government that drove the shah from power a quarter of a century later).
- It would not have orchestrated the destruction of democracy in Guatemala in 1954.
- It would have recognized the right of the Cambodian, Laotian, and Vietnamese people to choose their own future, and hence avoided the war that claimed some 50,000 American lives and as many as 4 million Indochinese.
- It would not have opposed until the very last moment the black liberation struggles in southern Africa.
- It would not have looked the other way (to put the best face on the matter) when the Indonesian military seized power in 1965 and massacred a million "communists."
- It would not have aided and abetted the establishment of military rule of monumental savagery throughout most of Latin America in the 1960s and 1970s (among other places in Chile, where Nixon/Kissinger deliberately undermined Latin America's most deeply established democracy, setting the stage for that "other 9/11"—the Pinochet coup in 1973).
- It would not have embraced the Marcos dictatorship in the Philippines from its onset in 1972 until its next-to-last moment in 1986.
- It would not have bankrolled murderous armed struggles against the popular governments that came to power in the 1970s after overthrowing a hated dictator or a colonial power in Angola, Mozambique, and Nicaragua.

- It would not have given the green light to our trusted anticommunist ally, General Suharto of Indonesia, to invade newly independent East Timor and begin a reign of terror that claimed the lives of a third of the population.
- It would not have given covert support to the attempted coup against the democratically elected government of Hugo Chavez in Venezuela in 2002, a government that had been brought to power largely by the poor of the country, disgusted by both of its traditional political parties, and would not have remained hostile ever since.
- It would not have worked ceaselessly, to this very day, to destroy the one society in Latin America that has eliminated starvation and homelessness, namely, "communist" Cuba.

This is by no means an exhaustive list. The United States has backed many more antidemocratic regimes than enumerated here.[50] And the United States has not stood alone in its anticommunist crusade. Most of the major European countries have backed most of these policies. Body-count comparisons have an obscene feel about them, but still it should be noted that the wars, coups, killings, terror, and torture that have been justified in the name of anticommunism may have destroyed at least as many people as did Hitler or Stalin.[51]

It didn't have to be that way. Had we been a democracy and not merely a polyarchy, it would not have been.

5.3.2 A Note on Liberty

Economic Democracy may be more democratic than capitalism, but what about liberty? Political theorists are fond of pointing out that democracy in and of itself does not guarantee that cornerstone value of modernity. Liberty, encompassing freedom of conscience, freedom of religion, freedom of speech, freedom of assembly, habeas corpus, the rule of law, and so on, can be abridged by an overzealous majority as well as by a tyrant. Might not Economic Democracy be *too* democratic?

The historically developed check to majoritarian abuses is a constitution guaranteeing basic civil and political rights to all citizens. There is no reason why such guarantees cannot be provided under Economic Democracy. A mass movement dedicated to establishing real as opposed to pseudo democracy is not going to trample on the genuine advances the previous order has achieved.

Political theorists also point out that civil and political rights are hollow if individuals do not have the ability to exercise them. Specifically, if the government controls all the media and all the employment in society—as it did in

Soviet-style societies—then formal freedoms remain empty, since dissident views cannot be promulgated. This argument has no force against Economic Democracy, since the government of such a society does not control all the media or all the employment. Economic Democracy is a market economy. There are many employment opportunities in the market sector, and there are many forms of profit-oriented media. Therefore, if there is a significant market for your ideas, there will be publishing houses willing to publish them. If you have difficulty finding a publisher, you and your friends can start your own publishing company, with your own funds or with the help of an investment grant from one of the community banks, all of which are on the lookout for possibilities to fund new, employment-generating businesses.

Another objection to the alleged compatibility of Economic Democracy with liberty concerns the size of government. It will be asserted that since Economic Democracy extends the scope of governmental activities, it will give rise to a massive bureaucracy that will inevitably erode our meaningful freedoms.

This assertion rests on two false assumptions. First, it assumes that Economic Democracy greatly increases the power of government. On the contrary, Economic Democracy does not so much increase the power of government as redistribute the power citizens have over government—by greatly curbing the political clout of money. Secondly, the assertion assumes that the bureaucracy under Economic Democracy will be significantly larger than under capitalism. This need not be the case. Certain government functions will be cut back under Economic Democracy. Since it will no longer be necessary to make the world safe for capitalist investment, the truly grotesque military budgets of the world can be scaled back drastically. So too can those bureaucracies now in place to control that portion of the population constituting capitalism's "reserve army of the unemployed" and those people rendered more or less permanently redundant by the system. Governments will remain large, since there is much for government to do, but there is no reason to think that a large government, suitably held in check by a system of constitutional guarantees and accountable to the electorate, will pose a genuine threat to political freedom.

5.3.3 A Note on Political Parties

Political parties under capitalism have historically represented different class interests: slave owners versus employers of wage labor, landed capital versus industrial capital, farmers versus urban dwellers, capital versus labor. Of course, parties must always cast themselves as representing universal interests and must appeal to an electorate beyond the narrow bounds of class, but the longevity and stability of political parties, when they *are* long-lived and stable, have depended on their representing distinct and enduring class interests. (In the absence of such interests, religion or ethnicity often substitutes—as we have witnessed so often and so tragically in recent years.)

If political parties tend to be class based, it is not altogether clear that political parties—as opposed to temporary and shifting voter alliances—would remain a feature of politics in postcapitalist society. This is not to say that political parties should be banned, but the class-based nature of traditional political parties suggests that various functions served by political parties in capitalist societies might be better served by other means.

What functions, exactly, do political parties perform? Two stand out. First of all, political parties raise money for electoral campaigns. The second function is less obvious but equally important. Political parties provide a safety net of sorts for people interested in a political career. Electoral politics under capitalism is hazardous. Not only must you devote considerable time and energy to campaigning (to say nothing of fundraising), but if you lose the election, you get nothing. This prospect is particularly distressing to incumbents, who have perhaps given years of their lives to politics. It should surprise no one that incumbents try to rig the rules to ensure their own reelection and try to make deals while in office that can be parlayed into lucrative private-sector employment should they lose an election. Political parties lessen the insecurity, since, if all else fails, the party will find a place for you in its ongoing organization.

Clearly, the party system dovetails nicely with interests of capital. It is good to have individual candidates for office always in need of campaign funds and ever on the lookout for a comfortable private-sector place to land if an election turns sour. Moreover, the political parties themselves—employers of last resort for defeated candidates—are also beholden to wealthy contributors, so all the bases are pretty much covered.

Economic Democracy will have to face the career-risk problem creatively if it is to draw good people into politics. One possible solution is a reemployment guarantee: If you decide to run for public office but lose, you may, if you so choose, return to your former place of employment at your old salary. If you win the election, the option always remains of returning to your former place of employment whenever you please, and at an income and position comparable to what you would likely have had, had you remained with the enterprise. Your former place of employment may have to make some adjustments to find a suitable spot for you, but such difficulties would seem a small price to pay toward ensuring good government. (Even under capitalism, governments during wartime usually make such arrangements for employees called to active duty.)

Needless to say, all elections in Economic Democracy will be publicly financed. Another small price to pay for an effective, genuine democracy.

6

Getting from Here to There

According to the criteria set out in chapter 1, successor-system theory
must not only specify and defend an alternative economic model; it
must also employ that model to help us make sense of the present world
and to suggest a reform-mediated transition to a different world, a world
"after capitalism." The previous three chapters described and defended a
model of Economic Democracy. This chapter will employ that model in
the two ways just noted—to make sense of the present and to suggest a
reform-mediated transition to a qualitatively different future. Of necessity, the presentations here will be more schematic than what has come
before. The issues are too large and complex to be handled adequately in
one chapter of a short book, but the topics are too important not to be
broached at all.

6.1 Economic Democracy as an Orienting Device

One measure of the validity of a theory is its predictive power. In 2001, as I
was composing the first edition of *After Capitalism*, I constructed a diagram
purporting to explain, from the perspective of successor-system theory, the
contours of twentieth-century economic development. Most of the analysis is
historical, but some predictions are made. Let me first repeat here what I said
then, and then consider how the predictions have fared.

6.1.1 How the World Looked Then (2001)

The twentieth century, particularly the latter half, was a time of remarkable large-scale economic experiments, whole countries reorganizing their economies, always in response to felt contradictions, hoping to create a new and better way of life. Without exception, these experiments have generated their own contradictions, leading either to hopeless dead-ends or to further creative adjustments. (This process reflects that basic tenet of historical materialism discussed in chapter 1: we are a pragmatic, creative species that refuses to submit passively to the difficulties of material and social life. We try new solutions, and although we often fail, although even our successes often have unintended consequences, we learn from our mistakes, we push on.) If we look at these experiments through the lens of capital, we see all paths converging on the model of neoliberalism—the glorious or inglorious (choose your adjective) "end of history." But if we look at these experiments through the lens of Economic Democracy, we see something rather different.

Let me offer a sweeping, oversimplified illustration of this second perspective. (See the accompanying diagram, figure 6.1.) The extent to which this sketch helps us see things in new and fruitful ways is a measure of the orienting power of the concept of Economic Democracy.

This diagram is essentially about the post–World War II period, although the great split in the twentieth century occurred in 1917, when socialism, for the first time, moved from theory to practice. A socialist "Second World" came into being to challenge a capitalist "First World" that had by then colonized most of the planet.

The economic disruption and insane destructiveness of World War I rendered First World capitalism highly vulnerable. Workers and peasants everywhere began to stir. By way of reaction, we got fascism in Italy, and "National Socialism" in Germany—experiments in authoritarian capitalism aimed at preventing the radical left from coming to power. As economic experiments, fascism and Nazism failed. They were too aggressively militaristic to avoid self-destructive war—but they did buy capitalism the time needed to find a better solution. The threat (and example) of fascism-Nazism justified a much larger role for government in economic affairs than laissez-faire orthodoxy countenanced, as well as the massive amounts of deficit spending that managed to pull the Western economies out of the Great Depression into which they had fallen. (World War II not only saved democracy from fascism; it saved capitalism from itself.)

Let us pick up the postwar story and trace the capitalist branch of the diagram. Following the great decolonization movements of the postwar period, the capitalist world split into two parts, as newly independent "Third World"

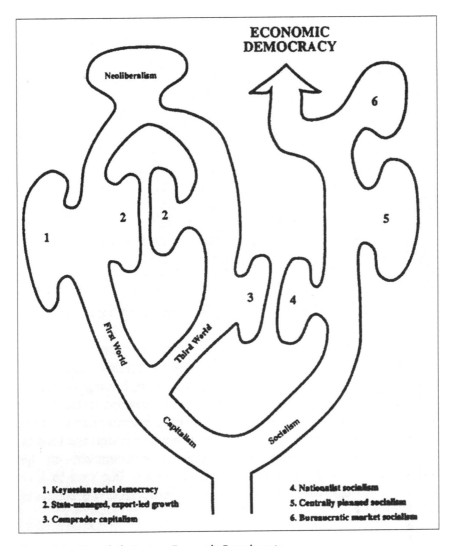

Figure 6.1   Twentieth-Century Economic Experiments

countries broke away from their colonial masters. If we trace the development of the First World branch, we find two distinctive forms of capitalism making their appearance. The first form is "Keynesian liberalism," so called because it takes its theoretical orientation from Keynes's radical revision of neoclassical orthodoxy. This form became dominant in the United States, Canada, Australia, New Zealand, and Western Europe. A large state was deemed necessary to ensure the social security of the citizenry and to mediate the conflicts between ever-more-organized labor and ever-more-concentrated business. High levels of government spending and high wages counteract the Keynesian problem of deficient demand.

For several decades, this model was solidly successful—rapid growth, rising real wages, low unemployment, economic stability—capitalism's "Golden Age." However, as time passed, the internal contradictions of the model began to intensify. Since negotiated wage settlements could be passed on to consumers by near-monopoly corporations, inflationary pressures began to build. Moreover, as these enterprises became hard pressed to sell all the goods they were producing, they became reluctant to engage in large amounts of new investment. Western countries found themselves strapped with "stagflation"—rising unemployment *and* inflation.

Laissez-faire conservatism, seemingly buried forever by Keynesian liberalism, came roaring back (under the auspices of Margaret Thatcher and Ronald Reagan) with its proposals to privatize, deregulate, cut back the welfare state, and open up domestic economies to more globalized competition. This new-old set of policy prescriptions, which we now call neoliberalism, eclipsed Keynesian liberalism and soon became what it remains today, the dominant economic ideology of Western policy-making elites.

The other great postwar experiment in advanced capitalism took place in Japan. In this second alternative to laissez faire, the state also played a much larger role than neoclassical orthodoxy would allow, but of a different nature than under Keynesian liberalism. Here the state makes a conscious decision to pursue a policy of export-led growth. Consumer credit is kept tight, and pensions and other welfare provisions are kept low, both measures aimed at securing a high rate of private savings. The government then targets certain industries for global expansion and provides them with easy access to these savings while engaging in heavy protectionism to allow the less-favored sectors of the economy to survive.

This model also proved to be remarkably successful. The world witnessed a "Japanese miracle"—a rate of growth that resulted in a fifty-five-fold increase in GDP over the space of thirty years (1946–1976). By the late 1980s, there was concern in the West that "Japan, Inc." would soon become globally dominant. However, this was not to be. The Japanese economy stalled—and remains stalled. Japanese exports now have to compete globally with lower-cost exports from other Asian countries. Their banking system has become overloaded with bad loans. Domestic demand, despite increased government expenditures, has been insufficient to pull the economy out of its doldrums. So the pressure is on Japan to reform: deregulate, open its markets to foreign competition, reduce the role of government planning—in short, to also adopt the neoliberal agenda.

If we look now at Third World capitalism during the postwar period, we also see two basic models. The first is the one most widely adopted in the wake of formal decolonization. A local elite takes the reins of political power and opens their country to transnational penetration. A regime of "comprador capitalism" is established. The local elite form domestic monopolies and connect to transnational capital. The country serves primarily as a market for First World goods and as a source of raw materials and exotic foodstuffs for First World buyers.

A few countries adopting this model experienced spurts of economic growth, but even in these cases the wealth did not "trickle down." The mass poverty endemic to all comprador-capitalist countries intensified. There were protests. When these protests threatened to become insurrectionary—as they often did—martial law or outright military rule was established. These Third World equivalents of the fascist-Nazi experiments, heavily assisted by the United States and utilizing all the means of torture and terror at their disposal, were usually able to check the revolutionary movements, but these militarized-capitalist regimes, like their First World predecessors, failed as economic models. So, when the threat of a revolutionary Left receded, most of them were overturned and replaced by more "democratic" governments. These new regimes, currently in place, are now advised, cajoled, and often heavily pressured (notably by the international lending agencies) to jump onto the neoliberal bandwagon.

The second model of Third World capitalism was considerably more successful than the comprador model. Taiwan and South Korea, the "baby tigers" of Southeast Asia, are the key examples. We have here a Third World version of the Japanese model. (Hence this model's placement next to the Japanese model on the diagram.) Since these countries were to serve as showcase alternatives to Chinese and North Korean communism, they were not only given substantial financial support by the United States, but they were also allowed a degree of economic independence uncommon in the Third World. The political elites of Taiwan and South Korea (in both cases, newly established) used this independence to institute large-scale land reform (thus breaking the power of the older elites) and to discipline capital as well as labor. Production for export was emphasized, allocation of capital was overseen by the state, and protectionist barriers were set up to shelter local industries.

Late in the game, numerous other Third World countries began to embrace export-led growth as their developmental strategy (although without as much regulation as Taiwan or South Korea). Then came the Asian meltdown of 1997–1998, which rocked South Korea as well as Indonesia, Thailand, Malaysia, and the Philippines. Local corruption and too much government was blamed. All countries were told to cut back on governmental expenditures, governmental regulation, governmental direction, and cast their lot with the wholly free market.

Thus, all roads lead to neoliberalism, at least in the view of our global policy makers. For the first time in history, a single strategy is being pressed on First and Third World countries alike. All are being urged to cut social spending, deregulate, privatize, and reduce as many barriers as possible to the free flow of goods and capital.

Let us now look at the socialist branch of the tree. Shortly after the Second World War, various experiments in non-Marxist "nationalist socialisms" (not to be confused with Hitler's "National Socialism") were attempted—Egyptian socialism, Algerian socialism, Indonesian socialism, Guyanian socialism, and so forth. Widespread nationalization of private businesses took place, and large state bureaucracies were created. The party in power attempted to direct the economy.

Unfortunately, little in the way of genuine development occurred under regimes of this sort. These experiments soon enough came to resemble, or revert to, comprador capitalism (hence their placement on the diagram).

Far more important—and far more successful—is the model of centrally planned socialism pioneered by the Soviet Union, then imposed on Eastern Europe. This became the developmental model for China, Cuba, North Korea, and Vietnam, and inspired Third World revolutionary movements everywhere. The model was, for a while, compelling. The Soviet Union changed its status from semifeudal backwater to global superpower in four decades. China moved from being the "sick man of Asia" to a great power in even less time. Cuba proceeded to eradicate illiteracy and poverty in so short an order that its example became a hemispheric "threat" to the comprador capitalist regimes of the region, against which the United States mobilized (and continues to mobilize) its vast resources.

But this model too ran up against internal contradictions. Centralized planning is able to provide for basic needs, but its incentive structures are too perverse to yield efficient and dynamic development. Hence, reformers began to experiment with ways of combining market mechanisms with collective ownership of means of production, first in Yugoslavia, then elsewhere. In Eastern Europe and Russia, these experiments were cut short by the events of 1989–1991. (These experiments did not spontaneously abort as a result of the political upheavals. Local elites and Western advisors had to work hard to discredit market socialism as a viable option.[1])

In China, however, they have borne remarkable fruit. Not all of it has been sweet, particularly in recent years, but the fact remains that the Chinese experiment with market socialism, begun in 1978, dramatically raised the standard of living for most of its 1.2 billion inhabitants and sustained a growth rate over the past two decades that is unmatched by any other country on the planet. Over the past twenty years, real per capita income has more than tripled, housing space has doubled, the infant mortality rate has been cut by more than 50 percent, the number of doctors has increased by 50 percent, and life expectancy has gone from sixty-seven to seventy. In 1978, there were 262 million people living in poverty in China. Twenty years later there were 74 million.[2] Whatever the shortcomings of the Chinese experiment, it cannot be denied that never before in human history have so many people been lifted out of poverty so quickly.

The Chinese experiment is enormously complex and its trajectory is far from certain, but at present, China should be regarded as a form of market socialism. There is at this time much theorizing and much practical experimentation going on in China. There are factions pushing for capitalist restoration while others remain committed to a "socialist market economy with Chinese characteristics"—as the economic structure is officially described. There is considerable concern about rising unemployment, a problem that capitalism cannot resolve, and considerable concern about increasing regional inequalities, a problem that market-determined investment flows will only exacerbate. There is considerable experimentation with various forms of workplace organization, including those that give ownership rights to workers. It is possible that the next move forward will be toward something like Economic Democracy.

Successor-system theory does not allow us to make confident predictions about the actual evolution of the Chinese Revolution or the reforms underway now in Cuba and Vietnam, but it allows us to be hopeful. It also suggests that in Russia, or perhaps elsewhere in Eastern Europe, a market-socialist evolutionary trajectory might be resumed, now that the huge costs and meager benefits of the attempted capitalist restoration have become apparent. In most of these countries, the ruling class lacks legitimacy, since everyone knows that the successful "capitalists" are mostly criminals who have looted the national patrimony. Successor-system theory suggests that there are more possibilities latent in that part of the world than conventional wisdom would allow.

6.1.2 How the World Looks Now (2011)

Ten years after the above was composed, how do things look? Consider first the global North. I argued that Japan was under pressure to adopt neoliberal reforms. In 2001 Junichiro Koizumi became prime minister, and launched a neoliberal program. It has failed. The economy continues to stagnate, inequality has worsened, young people can't find regular jobs, and Japan's ratio of debt to GDP, nearly 200 percent, is the highest among developed countries (more than twice that of the United States).

In Europe and the United States pressure is being exerted everywhere to cut back on public expenditures for health, education, unemployment insurance, pension provisions, and the like, now deemed "unaffordable"—despite the fact that, given ongoing productivity gains, these societies are significantly richer now than they were at the height of the welfare state. We are just going to have to get used to the "new normal"—high unemployment and reduced social services—so we are told.

In 2001 I argued that "all roads lead to neoliberalism," and yet (to quote myself):

> The neoliberal road is surely a dead-end. As the analysis of the previous two chapters makes clear, it is lunacy to entrust the health of the global economy to the animal spirits of private investors. Regional boom-bust cycles will intensify, as unregulated capital shifts rapidly from one country to another, looking for a quick fix, fleeing in panic when alarm bells go off. Long term, the Keynesian problem is bound to appear in ever more serious form. Competitive pressures compel enterprises everywhere both to cut costs, thus attenuating global effective demand, and to introduce the newest technologies, thus expanding productive capacity. The supply-demand gap will grow ever wider. The threat of a globalized overproduction crisis will grow ever more serious.
>
> It is by no means clear that globalized capitalism can pull back from the trap it has set for itself. Stagnation, together with gradually rising global unemployment and steadily worsening inequality within and among countries, may be the best that can be hoped for—short of radical transformation. Or the roof might cave in. A deep and enduring global depression is a real possibility.

I trust the reader will agree: not a word needs to be changed. This is precisely our situation today.

The analysis put forth concerning the socialist branch of the tree also remains valid. I argued that the market socialism that had developed in China was a positive development. The subsequent decade has borne this out. The Chinese economy has continued to develop rapidly, and now constitutes the second largest economy in the world. (It was the sixth largest in 2001.) When Hu Jintao and other "fourth-generation" leaders assumed power in 2002, they began applying a cautious brake to the unrestrained capitalism that had developed in certain sectors, stressing sustainable, balanced development instead, and have been openly concerned about growing inequality, environmental degradation, and corruption.

Policies put in place to correct excesses have not caused growth to slow. Moreover, since China's economic structure has proven to be far more resilient to the global turmoil of the past several years than have the capitalist economies of the United States, Europe, and Japan, those influential voices within China who had been calling for ever more "market liberalization" have suffered a setback. (More on China in the subsequent "Note.")

Vietnam's "socialist market economy" also continues to thrive, growing at 7 percent per year during the first eight years of the decade, before slowing during the global crisis, which cut into export markets. According to the 2010 *CIA World Factbook*, since 2003 "deep poverty [in Vietnam] has declined significantly."[3] (An interesting side-note: Vietnamese workers have been quite aggressive in pressing their demands in recent years, hundreds of strikes erupting—some 762 in 2008 alone. Moreover, according to the beleaguered Taiwanese investors who own many of the factories, "The authorities are supposed to come to mediate but basically they are here to fight for the workers. It's all one-sided." [Not something one would ever hear said in a capitalist country.])

Cuba has recently moved to increase the size of the market sector of its economy so as to provide employment for the large number of state employees that are being removed from government payrolls to promote efficiency. (President Raul Castro has remarked, "We have to remove once and for all the notion that Cuba is the only country in the world where you can live without working."[4]) Special emphasis is being given to food production, land being leased to those who will farm it productively and sell their products in farmers' markets. (Cuba, it is worth noting, currently ranks 17th of 171 countries on a composite United Nations Development Programme index of health and education, ahead not only of all other low-income countries, but also ahead of Greece, Italy, and the United Kingdom.[5])

The biggest surprise of the decade, not hinted at in the diagram (although not inconsistent with the accompanying analysis), has been the rise of the Left, via democratic means, in Latin America. In 1998, in Venezuela, an army officer who had been imprisoned for fomenting a revolt against a sitting president was swept into power with 56 percent of the vote, trouncing the candidates from the two traditional parties that had ruled the country for four decades. Surprising at the time—but who could have imagined, a decade ago, that Hugo Chavez would survive a coup attempt covertly supported by the United States in 2002, easily win a conservative-initiated recall-referendum (59–41 percent) in 2004, win another election in 2006, galvanize the poor of the country with community councils and Bolivarian circles to address basic needs, nationalize one of the country's major banks, and encourage the setting up of cooperatives throughout the country? Who would have expected him to declare, in 2005, his support for "a socialism for the twenty-first century," and begin constructing ALBA (Bolivarian Alternative for Latin

America) in opposition to Washington's "Free Trade Area of the Americas," an alternative alliance that now includes Cuba, Nicaragua, Bolivia, Ecuador, and many of the small Caribbean nations?

Indeed, who would have predicted the number of left or center-left leaders coming to power democratically throughout Latin America during the first decade of the twenty-first century: Ricardo Lagos in Chile and Luiz Ignácio "Lulu" da Silva in Brazil in 2002, Néstor Kirchner in Argentina in 2003, Tabaré Vásquez in Uruguay in 2005, Michele Bachelet in Chile, Evo Morales in Bolivia, Rafael Correa in Ecuador and Daniel Ortega in Nicaragua in 2006, Cristina Fernández in Argentina and Álvaro Colom in Guatemala in 2007, Fernando Lugo in Paraguay in 2008, and Mario Funes in El Salvador in 2009?[6] Of course few of these leaders are as "radical" as Chavez, and in no case has any of them engaged in wholesale nationalization of means of production, large-scale land redistribution or any other head-to-head confrontation with the economic elites of their countries—although in most cases cooperatives have been encouraged, and the governments have tried to gain some control over investment allocation.[7] The capitalist classes in all these countries remain entrenched. Still . . . something quite unexpected has happened. How it plays out remains to be seen.[8]

6.1.3. A Note on China

The Chinese economy has become the second largest in the world. China recently surpassed the United States as the leading producer of carbon dioxide on the planet. We are flooded these days with books, articles, and news commentaries about "the rise of China," most aimed at provoking anxiety and fear. ("Sweetie, are you having nightmares about China again?"—Cartman's mother to her son, in an October 28, 2008, episode of *South Park*.[9])

It is not so often noted, however, how remarkably *different* China's rise has been from that of other dominant powers: Unlike the major European states, it has not tried to colonize areas of the world poorer or weaker than itself. Unlike pre–World War II Japan, it has not waged ruthless warfare against its neighbors to enhance its economic "sphere of influence." Unlike the United States, it has not set up military bases all over the world, toppled governments deemed "unfriendly," or sent in troops whenever "security interests" seemed threatened. Unlike the Soviet Union, it has not engaged in a massive arms race with the world's other "superpower," nor has it installed client governments in nations on its border.[10]

China's rise has been what it has proclaimed it to be: a peaceful rise. (It is interesting that those predicting a military confrontation between the United States and China often point to "resource wars." These resources, of course, are not the resources within our own borders, but those resources in other parts of the world to which we feel entitled.)

This is not to say that there is nothing wrong with China. There's plenty wrong with China: the income gap is large and widening; there are lots of sweatshops providing the Wal-Marts of the world with cheap manufactured goods; corruption, particularly at the lower levels of government, is rampant; dissent is often suppressed; environmental degradation is severe. Consider the comments of Pan Yue, China's deputy environmental minister:

> Our raw materials are scarce, we don't have enough land and our population is constantly growing. . . . Cities are growing, but desert areas are expanding. . . . Five of the most polluted cities in the world are in China; acid rain is falling on one third of our territory; half of the water in China's seven largest rivers is completely useless, a quarter of our citizens lack access to clean drinking water.[11]

These facts present a grim picture. And yet—there are these "optimism" reports: A Pew Research Center survey in 2005 found China to be "the world leader in hope for the future"—the most optimistic of the seventeen nations surveyed. Not only was personal optimism high, but China led the list regarding "satisfaction with national conditions." Fully 72 percent indicated satisfaction, as opposed to 19 percent dissatisfied. This compares with only 39 percent in the United States indicating satisfaction, 57 percent dissatisfied. (And that was *before* the financial meltdown.) It is noteworthy, too, that the young Chinese, ages eighteen to twenty-nine, are the most optimistic of all, 78 percent anticipating a "very positive future."[12] More recent surveys by Gallup indicate continued optimism in China (78 percent), much more than in the United States (52 percent), UK (43 percent) or Japan (23 percent). (The UK figure is on the high side for Europe, France registering 33 percent, Germany 30 percent, Italy 23 percent, Greece 10 percent).[13]

What is going on in China? How does China appear from the perspective of successor-system theory, which posits Economic Democracy as a path forward for humanity? Is China simply *Capitalism with Chinese Characteristics* (the *Economist*'s "Book of the Year" in 2008), or is it something different?[14] That China has "gone capitalist" is certainly the dominant view across the political spectrum, left, right, and center—but is this true?[15]

First, from the perspective of successor-system theory, some double-negatives:

- The fact that China has given a large scope to the market in its economy does not mean that China is not a socialist society. As successor-system theory makes clear, a viable, desirable socialism requires a suitably regulated market mechanism to allocate most goods and services.

- The fact that there is considerable inequality in China does not mean that China is not a socialist society. If there are markets, there will be inequalities that have nothing to do with individual effort. Some enterprises will be luckier than others. Some will be better run. Within enterprises inequalities will persist, since financial incentives will be employed to attract and retain skilled technical and managerial personnel.
- The fact that there are some very rich capitalists in China does not mean that China is not a socialist society. As we have seen, a viable, desirable socialism might want to include a capitalist sector—certainly a sector of small businesses, but perhaps even a sector of large, entrepreneurial capitalists. Entrepreneurial capitalists could play a useful role in fostering innovation and providing much needed employment, particularly in a developing country. It should not be presumed that such a sector will inevitably become the dominant sector, certainly not if wages and working conditions are regulated, these firms are unionized, and a large alternative sector of public firms exists.

Successor-system theory urges us to look for positive signs as well. What about workplace democracy in China?

We observe that formal institutions are in place in many enterprises, backed by official rhetoric. The language of "democratic management" is widely used in China. The Chinese Constitution proclaims that "state-owned enterprises practice democratic management through congresses of workers," which are empowered to "decide matters concerning the well-being and benefits of the workers," and even to "elect the factory director or manager according to the arrangement of the competent governmental department."[16] Even nonpublic enterprises are supposed to be "conducive to developing democracy, giving voice fully to the workers' ideas and demands, and allowing the workers to take part in their enterprises' democratic management"—at least according to Politburo member Wei Jianxing.[17]

Even if they are not yet effective—which they are not—the fact that formal institutions are in place and supported by the prevailing ideology is not insignificant. A revitalized labor movement could well make use of them. There is class struggle going on in China right now. How it will be resolved remains undetermined.

What about social control of investment in China? Again, formally, the situation is promising. Financial institutions in China are overwhelmingly public institutions. The Chinese government has control over its investment funds in ways that governments in capitalist countries do not. Banks, which are virtually all public, control 75 percent of the capital of the country, as compared with less than 20 percent in "developed" countries. Stock and bond markets in China are among the smallest in the world—and these are used almost exclusively by state-owned enterprises. Strict capital controls prevent citizens from investing in foreign financial markets or securities.[18]

Another consideration concerning social control of investment: the invisible hand of the market does not dictate the future. China still plans. It sets out goals and it commits resources to realize them. Among the current goals: to create a moderately well-off "harmonious socialist society," a sustainable, "green" economy, and "new socialist countryside."

(A brief comment on this last goal. The Chinese government is deeply concerned about the widening gap between town and country, which could trigger a truly massive migration from the countryside to cities. As it is, current migration is huge, but what is going on now could be dwarfed by what might come. Hence plans are being made to forestall this, derived at least in part from a call frequently heard from the Chinese New Left for "an alternative conception of modernity," one that brings modernity to the countryside, rather than modernizing through urbanization. This is an extraordinary concept, one with world-historic implications, given that well over half of the world's poor still live in rural areas.)

Are the references to socialism by China's ruling class merely verbal ploys, or do they reflect the fact that China is not (at least not yet) a capitalist country? We have defined "capitalism" as a market economy in which the bulk of the means of production are in private hands and the bulk of the workforce are wage laborers. But in China nearly half of the Chinese labor force is engaged in agriculture, and the land has not been privatized. Moreover, although the share of the output of state-owned enterprises in the economy has declined dramatically over the past several decades, it still makes up a substantial part of the national economy—controlling roughly 30 percent of the total secondary and tertiary assets, and over 50 percent of total industrial assets.[19] Given this definition, it would seem that China is not (yet) a capitalist country.

It also seems clear that the capitalist class, although influential, is far from dominant. Let me offer three reasons for thinking that they will remain subordinate, that is, three reasons for thinking that China will not "go capitalist":

- Capitalism cannot solve China's fundamental problems—and its ruling class knows this. China's political class is not stupid. Singapore's longtime ambassador to the U.N., Kishore Mahbubani, has remarked that "after more than a hundred years of anarchy and misrule, China has amassed the best governing class it has seen in generations."[20] None of the problems noted above—widening income inequality, environmental destruction, etc.—is news to the Chinese. These are discussed incessantly in the press and debated at the highest levels of government. The Chinese ruling class is well aware that unbridled capitalism will exacerbate inequalities, create more unemployment, and wreak ecological havoc. This was clear to most even before the Great Global Recession. It is even more obvious now.

• There is considerable pressure from below opposing the capitalist trajectory, pressure from workers and peasants, who have ideology on their side. Protestors often appeal to socialist values, and are supported by significant party officials and intellectuals. Chinese workers and peasants are far from passive. A new law was passed in 2008, the Labor Dispute Conciliation and Arbitration Law, in response to skyrocketing numbers—some 317,000 disputes in 2006, of which 14,000 involved demonstrations or strikes, sometimes even violence.[21] Although workers and peasants appear to hold the central government in high regard, there is deep discontent with local officials, who are often (correctly) perceived as corrupt and bent on appropriating for themselves and their allies public lands and state assets.

• This pressure generates deep concern about instability on the part of the political class, who, given recent history, are particularly sensitive to this issue. China has experienced massive upheavals during the century just past: anticolonial struggles, civil war, Japanese occupation, a Communist revolution, the Great Leap Forward, the Cultural Revolution, Tiananmen Square. The leadership knows that things can spin out of control. (The Chinese ruling class is haunted by the specter of instability in ways that Western ruling classes are not. Our ruling classes do not have to pay attention to the poor. They've been wholly marginalized. Chinese workers and peasants are by no means marginal—and they have ideology on their side.)

This concern on the part of China's rulers is wholly understandable. Members of the political class want to preserve their own place in society. Such is the concern of every political class. But there is a second factor that is far from irrelevant. They want to preserve the *collective accomplishments* of China—and their own place in *history*. Astonishing successes have been recorded, accomplished by the Chinese themselves without significant external aid or advice. China's rulers do not want to see these successes unravel, as could happen if popular grievances and environmental issues are not addressed.

It is by no means clear that China will succeed in dealing with the immense problems the country faces, above all on the environmental front. If it does, it will have invented a new kind of socialism. In any event, we should wish them well—workers, peasants, and also those honest entrepreneurs, New Left intellectuals, social critics, and noncorrupt party members, who are currently engaged in one of the momentous projects of our species: an attempt at creating a moderately well-off, sustainable, harmonious society for a fifth of the world's population, a fifth that had been, barely a half-century ago, among the poorest on earth. The stakes are very high. World-systems theorist Giovanni Arrighi sums up his detailed, careful study of China:

> If China's reorientation [away from the energy-consuming Western path, toward a more balanced and ecologically-sustainable development] succeeds in reviving and consolidating China's traditions of self-centered market-based development, accumulation *without* dispossession, mobilization of human rather than non-human resources, and government through mass participation . . . China will be in a position to contribute decisively to the emergence of a commonwealth of civilizations truly respectful of cultural differences. But, if the reorientation fails, China may well turn into a new epicenter of social and political chaos that will facilitate Northern attempts to re-establish crumbling global dominance, or . . . help humanity burn up in the horrors of the escalating violence that has accompanied the liquidation of the Cold War world order.[22]

6.2 An Economic Democracy Reform Agenda

The diagram discussed above (figure 6.1) is a heuristic device that oversimplifies the real world, and hence might be misleading in certain respects. For example, it might be read as indicating that there is no path from capitalism to Economic Democracy. Successor-system theory does not draw that conclusion, although it does suggest that the transition to Economic Democracy might be easier for a country that had earlier taken a socialist road.

The diagram also leaves out an important consideration: the degree to which elements of Economic Democracy have been established within capitalism itself. Marx liked to speak of the institutions of the new society developing within the womb of the old. These institutions, many of them already in existence in some form, point to a reform agenda for an advanced capitalist society. These reforms, if implemented, would fall short of full Economic Democracy, but they can be seen as steps along the way—much as the reforms proposed by Marx and Engels in their historic *Manifesto* fall short of their hoped-for communism.

Let me advance a relatively short list (not intended to be definitive), grouping them under the headings suggested by the institutional framework of Economic Democracy. Marx and Engels listed ten reforms. I will list twelve, with brief comments, grouping them under five headings. I should say, as Marx and Engels did of their list: "These measures will of course be different in different countries. Nevertheless, in most advanced countries, the following will be pretty generally applicable."[23] In constructing this list, I am thinking of the United States.

6.2.1 Democratizing Labor

Since the goal of Economic Democracy is to have most enterprises worker run, let us offer assistance to those workers trying to set up such enterprises today. Let us also push to extend the two basic tenets of worker self-management, participation and profit sharing, to workers in existing enterprises. Let us consider giving workers the right to buy their company, if they so choose. Let us insist that nationalized companies be worker-self-managed. Hence, four proposals:

- *Public financial and technical support for producer cooperatives and for worker buyouts of capitalist firms.*
  The time is right to push for cooperatives. On December 21, 2009, the United Nations General Assembly declared 2012 to be the "International Year of Co-operatives," and has urged "governments to establish policies, laws and regulations conducive to the formation, growth and stability of cooperatives." Earlier that year the International Labour Organization released a report on the "Resilience of the Cooperative Business Model in Times of Crisis." On October 27, 2009, the United Steelworkers (USW)—the largest industrial union in North America—and Mondragon Internacional, S.A., announced a framework agreement for collaboration in establishing Mondragon cooperatives in the manufacturing sector within the United States and Canada.[24]
- *Legislation mandating, or at least encouraging, profit sharing and more worker participation in capitalist firms.*
  Current Employee Stock Ownership Plan (ESOP) legislation in the United States encourages firms, by means of tax breaks, to provide employees with stock in their company, but it does not guarantee workers control over the company commensurate with their degree of ownership. A reform of this legislation is in order, to develop further its progressive potential. "Codetermination" along German lines, requiring worker representation on corporate boards, should also be pushed.
- *Legislation giving workers the right to buy their company if they so choose.*
  Such a law has been proposed by economist Gregory Dow, to be applicable to all limited liability companies traded on a public stock exchange. If workers so desire, a referendum is held to determine if the majority of workers want to democratize the company. If the referendum succeeds, a labor trust is formed, its directors selected democratically by the work-

force, which, using funds derived from payroll deductions, purchase shares of the company on the stock market. In due time, the labor trust will come to own the majority of shares, at which time it takes full control via a leveraged buyout, that is, by borrowing the money to buy up the remaining shares.[25] (Since worker-owned firms tend to be more productive and more stable than capitalist firms, local, state, and/or national subsidies might be in order so as to help workers acquire shares and/or to providing low-cost financing for the final buyout.)

- *Legislation stipulating that when a major corporation goes bankrupt, but is bailed out by the government, the government should nationalize the company and restructure it as a worker self-managed enterprise.*
Restructuring a firm to be worker self-managed entails replacing the corporate board of directors with a democratically elected workers council and instituting profit sharing for all workers. The company should not be returned to the private sector when it becomes profitable. (Such a procedure could have been followed when General Motors went bankrupt in 2009. The government did, in effect, nationalize the company, receiving 60 percent of the stock in the "new GM" that was created when the "old GM" collapsed.)

6.2.2 Democratizing Capital

To replace private control over investment with social control is a key tenet of Economic Democracy. There are at least four reforms we might undertake that move us in that direction.

- *Democratization and reregulation of the banking system, to make the Federal Reserve System more accountable to the electorate and local banks more accountable to their communities.*
The Federal Reserve, like central banks in almost all capitalist countries, is now run primarily for the benefit of the financial class—hence, the obsessive concern with inflation. The Federal Reserve (and eventually all banks) should be managed so as to enhance the well-being of the democratic community, which means employment creation should be as serious a goal as keeping inflation within reasonable bounds.
- *The establishment, at the local, state, and perhaps even the national level, of public banks to compete with banks in the private sector, with their profits dedicated to job creation.*
Many citizens might well prefer banking with an institution committed to helping local businesses create jobs to banking with banks oriented to maximizing shareholder value. (Local support for a bank committed

to increasing employment in the Basque region has been a key reason for the success of Mondragon's Caja Laboral.) One such bank already exists in the United States, the Bank of North Dakota (founded by socialist A. C. Townley in 1915). It has fared so well during the Great Recession that a number of other states are now considering doing something similar.[26]

- *Replace the corporate income tax with a capital assets tax, the proceeds to be used for community capital investment and to increase employment.*
  This tax can be justified on two distinct grounds. First, it would redress a current imbalance that even neoclassical economists should agree decreases efficiency and creates unemployment. At present, companies are taxed for the labor they employ (payroll taxes) but not for the capital they use. Thus, companies use relatively less labor relative to capital than they otherwise would.

  Secondly, it would make corporate tax avoidance far more difficult than it now is. Currently, corporations have become so adept at tax avoidance that companies making vast profits often pay no taxes at all. (In 2009, neither ExxonMobil nor General Electric, nor Bank of America paid any corporate income tax in the United States, despite net incomes of $45 billion, $10 billion, and $4.4 billion respectively.) The share of revenue coming from the corporate income tax has dropped from about one-third in the early 1950s to less than one-sixth in 2008. In contrast, payroll taxes provided more than one-third of the revenues in 2008, compared with just one-tenth in the early 1950s. Warren Buffett's celebrated remark is surely on the mark: "There's class warfare, all right, but it's my class, the rich class, that's making war, and we're winning."[27]

  A capital assets tax would be simple and transparent. The tax base would be the share price on January 1 of the tax year, multiplied by the number of outstanding company shares, that total multiplied by the fraction of sales the company made in the United States. The tax rate should be small at first, but it can be raised over time, revenues going into a collective investment fund.

- *Reregulation of transnational capital flows.*
  Beginning with a "Tobin tax" (i.e., a small tax on all transnational financial market transactions), we need reforms aimed at discouraging the rapid, speculative, destabilizing movement of massive amounts of funds from one market to another.[28] Our ultimate goal is to *halt* market-driven cross-border flows, not merely to slow them down, but reregulation is a step in the right direction. An important side benefit of a Tobin tax would be the generation of substantial revenues, which could be used to fund other parts of the reform agenda.

6.2.3 Toward Full Employment

Make the government the employer-of-last-resort. In chapter 4 I argued that full employment is impossible under capitalism because the threat of unemployment is the disciplinary stick that keeps the workforce in line. Economists shy away from mentioning the disciplinary effect of unemployment, but most believe that when unemployment gets too low, bad things happen. We get inflation, they say, which, if not checked, can accelerate out of control.

Most economists believe this, but not all. L. Randall Wray and other researchers at the Center for Full Employment and Price Stability at the University of Missouri–Kansas City, as well as researchers at the Australian Centre of Full Employment and Equity, have long argued for ELR (government as employer-of-last-resort), and have presented various proposals for how such a program could be implemented. In general, these proposals would have the government offer a job at minimum wage, or perhaps slightly below current minimum wage, to any able-bodied person wanting one. Funds for job creation would come from the national government, but the programs would be administered locally. Proponents argue that, since the wage rate is low, ELR will not be inflationary, will not compete with private-sector hiring, and is easily affordable. They also argue that such a program will stabilize the economy, for it will prevent the mass unemployment that so exacerbates and prolongs a recession, and will automatically increase government spending at such time, which is exactly what Keynesian economic theory prescribes.[29]

Since ELR is one of the key institutions of Economic Democracy, proponents of Economic Democracy should support wholeheartedly such a program, whatever reservations one might have as to its ultimate compatibility with capitalism, or however short of *full* employment it falls; for example, "The 21st Century Full-Employment and Training Act," which Representative John Conyers introduced in May 2010. (The program is to be financed by a "Tobin Tax"—designated FTT: financial assets trading tax.) This bill mandates government creation of jobs when unemployment gets too high, although—in keeping with the realities of capitalism—it accepts 4 percent unemployment as "full" employment.

6.2.4 Toward Fair Trade

Make no mistake: free trade is a fool's game for the underdog—for workers in contest with capitalists, for poor countries when dealing with rich countries. Not all anti-free-trade programs are progressive, but progressives should not cede protectionism to the reactionaries. Properly constructed fair trade can greatly benefit working people of all nations. To this end, we should adopt a fair trade proposal along these lines:

- *Tariff-based fair trade, not free trade, when there are significant wage and environmental-regulation disparities between the trading countries.*
  Tariffs should be imposed to make it impossible for countries to gain competitive advantage simply by paying their workers less or being less stringent with environmental regulations.
- *All proceeds from the fair-trade tariffs to be rebated to appropriate worker-friendly organizations or agencies, private or governmental, in poor countries.*
  Free-trade advocates love to argue that tariffs are selfish, hurting both consumers and poor-country workers. Poor-country trade representatives often concur. It is important to undercut this argument. Rich-country consumers will indeed pay more for poor-country products— but the higher prices will help, not hurt, poor countries, and will protect our own workers as well. (It should be noted that these reforms fall short of the full-bodied "socialist protectionism" of Economic Democracy, since it only targets those commodities that compete with locally produced ones. Under Economic Democracy, *all* commodities from poor countries would be subject to a tariff, which is rebated to the poor country, so as to ensure them a fair price for their goods.)

6.2.5 Democratizing Democracy

As the great novelist/essayist/activist Arundhati Roy has observed, democracy is in crisis:

> Modern democracies have been around long enough for neo-liberal capitalists to learn how to subvert them. They have mastered the techniques of infiltrating the instruments of democracy—the "independent" judiciary, the "free" press, the parliament—and molding them to their purpose. The project of corporate globalization has cracked the code.[30]

What might be done? There are two strategies a reform movement might employ, one aimed at reducing, at least to some degree, the massive concentration of wealth that presently exists, the other aimed at reducing the impact of private wealth on the democratic process.

The first strategy employs a *wealth tax.* Conservatives, who so often invoke "human nature" as a reason to doubt that socialism could ever work, seem never to notice how that same defective "human nature," when coupled with wide disparities of wealth, will inevitably undermine democracy. For it is "human nature" for those with money to do whatever they can to preserve and enhance their financial situation. Since a democratic government *could* redistribute their wealth, it is utopian to think that the financial resources that can be mobilized by the wealthy will not be deployed to control the political process, so as to make sure that tax policies aimed at keeping the rich from becoming *too* rich will never be enacted.

Still, the attempt must be made. Of course it is much more difficult to take wealth away from the rich than to keep them from becoming too rich in the first place. In the aftermath of World War II, given the egalitarian spirit of that time, it did not seem unreasonable to most people to tax income in excess of $200,000 (about $2 million in today's dollars) at 91 percent. And so we lived in a far more egalitarian society then than we do today. But then came the tax-cutting sprees of Reagan and Bush, so that the top rate is now only 35 percent, and much of the income of the ultra-rich gets classified as "capital gains," and taxed at only 15 percent. The wealth of the wealthy has soared. (Paul Krugman notes that if we define a "billionaire" as someone whose wealth is greater than the output of 20,000 average workers [$1 billion in the mid-1990s], there were sixteen in 1957, thirteen in 1968. There are 160 now.[31])

If we do the math, we see that the only way, short of expropriation, to bring the giants down to more human size is a *wealth tax*. A high *income tax* won't do. Consider: if a billionaire makes 6 percent on his fortune, he receives from his "investments" alone, apart from any work he might do, $60 million a year. If 90 percent of that were taxed away via an income tax, he'd still have $6 million to live on. Assuming he is able to live within his means—that is, spend less on personal consumption than the $6 million plus his salary—his $1 billion stash remains untouched. Indeed, if he spends less than $6 million plus salary, his wealth will grow!

A *wealth tax* of 10 percent, on the other hand, would require that he pay $100 million, leaving him with $900 million. His wealth would begin a (slow) descent down from the stratosphere. In short: if taxation is to be used to chip away at accumulated wealth, it cannot be an income tax. It must be a wealth tax.[32]

It should be noted that there are two distinct reasons for imposing a wealth tax: (1) To acquire an additional source of revenue to pay for needed social and environmental programs. In this case, we are asking those who have benefited so immensely from the current system to give back to society a portion of those gains. (2) To reduce the disparity between the average citizen and the really rich, a disparity that undermines democracy. The first argues for the imposition of a wealth tax of some sort; the second for a wealth tax *high*

enough to actually reduce the accumulated wealth of the ultrarich. It is probably advisable to push initially for a small wealth tax, appealing to the first
reason. Later, if the progressive movement gains sufficient strength, the rate
can be raised—and the second reason made explicit. (Even a modest wealth
tax would generate a large amount of revenue, since wealth is so massively
concentrated in the United States. The upper 1 percent owns more than a
third of all net household wealth, that is, about $20 trillion. A mere 2 percent
wealth tax on the top 1 percent would thus net $400 billion—roughly the
entire cost of Medicare for the country.[33])

Campaign finance reform is the second strategy and is high on the agenda
of all progressive reform advocates. Needless to say, meaningful reform is
difficult to achieve, since the politicians who must craft the reform legislation are, for the most part, beneficiaries of the current system. Limited
reforms have been instituted in the past, notably in 1974 (in response to the
Watergate scandals) and McCain-Feingold in 2002, but the Supreme Court,
in its notorious *Citizens United* decision, has pretty much nullified whatever (minimal) effectiveness these laws had. Still, campaign finance reform
must be a site of struggle, since the likelihood of enacting *any* of the above
reforms depends in no small part on curbing the power of wealth to control
the legislative process.

One particularly imaginative and well-developed two-part proposal has
been offered by Yale Law School professors Bruce Ackerman and Ian Ayres,
designed to avoid constitutional (and popular) objections.[34]

- Part 1: All voters are given publicly funded credit cards (called "Patriot
  cards") worth fifty dollars, which can be used (only) to make campaign
  donations to candidates or parties. The fifty dollars may be split among
  as many candidates as one chooses.
- Part 2: All donations, those from the Patriot cards *and* all other private
  contributions, must be made *anonymously* to a blind trust operated by
  the Federal Elections Committee, which credits the candidates' accounts.
  This provision blocks the notorious quid pro quo giving that has so cor-
  rupted our political process. Candidates know how much money they've
  received, but not who gave it to them.

Such a program would not be terribly expensive. If *all* of the 200 million or so citizens eligible to vote used their Patriot card to donate to the
campaigns of their choice, the total would be only $10 billion, less than 0.3
percent of the federal budget for 2010. Yet $10 billion—or even half that
amount—would more than offset all the campaign spending of corporations and the ultrarich—which, in 2010 was some large fraction of the $4.2

billion spent that year. (This amount was a midterm election record, and yet, as conservative *Washington Post* columnist George Will rightly pointed out, "That is about the what Americans spend in one year on yogurt, but less than they spend on candy in two Halloween seasons, and . . . much less than they spend on potato chips, $7.1 billion in a year."[35]) To match the publicly funded contributions of ordinary voters, the wealthy would have to double their current campaign spending, and yet, in light of Part 2 of the reform proposal, have no guarantee that recipients of their largesse would even know who had given them the money.

Not only would such a reform greatly reduce the power of the wealthy to dominate the political realm (without in any way restricting the amount of money they can contribute), but it would doubtless revitalize citizen participation in the electoral contests. With fifty dollars to contribute to whichever candidates, of whatever party one chooses (including third parties[36]) a major incentive exists to pay attention to politics, follow the news, and scrutinize the candidates—as is supposed to happen in a genuine democracy.

6.3 From Reform to Revolution

The reform agenda outlined above, even if fully implemented, would not be Economic Democracy. These reforms would give us a kinder, gentler capitalism, but it would still be capitalism. It would be an unstable capitalism, however. With it becoming ever clearer that workers could run enterprises effectively and that investment funding could come from the state, the role of the capitalist class would be subjected to increased scrutiny. Workers would likely become ever more assertive, capitalists ever more nervous. With worker participation and profit sharing widespread, a capital assets tax in place, and with capital's freedom of investment ever more circumscribed, the stage would be set for a decisive confrontation. But how can we imagine such a confrontation working its way through to a happy ending? How can we imagine "revolution"?

Let me tell three stories. The first I'll call "radical quick"—an imaginary, abrupt transition from contemporary capitalism to Economic Democracy. The second story modifies and complicates the first by taking into account the fact that, at least in the United States, millions of ordinary citizens now have ties to the financial institutions that would be abolished in the "radical quick" transition. In both cases, the result is Economic Democracy—the successor-system to capitalism. The third is more gradual, not presupposing a major financial meltdown. In all three cases, I am thinking of the United States.

One of the "conditions," if there is to be a relatively peaceful transition from capitalism to socialism, is the coming to power of a Left political party with a radical agenda. This condition will be presupposed in the stories I will tell.

6.3.1 Radical Quick

Suppose, perhaps as a result of a severe economic crisis that destroys the credibility of the existing ruling class, a Left political party is swept into office in a landslide election and is thus empowered to enact whatever reforms it deems necessary. Let us set aside concerns about constitutional protections of property rights. We have an overwhelming mandate to move beyond capitalism to something better, to this "Economic Democracy" we have been promising. What would we do?

Let me say at the outset that I do not propose this as a realistic scenario. The "revolution" is not in fact going to happen this way, at least not in the United States. However, imagining an abrupt transition will give us a simple model, which can later be modified and made more credible.

In fact, the basic institutional reforms are not hard to specify, nor is it hard to imagine their peaceful implementation. We don't have to talk about seizing the estates of the wealthy, or replacing capitalists by dedicated cadre, or creating hosts of new institutions. We do not find ourselves in Lenin's predicament, trying to figure out how to create a wholly new society. Four simple reforms would bring us to Economic Democracy.

- First, we issue a decree abolishing all enterprise obligations to pay interest or stock dividends to private individuals or private institutions. This decree will need no enforcement, since enterprises are not going to insist on paying what they are no longer legally obligated to pay.
- Second, we declare that legal authority over all businesses employing more than N full-time workers (where N is a relatively small number) now resides with those workers, one-person, one-vote. Workers may keep the same managers that they now have, or replace them. The authority is now theirs—to determine what to produce, how to produce it, at what price to market it, how to distribute the profits among themselves, and so forth. Guidelines will be issued concerning the formation of worker councils (in those companies where such councils do not already exist), but the only restriction placed on the workforce is the obligation to keep intact the value of the capital assets of the business. These are now regarded as the collective property of the nation and are not to be looted or squandered.

- Third, we announce that a flat-rate tax will be levied on each firm's capital assets, all the revenue from which will go into the national investment fund. Firms may object to this new tax, but it will be pointed out that they are no longer paying dividends to their stockholders or interest on loans they have accumulated. This tax is the rent they pay for the use of assets now regarded not as the private property of owners but the social property of the nation. (If a capital assets tax has already been implemented under capitalism, as a part of the reform process, the mechanisms for calculating and collecting the tax will already be in place. The rate need merely be raised.)
- Fourth, we nationalize all banks. These now-public banks will be charged with reviewing applications for new investment grants and with dispensing the funds generated by the capital assets tax according to the double criteria of profitability and employment creation. Nationalizing banks is not as "revolutionary" as one might think. Both Norway and Sweden nationalized theirs (temporarily) during crisis periods in the early 1990s. The decidedly non-left *Far Eastern Economic Review* proposed nationalization to resolve Japan's banking crisis.[37] Nationalization was discussed by various economists and policymakers in the United States when the financial system began to melt down in 2007. In our scenario, commercial banks would no longer be viable as private institutions anyway, since there is no longer any interest revenue coming in from their loans, so the government would have no choice but to take them over. These institutions, which now oversee the distribution of the investment fund, will still have a vital role to play under Economic Democracy, although they will no longer be profit-making institutions.

That's it—four simple reforms. The day after the revolution, virtually all businesses keep doing exactly what they did before, so the production and distribution of goods and services need not be disrupted. Workers still work, managers still manage, businesses still compete. Enterprises begin setting up new governing structures; the IRS puts into place a new tax code; banks begin the process of restructuring. The Federal Reserve may have to provide these banks with some liquidity to tide them over, but since it is authorized (even now) to create new money, it can readily do so.

Of course, the financial markets will crash—if they haven't already. Capitalists will try to cash in their stocks and bonds, but these will be worthless, since there will be no buyers. Huge amounts of paper wealth will evaporate—but the productive infrastructure of the nation will remain wholly intact. That's the lovely part. Producers keep producing; consumers keep consuming. Life goes on—after capitalism.

6.3.2 Radical Slower (with Concern for Stockholders)

Too simple? Of course. The above is not meant to be a realistic scenario. Above all, it fails to take into account the fact that millions of ordinary citizens (not only capitalists) have resources tied up in the financial markets. People with savings accounts or holdings in stocks and bonds have been counting on their dividend and interest checks. (Nearly half of all American households have direct or indirect holdings in the stock market, mostly in pension plans.) Eliminating all dividend and interest income—which is what Radical Quick does—will not strike these fellow citizens as a welcome reform. Let us run through our story again, this time complicating it to take into account their legitimate concerns.

Let me first set the stage a little more fully than I did with Radical Quick. Let us suppose that a genuine counterproject to capitalism has developed, and that, gradually gaining in strength, it has been able to elect a Left government that has put most of the reforms outlined earlier in this chapter on the table and has secured the passage of some of them. Suppose investors decide they've had enough and begin cashing in their stock holdings so as to take their money and run to greener pastures. A stock-market crash ensues. In reaction, the citizenry decide that they too have had enough—and give their Left government an even stronger mandate to take full responsibility for an economy now tumbling into crisis—not to bail out the banks this time (which, they now know will not solve the underlying problem), but to engage in a radical restructuring of the economy.

Our new government declares a bank holiday, pending reorganization (as Roosevelt did following his election in 1932). All publicly traded corporations are declared to be worker controlled. This control extends only to corporations, not to small businesses or even to privately held capitalist firms. It is decided that it will be sufficient to redefine property rights only in those firms for which ownership has already been largely separated from management.

All banks are nationalized, as in Radical Quick. Individual savings accounts are preserved, as are consumer loan obligations, including home mortgages (so long at the institutions making the loans did so conscientiously and without deception). They remain in, or are transferred to, those banks now designated as Savings and Loan Associations. These will continue to accept savings and make consumer loans, paying interest on the former, charging interest on the latter. Other banks are designated as commercial banks. These will facilitate short-run business transactions and will serve to distribute society's investment fund.

Funds for the commercial banks will now come from the capital assets tax. If such a tax is already in place as a result of prior reforms, it need only be raised sufficiently to compensate for that portion of the investment fund previously coming from private savings. If no tax is in place, the government can use the total value of a company's stock, as recorded on some specified date before the crash, as the value of the enterprise's capital assets, and set the tax rate so as to generate the desired quantity of funds.

At this point, the basic structure of Economic Democracy is in place. We have what we had with Radical Quick, except that worker self-management has been extended only to corporations, not to the rest of the private sector. One major issue still needs resolution—what to do with all those people who have relied on the income from their stocks and bonds to maintain or supplement their existing incomes, particularly retired people who have been depending on their private pension-fund investments.

In point of fact, most of these people will be desperate at this point, and looking to the government for help, because the stock market has just crashed, thereby wiping out their portfolios. A solution is straightforward. Our government will exchange all outstanding stock certificates and corporate bonds for long-term government annuities—guaranteeing a steady income to each holder for the rest of the person's life. The value of each portfolio will be set at the value of the person's stocks and bonds at a determined pre-crash date. The annuity income will be a fixed percent of the portfolio value, with a cutoff of, say, the salary of the highest-paid public official (at present, $400,000). In effect, we are nationalizing the corporate sector of the economy with compensation—generous compensation, since the stock market crash has rendered most stock certificates and corporate bonds almost valueless. In effect, our socialist government is preserving the income flows of everyone invested in the financial markets, capitalists included—up to (a rather generous) maximum.

To those who find it obscene that former capitalists should continue to maintain lifestyles far beyond the means of ordinary people (an understandable reaction), we should stress that the capitalist qua capitalist is not an inherently immoral person, deserving of punishment. To be sure, many, perhaps most, will have used their resources to block the coming into being of a genuinely democratic society, but most have made their fortunes by playing by the rules. Of course these rules have been made, for the most part, by that capitalist class (via the politicians whose campaigns they fund)—but not by *all* of the individuals who comprise this class. Economic Democracy has some leeway for generosity.

We should also remember that this annuity subsidy is not open-ended (as is, under capitalism, the income stream from wealth). It ceases with the death of the recipient. It does not pass on to his heirs.

Lest our proposal for "the euthanasia of the capitalist class" seem too far-fetched, it should be noted that John Maynard Keynes predicted "the euthanasia of the rentier" as capital became ever more plentiful,[38] and that John Kenneth Galbraith, four decades later, proposed the "euthanasia of the stockholder." Galbraith's proposal is quite similar to the one presented here:

> Convert the fully mature corporation . . . into fully public corporations. Assuming the undesirability of expropriation, this would mean public purchase of the stocks with fixed interest-bearing securities. This would perpetuate inequality, but it would no longer increase adventitiously with further increases in dividends and capital gains. In time inheritance, inheritance taxes, philanthropy, profligacy, alimony and inflation would act to disperse this wealth.[39]

Galbraith justifies the nationalization of publicly traded corporations for essentially the same reasons we have offered:

> In its mature form the corporation can be thought of as an instrument principally for perpetrating inequality. The stockholders, as we have seen, have no function. They do not contribute to capital or to management; they are the passive recipients of dividends and capital gains. As these increase year to year, so, effortlessly, do their income and wealth.

6.3.3 Slower Still (without a Financial Meltdown)

The preceding two scenarios presuppose a stock market crash that makes dramatic, transformative change economically feasible and politically possible. But a more gradual transformation can be imagined that doesn't presuppose a sudden, massive financial crisis.

In 1976 Rudolf Meidner, chief economist of the LO, Sweden's largest trade union federation—and coauthor with Gosta Rehn of the Swedish welfare state—presented a plan to the labor federation for the gradual takeover of the Swedish economy by its working class. It was adopted enthusiastically, the vote result greeted with a standing ovation and the singing of the *International*. The *Meidner Plan* was quite simple. Every company with more than fifty employees would be required to issue new shares of its stock each year equivalent to 20 percent of its profits. Since the issuing of new shares does not cost the firm anything, this does not interfere with operating expenses or investment plans. (It merely increases the number of claimants to the percent of profits the firm sets aside to pay out in dividends to its shareholders. That is to say, it cuts into the income accruing to passive shareholders.)

These shares would be held in a "labor trust," collectively owned by all wage earners. Shares would not be sold. In due time—Meidner estimated thirty-five years or so—most firms would come to have the majority of their stock owned by the trust, that is, collectively by Swedish workers. The Swedish capitalist class, as might be expected, was horrified. It launched a counter-offensive that saw the Swedish Social Democratic Party, which had governed Sweden since the Great Depression and was closely tied to the LO, voted out of office.[40]

Some version of such a plan could be adopted by a Left government committed to establishing Economic Democracy—if it was strong enough to get the requisite laws passed and entrenched enough to keep them on the books until their end is accomplished. As individual firms become, over time, majority worker owned (owned by the working class collectively, via the Labor Trust, not by the firm's own workers), the government could purchase the remaining privately held shares, then turn the enterprises over to the workers of those enterprises to be run democratically. (The dividends paid to the Labor Trust over the years could be used to finance the final buyouts.) Following a buyout, the firm would no longer pay dividends but would pay a capital assets tax instead—the leasing fee the firm's workers pay for use of the firm's (now publicly owned) assets. The other institutions of Economic Democracy—a public banking system for allocating investment funds, private or cooperative savings and loan associations, and the government as employer-of-last-resort—could be developed over the several decades the transition to workplace democracy was underway.

As with the original Meidner plan, the capitalist class would certainly oppose such a proposal vigorously, but, to the extent that we are able to move toward genuine democracy . . . who knows? The bad guys don't *always* win.

6.4 A New Communism?

The various programs for revolutionary structural reform sketched above could be brought about peacefully if conditions are right. One of these "conditions" is the coming to power of a Left political party with a truly radical agenda. But how, given the enormous power of the capitalist class, could this ever happen?

Clearly, the ground must be prepared. A sudden economic crisis will not suffice. Unless the counterproject is well developed, the state will simply bail out the capitalists again, squeezing the majority further—which could breed calls for simpler, uglier solutions that will not, of course, be real solutions. Fortunately, the failure of racist, fascist, and militaristic experiments is well known, and this historical memory—which must be kept alive—provides an important counterweight to reactionary tendencies. But without a well-developed counterproject, this counterweight may prove insufficient. Although a moderate economic crisis might provide opportunities for meaningful reform, a severe crisis, too early, before the counterproject has become self-conscious, could give us fascism, not socialism.

As indicated in chapter 1, the counterproject must bring together, at least in collective spirit, the various movements now struggling, often in isolation from one another, for progressive social change: movements for gender and racial equality, ecological sanity, and peace; struggles against poverty, homophobia, militarism, and against prisons and executions as solutions to our social problems.

It is clear that the labor movement must play a central role, since changing the nature and structure of the workplace is fundamental to the economic dimension of the counterproject. It is hard to imagine any of the economic reforms listed on our reform agenda being adopted without strong pressure from a revitalized labor movement.

Of course, economic issues are not solely the province of the labor movement, nor are issues of race, sex, ecology, peace, or prisons outside the purview of labor. None of these issues in fact can be treated in isolation from the others, although various movements will doubtless have distinctive emphases.

How are we to achieve unity in diversity, a dialectical unity that involves a genuine commonality of interests (and not just tactical alliances) but avoids the reductive subordination of one movement to another? Let us dream a little. Let us return to that short text that is still find so provocative and inspiring, written 150 years ago by those two young men who had been drafted by their comrades to draw up a manifesto for their little, short-lived "Communist League." Let us dream of a New Communism.

> Communists do not comprise a separate political party opposed to other working class parties. They have no interests separate and apart from those of the proletariat as a whole. They do not set up any sectarian principles of their own, by which to shape and mold the proletarian movement.[41]

This, we observe, is something very different from the Leninist model that came to be dominant on the Left. There is no talk here of democratic centralism, of a tightly organized, tightly disciplined party with an unshakable confidence in its doctrinal correctness. "New communists" would be concerned not only with the "proletarian movement" but with the entire counterproject.

Communists, say Marx and Engels, must be both internationalist and nationalist.

> In the national struggles of the proletarians of different countries, [communists] point out and bring to the front the common interests of the entire proletariat, independently of all nationality. . . . [However,] the proletariat must first of all acquire political supremacy, must rise to be the leading class of the nation, must

constitute itself as the nation. . . . The first step in the revolution by the working class is to . . . win the battle of democracy.[42]

Although communism is envisaged as an international movement, Marx and Engels do not call for the abolition of nation-states, nor do they declaim on the futility of national struggles. On the contrary, they insist that the essential struggles must take place on precisely the terrain of the nation-state—and can be won only insofar as genuine democracy is truly established.

As the *Manifesto* makes clear, Marx and Engels are "reformists." They not only endorse a reform agenda, but they see such reforms as essential means to radical transformation. At the same time, they remain clear-sighted about the insufficiency of "mere" reforms.

> The proletariat will use its political supremacy to wrest by degrees all capital from the bourgeoisie. . . . In the beginning, this cannot be effected except . . . by means of measures which seem economically insufficient and untenable, but which, in the course of the movement, outstrip themselves, necessitate further inroads upon the old social order, and are unavoidable as a means of entirely revolutionizing the mode of production.[43]

To summarize: The conception of a revolutionary movement that emanates from the pages of the *Communist Manifesto* is something different from the kinds of revolutionary movements that emerged in the twentieth century. Marx and Engels advocate an international association of committed activists who share a common global vision, who represent the most progressive elements of all progressive organizations and parties, who work primarily within the confines of their own nation-state, but who keep the international dimensions of the struggle in focus, and who recognize that many reforms are possible and desirable before global capitalism gives way to socialist reconstruction.

Might not some such concept of a revolutionary movement once again take root? If we assimilate sufficiently the lessons of our history, we will be on guard against excessive dogmatism, reductionism, and sectarianism. We will also assimilate the positive as well as negative lessons of the other monumentally important movements of our century: feminism, antiracism, environmentalism, pacifism, movements for human rights, and struggles everywhere against degrading and exploitative conditions. Perhaps this new revolutionary movement will see itself as something other than a "new communism." Perhaps it will want to eschew the word "revolution." The terms here are not important. What is important is that people regain that sense, which arises every so often in human history, that we are faced with a collective task that will require the combined efforts of masses of people in all walks of life, and that will, if successful, change the world.

6.5 A New World

> The need for another revolution should be obvious to all those who are not
> willfully blind. It is not, I fear, probable. But without doubt it is possible.

So wrote Brian Barry, Lieber Professor of Political Philosophy, Columbia
University, and professor of political science, London School of Economics,
the closing words of his beautiful, angry book, *Why Social Justice Matters*
(2005)—his last book. (Barry died in 2009.) These words were foreshadowed
by his remarks in the book's preface:

> One thing can be stated with certainty: the continuation of the status quo is
> an ecological impossibility. The uncertainty lies with the consequences of this
> fact. It is quite in the cards that the response will be the further retrenchment
> of plutocracy within countries and an ever more naked attempt by the United
> States, aided and abetted by a "coalition of the willing," to displace the costs onto
> poorer countries. Whether it succeeds or fails, the results will be catastrophic.
> But I shall argue that there are some grounds for hope, which include growing
> discontent within rich countries with politics as usual.[44]

6.5.1 Compelling Visions

We need a revolution. Not a violent revolution, which, as pointed out in chapter 1, cannot possibly succeed, but a democratic movement that can introduce
fundamental structural changes to the economy. But a new revolutionary
movement, if it is to take hold and gather wide support in an advanced capitalist society, must do more than criticize the existing order. It must also propose
economically viable structural changes that would take us beyond capitalism—
as has been done in this book. It must dispel the lie that "there is no alternative."

But these two moments—critique and the presentation of a structural alternative—are still insufficient. We also need a dream, a vision of a new way
of life. This new way of life should be defined by more than what it negates,
supplemented by reform proposals. Yes, we want a world without war, racism, sexism, or homophobia, a world in which our basic economic institutions are under democratic control—but we want more than that. We need to
make this clear. We need to articulate concretely our dream of a new world,
so as to kindle the imagination, inspire hope, and motivate action. (I am using
"we" here, for I am presuming that readers who have made it this far have
been persuaded that "another world" is both necessary and possible, and are
concerned about making this possibility a reality.)

Of course there is no *one* monolithic, all-encompassing vision. What
should be embraced is a kaleidoscope of visions, not contradictory, but

emphasizing different features, each beautiful in its own way. Let me survey several that I find compelling. There are others. The culture of a revolutionary movement should keep alive past dreams as well as create new ones.

We've already encountered one, coming from the "natural capitalists":

> Imagine for a moment a world where cities have become peaceful and serene because cars and buses are whisper quiet, vehicles exhaust only water vapor, and parks and greenways have replaced unneeded urban freeways. OPEC has ceased to function because the price of oil has fallen to five dollars a barrel, but there are few buyers for it because cheaper and better ways now exist to get the services people once turned to oil to provide. Living standards for all people have dramatically improved, particularly for the poor and those in developing countries. Involuntary unemployment no longer exists, and income taxes have been largely eliminated. Houses, even low-income housing units, can pay part of their mortgage costs by the energy they *produce*.[45]

This won't happen under capitalism (so I've argued), but it is a worthy, inspiring vision, focusing on cities that have become "peaceful and serene." Another vision, not contradictory, but emphasizing different elements, can be found in Marx, particularly in his early writings, but also in *Capital*. Consider some of the elements:

Unalienated labor. Labor is *the* central concept in Marx's work: his indignation at the alienation and exploitation of labor under capitalism, his sense of the way the world could be if we produced as fully human beings. In a truly human world "labor would be a free manifestation of life and hence an enjoyment of life":

> In my production I would have objectified my individuality, and experienced the individual joy of knowing my personality as an objective, sensuously perceptible and indubitable power. In your satisfaction, I would have had the conscious satisfaction that my work satisfied a human need. . . . You would have experienced me as a reintegration of your own nature and a necessary part of yourself. I would have been reaffirmed in your thought as well as your love; in my individual life, I would have confirmed my true human nature.[46]

A breakdown of the division between mental and manual labor—at work, but also in education. To develop oneself fully, one should develop both mental and manual skills. Indeed, education itself should go beyond "the monotonous and uselessly long school hours of children of the upper and middle classes. . . . It should combine productive labor with instruction and gymnastics . . . the only method of producing fully developed human beings."[47]

An end to a division of labor requiring permanent, lifelong specialization. Not only should each job be humanized and made meaningful, but people should not be confined to only one job or career. For we are all capable of many occupations, each of which can contribute to the development of our capacities and the broadening of our horizons. "In a communist society, where nobody has an exclusive area of activity . . . I can hunt in the morning, fish in the afternoon, breed cattle in the evening, criticize after dinner, just as I like, without ever becoming a hunter, a fisherman, a herdsman or a critic."[48]

An end to the antagonism between town and country. Not only does this division "make one man into a narrow town animal, another into a narrow country animal, and everyday creates a conflict between their interests," but it is also ecologically destructive. When populations are concentrated in large cities, "it disturbs the circulation of matter between man and the soil, i.e., prevents the return to the soil of its elements consumed by man . . . ; it therefore violates the conditions necessary for the lasting fertility of the soil." What is called for is "its restoration as a system . . . under a form appropriate to the full development of the human race."[49]

The emancipation of the senses. In a fully human society, we will cultivate and refine our senses. We will taste subtle flavors, hear the complexity of music, see the colors and shades and textures in works of art. To do so, we need other people—people to teach us how to taste, hear, and see, people who can fill in the cultural and historical details of what we are sensing, so that we *experience* it more fully. Moreover, our senses are "not only the five senses, but also the so-called spiritual senses (will, love, etc.)." We will become attuned to the human and nonhuman world in a human way.[50]

People "rich in human needs," aware of their dependence on others. Wealth and poverty, says Marx, will mean something different in a fully human society than they do today. "The rich man is one who *needs* a totality of manifestations of life," that is to say, a person who *needs* not only adequate food, clothing and shelter, but art, music, friendship, love, play, a connection with nature, and who feels the absence of such things as a lack. The person also recognizes his *poverty*, his utter dependence on other human beings, but he experiences this "passive bond," this "poverty," as simultaneously "the greatest wealth, the *other* human being, as need."[51]

Sufficient free time to develop the capacities that work does not develop, and to enjoy the satisfaction of our human needs. It is not enough that our labor be unalienated. It must not be excessive. Work will always be necessary, but for "that development of human energy which is an end in itself, the true realm of freedom, to blossom forth, . . . the shortening of the working day is its basic prerequisite."[52]

In sum, the Marxian vision of a new world is one in which the work I do—the work we all do—is both challenging and satisfying. Through work I develop my skills and talents, and have the pleasure of contributing to the well-being of others. The work that I do involves my body as well as my mind, physical dexterity as well as intelligence—capacities that have been nurtured through education. I do various kinds of work over the course of my life. I have regular contact with nature, in harmony with which we all live. I have good work, but also enough free time to develop an appreciation for good food, art, music, dance, whatever. I may want to develop my creative abilities in some of these areas. I have time, too, for real and lasting friendships, for love and affection. It won't be heaven. There will still be disappointments, broken hearts, jealousy, not to mention pain and disease and death. We are, after all, finite, imperfect beings. But available to all: a rich, full, *human* life, for which "the free development of each is a condition for the free development of all."

Marx's vision is remarkably similar to that of another visionary, E. F. Schumacher, whose *Small Is Beautiful: Economics as if People Matter* had a powerful influence on the counterculture of the early 1970s, particularly among those (like me) thinking seriously about moving "back to the land." (Schumacher, a German-born economist, served for twenty years as the chief economist to the British Coal Board. During this time he developed a scathing critique of contemporary economics and contemporary Western society, and a powerful alternative vision. In 1995 the *London Times Literary Supplement* ranked *Small Is Beautiful* among the one hundred most influential books published since the Second World War.)

Like Marx, Schumacher lays great stress on labor. Not only should we plan for full employment, that is, "employment for everyone who needs an 'outside' job," but the work should be *good work*.

> To organize work in such a manner that it becomes meaningless, boring, stultifying, or nerve-wracking for the worker would be little short of criminal. It would indicate a greater concern with goods than with people, an evil lack of compassion and a soul-destroying degree of attachment to the most primitive side of this worldly existence.[53]

More so than Marx, Schumacher emphasizes the importance of developing the right kind of *technology* to achieve full employment and good work. "Labor saving" should not be the paramount goal of technological development, because labor should not be regarded as a simple "cost of production" to be minimized. Technology should enhance labor, not eliminate it, and it should be, as far as possible, appropriate to small-scale, decentralized production.

> What is it we really require from the scientists and technologists? I should answer: We need methods and equipment which are

- cheap enough so that they are accessible to virtually everyone,
- suitable for small-scale application, and
- compatible with man's need for creativity.[54]

Like Marx, Schumacher is concerned about our management of *land*. Land is not, he insists, merely a productive resource. Our management of land "must be primarily oriented toward three goals—health, beauty, and permanence. The fourth goal—the only one accepted by the experts—productivity, will then be attained almost as a by-product."[55]

Moreover, we must do something to halt, then reverse, the massive, global migration of people from the countryside to the cities—"the collapse of the rural economy, the rising tide of unemployment in town and country, and the growth of a city proletariat without nourishment for either body or soul." We should be searching for policies "to reconstruct rural culture, to open the land for gainful occupation to larger numbers of people, whether it be on a full-time or part-time basis, and to orient all our actions on the land toward the three-fold ideal of health, beauty and permanence." (For a disturbing account of the still-rising tide of urban migration, see Mike Davis, *Planet of Slums*. For an account of what the corporatization of agriculture has done to rural America—heartbreaking to those of us who were part of the "back to the land" movement—see Nick Reding, *Methland: The Death and Life of an American Small Town*.)[56]

Of course, as one would expect, given the title of his book, Schumacher urges us to think in terms of human scale. Enterprises should not be "too big." Cities should not be "too big." Indeed, countries should not be "too big." "If we make a list of all the most prosperous countries in the world, we find that most of them are very small; whereas a list of all the biggest countries in the world show most of them to be very poor indeed."

> Imagine that in 1864 Bismarck had annexed the whole of Denmark instead of only a small part of it, and that nothing had happened since. The Danes would be an ethnic minority in Germany, perhaps struggling to maintain their language by becoming bilingual, the official language of course being German. Only by thoroughly Germanizing themselves could they avoid becoming second-class citizens. There would be an irresistible drift of the most ambitious and enterprising Danes, thoroughly Germanized, to the mainland in the south, and what would then be the status of Copenhagen? That of a remote provincial city.[57]

(Schumacher would not have endorsed the project for a European Union—which, as the current crisis makes clear, is deeply flawed. He would have applauded the breakup of the Soviet Union, the separation of Czechoslovakia into two countries, and the outcome of the recent referendum in Sudan.)

Schumacher also addresses an issue that Marx, writing before the era of large-scale advertising and mass consumption, could not have considered. "Standard of living" should not be measured, he says, by the amount of annual consumption, which assumes that a man who consumes more is "better off" than a man who consumes less. Rather, "the aim should be to attain the maximum of well-being with the minimum of consumption." If we break our addiction to relentless growth and live in relatively self-sufficient regions that are ecologically sustainable, there will be enough to go around. He quotes Gandhi: "The Earth provides enough for every man's need but not for every man's greed."[58]

Thus Schumacher's vision: a world in which everyone has good work that allows for human creativity and enough material goods to live well, a world in which many of us work the land, in which we all work in human-scale enterprises and live in human-scale, sustainable communities. (There would be cities in Schumacher's world, but not mega-cities. He suggests "something on the order of half a million inhabitants. It is quite clear that above such a size nothing is added to the virtue of a city."[59])

An impossible dream? Schumacher responds to this charge:

> Now it might be said that this is a romantic, a utopian, vision. True enough. What we have today, in modern industrial society, is not romantic and certainly not utopian. But it is in very deep trouble, and holds no promise of survival. We jolly well have to have the courage to dream if we want to survive and give our children a chance of survival.[60]

John Maynard Keynes had a dream. (Interestingly enough, Keynes intervened to have Schumacher released from a detention center in Britain, where he had been interred as a German alien at the outbreak of World War II. Keynes had been much impressed by a technical paper sent to him by the then young Schumacher.) Keynes noted in the final chapter of *The General Theory* that "the outstanding faults of the economic society in which we live are its failure to provide for full employment and its arbitrary and inequitable distribution of wealth and income." But he didn't think this unhealthy state would persist, for he thought capital would soon become so plentiful that interest rates would soon approach zero, which "would mean the euthanasia of the rentier, and, consequently, the euthanasia of *the cumulative, oppressive power of the capitalists to exploit the scarcity value of capital.*"[61] (Keynes's words, not Marx's. One can see why neoliberal economists have fought so hard to discredit Keynes.)

Above all, Keynes looked forward to the gradual replacement of increasing consumption by increasing *leisure*, and to the beneficent effects such a transformation would bring. In a remarkable essay, written just after the outbreak of what would become the Great Depression, he looked to the future:

> We shall use the new-found bounty of nature quite differently than the way the rich use it today, and will map out for ourselves a plan of life quite otherwise than theirs. . . . What work there still remains to be done will be as widely shared as possible—three hour shifts, or a fifteen-hour week. . . . There will also be great changes in our morals. . . . I see us free to return to some of the most sure and certain principles of religion and traditional virtue—that avarice is a vice, that the extraction of usury is a misdemeanor, and the love of money is detestable, that those walk most truly in the paths of virtue and sane wisdom who take least thought for the morrow. . . . We shall honor those who can teach us how to pluck the hour and the day virtuously and well, the delightful people who are capable of taking direct enjoyment in things.[62]

Keynes wrote these words in 1930, at a time when "the prevailing world depression, the enormous anomaly of unemployment, the disastrous mistakes we have made, blind us to what is going on under the surface."[63] His projection was for "a hundred years hence," that is, 2030—no longer the distant future. What he hoped for won't happen under capitalism—but it *could* happen.

The visions surveyed above focus on labor, leisure, and nature, but there is another element that needs to be made explicit. The philosopher Hannah Arendt, in examining the *vita activa* (the active life), identifies three components: labor, work, and action. The first two involve humans interacting with nature to produce things, not only things necessary for biological survival, but things that bestow permanence, durability, and beauty "upon the futility of mortal life." The third factor, however, transpires among humans without the intermediary of things, and is "connected to the human condition of natality: *the beginning of something new.*"[64]

The possibility of *action* is also crucial to our vision. It lies at the heart of our commitment to democracy. When one has a new idea, conceives of a better way of doing something, or when one sees something wrong and thinks we should change course, there exists the possibility of *acting*—of talking to others, joining together, initiating change, making things happen.

6.5.2 What Should I Do?

The possibility of action is crucial, not only as a feature of the world we want, but to achieving that world. In the last lines of his book, Schumacher writes:

> Everywhere people ask, "What can I actually *do*? The answer is as simple as it is disconcerting: we can, each of us, work to put our own inner house in order. The

guidance we need for this cannot be found in science or technology, the value of which utterly depends on the ends which they serve; but it can still be found in the traditional wisdom of mankind.

Not a lot of guidance, but more than Keynes provides, for Keynes is convinced (so it seems) that the capitalist class, those "rentiers," will quietly disappear as interest rates sink to zero. Marx harbors no such illusions, but, like Keynes, he thinks that history is on our side, the side of the vast majority, and that sooner or later "the expropriators will be expropriated."

We, today, can't be so optimistic. Our species has created the means of nuclear annihilation, as well as conditions that, if unchecked, will soon cause massive ecological devastation. It is hard to dispute Barry's grim assessment:

> It is quite possible that by the year 2100 human life will have become extinct, or will be confined to a few residual areas that have escaped the devastating effects of nuclear holocaust or global warming on a scale that has in the past wiped out almost all existing life forms.[65]

So—what is to be done? Let me close with my own thoughts—simple thoughts. (It's not the thinking that is hard, but the *acting*.) I would recommend three steps.

First, as Schumacher says, "get your own house in order." I take this to mean that one must change one's life, at least in some respects, so as to live a life that in some way prefigures the world we want. This means living more frugally, striving to reduce one's carbon footprint, shifting one's diet from more meat to less, or perhaps none at all (which happens to be a much healthier, as well as more ecologically sustainable, way to live). This means thinking about, and cultivating, the human and natural relationships that "the traditional wisdom of mankind" recommends.

Will a change of lifestyle change the world? No, of course not. As our earlier analysis makes clear, if everyone were to start consuming less, we'd plunge into economic crisis—unless structural changes are also made. But *one* is not *everyone*. *Your* reduced consumption will not, at this point in time, damage the economy, whereas it will likely make you a better person and will simultaneously validate—indeed help create—the attitudes and values necessary for a new world. Your example makes it easier for others to change.[66]

Step Two: Spend some time working with others to alleviate some concrete social problem. This means joining an organization or starting one. The possibilities are endless, for the problems are endless: local and global poverty, racism, sexism, homophobia, the many facets of ecological destruction, war, domestic violence, prisons, capital punishment, unemployment, our irrational food supply, hopelessness, and so on. None of these organizations, by themselves, will bring about the needed revolution. But we don't know that history is on our side. The needed revolution may never happen. However, we can be pretty sure—I say this from long experience—that getting involved in a good project will bring you into contact with good people, people often better (smarter, braver, more skillful at X or Y) than yourself, and this will in turn make you a better, indeed happier, person. As Frances Moore Lappé points out,

> We form ourselves in large part by the choice of whom we bring into our lives. So we can choose to associate with those more courageous than we. By observing them, we experience courageousness, and perhaps become more gutsy than ourselves. Pretty amazing.[67]

Step Three: As pointed out in the last section, we also need a large, coherent political movement. The capitalist class will not melt away, as Keynes hoped. If the deep structural changes that are needed are to come about peacefully, we need a political party—or perhaps a coalition of political parties—that is committed to deep structural change. How might we imagine such a party? Let me offer one example from which there might be much to learn.

Everyone knows that 1989 was the "Year of Revolution" in Eastern Europe. Not so many remember, if they were aware of it at all, that in 1989 a socialist steelworker came startlingly close to being elected the president of Brazil—Brazil, a poor country wracked by staggering debt and inequality, by economic and environmental crises, but also, at that time, the world's ninth-largest economy, the world's fourth-largest food producer, a country enormously rich in resources and containing one of the largest industrial centers of the global South. Luíz Inácio Lula da Silva was the candidate of a political party formed ten years before, *Partido dos Trabalhadores* (PT)—the Party of the Workers.

Lula (as he is commonly called) lost that year, but neither he nor the PT gave up. The party grew, won local elections, and then, in 2002, Lula was elected president of the country—then reelected in 2006. In 2010 the PT candidate won yet again, Dilma Rousseff becoming the first woman to ever head a government in Brazil. And the PT's national coalition, for the first time, achieved a broad majority in both the Senate and the Chamber of Deputies, something the Lula administration never had. (Dilma Rousseff, as a young Left activist opposing the military government then in power, was arrested, suffered torture by electric shock for twenty-two days, and spent nearly three years in prison.)

The PT was, at its inception, a most unusual party, bringing together elements of Marxism, feminism, and Catholic liberation theology. (Its founding conference in 1980 was held at Colégio Sion, a Catholic girls school in São Paulo.) The PT rejected the Leninist model of rigid discipline, and explicitly rejected armed struggle.[68] It affirmed a commitment to democracy: "Democracy, understood as the wide aggregate of citizens' rights to political participation and representation cannot be seen as a bourgeois value . . . [for] democracy became a universal ideal when it was taken by the working class."[69] It was also a party that wanted to participate in the construction of a powerful "civil society," and consciously structured itself to maintain organic links to the large variety of grassroots movements that have proliferated in Brazil. Its founding Political Declaration of 1979 proclaims:

> The idea of the Partido dos Trabalhadores arose with the advance and reinforcement of this new and broad-based social movement, which now extends from the factories to the neighborhoods, from the unions to the Basic Christian Communities, from the Cost of Living Movement to the Dwellers' Associations, from the student movement to the professional associations, from the movement of black people to the women's movement, as well as others, like those who struggle for the rights of indigenous peoples.[70]

Reflecting this declaration, all regular members of the PT were initially required to belong to a separate grassroots organization—an innovative idea, which (in my judgment) is well worth considering today.

It is true that Lula moved rapidly toward the center upon his election in 2002, making many compromises and concessions to the right-wing opposition and alliances with more progressive members of the moneyed elite, causing much criticism from within the party, and some defections to parties to the left of the PT. Nonetheless (or perhaps because of this), the Brazilian economy began to grow rapidly, weathered the global downturn of 2008, and is growing again. And the PT has implemented some important programs, land reform and Zero Hunger (now *Bolsa Familia*), which have greatly aided the country's poor. As Moisés Naím, writing for *Newsweek*, has observed:

> In Brazil a labor-union leader has presided over an amazing period of social and economic progress. It is also one of the few countries that have successfully managed to reduce economic inequality at a time when everywhere else inequities are deepening. Successive Brazilian governments have succeeded in improving education, health and the living standards of millions of impoverished citizens who have now joined a growing middle class. . . . In 1995, 15 percent of Brazilian school-age children did not go to school. In 2005, this fell to 3 percent, and today Brazil has practically achieved universal basic education.[71]

Of course we don't know how this hugely important historical experiment will play out, but the fact remains: Brazil now possesses a large, experienced political party that, under the right circumstances, could aim for more than mere reforms. (While Venezuela, which surprised the world—and shocked the United States—by electing and reelecting Hugo Chavez, appears to many on the Left a more inspiring example than Brazil, Venezuela, lacking a well-established political party comparable to PT, is far more dependent on one charismatic leader than is Brazil. It is also the case that the Brazilian economy is considerably more developed and more diverse than the Venezuelan economy, thus more closely resembling our own.)

What is possible for Brazil—or Venezuela—points to possibilities elsewhere. Recall Brian Barry's words:

> The need for another revolution should be obvious to all those who are not willfully blind. . . . Without doubt it is possible.

Recall Marx's eleventh thesis on Feuerbach:

> The philosophers have only *interpreted* the world in various ways. The point, however, is to *change* it.[72]

Notes

Preface to the Revised Edition

1. Paul Krugman, *The Return of Depression Economics and the Crisis of 2008* (New York: W. W. Norton, 2009), 14.

2. Joseph Stiglitz, "America's Socialism for the Rich," (Berkeley Electronic Press June 2009).

3. Krugman, *Return of Depression Economics*, 14.

4. Karl Marx, "Afterward to the Second German Edition," in *Capital*, vol. 1 (New York: International Publishers, 1967), 26.

5. Amartya Sen, *Development as Freedom* (New York: Knopf, 1999), 167. Emphasis added. (It must be said—this remark is buried rather deeply in the text, and not elaborated further.)

6. Amartya Sen, "Capitalism Beyond the Crisis," *New York Review of Books*, March 26, 2009, 27.

Preface to the First Edition

1. Isaiah Berlin, *Russian Thinkers* (New York: Penguin Books, 1978), 22. Berlin attributes the epigram to the Greek poet Archilochus, which he (Berlin) interprets as defining two kinds of thinkers.

2. Richard Rorty, "For a More Banal Politics," *Harper's*, May 1992, 16.

3. Nancy Holmstrom and Richard Smith, "The Necessity of Gangster Capitalism: Primitive Accumulation in Russia and China," *Monthly Review* 51, no. 9 (February 2000): 5. (I'm in basic agreement with Holmstrom and Smith regarding Russia, but not regarding China.)

4. E-mail received September 10, 1999, entitled, "With Her Eyes Opened—a Letter from Bulgaria," by Doncheva.

5. Quoted by Hans-Peter Martin and Harald Schumann, *The Global Trap: Globalization and the Assault on Democracy and Prosperity* (New York: Zed Books, 1997), 45. See pp. 40–46 for a gripping account of this near-disaster.

6. Alexander Cockburn and Jeffrey St. Claire, *Five Days That Shook the World: Seattle and Beyond* (London: Verso, 2000).

7. Michael Mann has labeled this latter phenomenon "combat fundamentalism." For an extended analysis, see his "Globalization and September 11," *New Left Review*, no. 12 (November–December 2001): 51–72.

8. Robert Friedman, "And Darkness Covered the Land: A Report from Israel and Palestine," *The Nation* 273, no. 1 (December 24, 2001): 13.

9. *Le Nouvel Observateur* (France), January 15–21, 1998, 76.

10. Cf. Benjamin Barber, "Beyond Jihad vs. McWorld," *The Nation* 274, no. 2 (2002): 11–18.

1. Counterproject, Successor-System, Revolution

1. See Roger Lowenstein, *When Genius Failed: The Rise and Fall of Long-Term Capital Management* (New York: Random House, 2000), for the less-than-edifying details.

2. My calculation, based on the *Forbes* list of the global billionaires in 2007. The $2.7 trillion fortune of the top 500 was equal to the 5.6 percent of the global income that year (which totaled $48 trillion) received by the bottom 60 percent. This result is consistent with the United Nations Development Programme report that in 1998 the top 225 individuals possessed wealth equal to the combined incomes of the bottom 47 percent of the world's population. United Nations Development Programme, *Human Development Report, 1998* (Oxford: Oxford University Press, 1998), 30.

3. Data on hedge funds from Nelson Schwartz and Louise Story, "Pay of Hedge Fund Managers Roared Back Last Year," *New York Times*, March 31, 2010. Data on poverty from the U.S. Census Bureau website. The poverty line (2010) for a family of four is $20,050.

4. Cited in Mancur Olsen and Hans Landsberg, *The No-Growth Society* (New York: Norton, 1974), 97.

5. Jeffrey Isaac, "Marxism and Intellectuals," *New Left Review*, n.s., 2 (March–April 2000): 114. Francis Fukuyama famously proclaimed liberal capitalism as the end of history in his *The End of History and the Last Man* (New York: Free Press, 1992).

6. Sent by Starhawk, from Genoa, July 21, 2001. Starhawk is an American author and activist who has taken part in numerous antiglobalization protests in recent years. You can check her website at www.starhawk.org.

7. For an on-the-spot account of the Seattle events, see Alexander Cockburn and Jeffrey St. Clair, *Five Days That Shook the World* (London: Verso, 2000). For an invaluable source of information about past and future antiglobalization protests worldwide, see www.indymedia.org.

8. Paul Hawken, *Blessed Unrest: How the Largest Movement in the World Came into Being and Why No One Saw It Coming* (New York: Viking, 2008).

9. Hawken, *Blessed Unrest*, 2.

10. Walter Benjamin, "Theses on the Philosophy of History," in *Illuminations* (New York: Schocken Books, 1969), 255.

11. Recently the Marxist philosopher, Slavoj Žižek has argued, "Yes, Christianity and Marxism should fight on the same side of the barricade . . . the authentic Christian legacy is much too precious to be left to the fundamentalist freaks." *The Fragile Absolute: Or, Why Is the Christian Legacy Worth Fighting For?* 2nd ed. (London: Verso, 2009).

12. For an elaboration of this distinction, see James Lawler, "Marx's Theory of Socialisms: Nihilistic and Dialectical," in *Debating Marx*, ed. Louis Pastouras (Lewiston, NY: Edward Mellen Press, 1994).

13. See Karl Marx, "Private Property and Communism," in his *Economic and Philosophical Manuscripts of 1844*, reprinted in Lawrence Simon, ed., *Karl Marx: Selected Writings* (Indianapolis, IN: Hackett, 1994), 68–79.

14. For a penetrating, hopeful analysis of events unfolding in Latin America, see Marta Harnecker, "Latin America and Twenty-first Century Socialism: Inventing to Avoid Mistakes," *Monthly Review*, 62, no. 3 (July–August 2010): 1–83. (The entire issue of the magazine is devoted to Harnecker's essay.)

15. Pierre Bourdieu, "A Reasoned Utopia and Economic Fatalism," *New Left Review* 227 (January–February 1998): 126.

16. For a more detailed consideration of the connection between historical materialism as an explanatory theory of history and its hopeful prediction, see my "Does Historical Materialism Imply Socialism?" in *Reason and Emancipation: Essays on the Philosophy of Kai Nielsen*, ed. Michel Seymour and Matthias Fitsch (Amherst, MA: Humanity Books, 2006), 196–207.

17. V. I. Lenin, *State and Revolution* (New York: International Publishers, 1932), 83–84.

18. Paul Samuelson, *Economics* (New York: McGraw-Hill, 1973), 883. Samuelson offered other scenarios as well, but did not take sides, claiming the various projections "represent the spread of best expert opinion."

19. Karl Marx, "Preface to a Contribution to the Critique of Political Economy," in Simon, *Karl Marx*, 211.

20. For an account of the G-7 strategy to thwart Mikhail Gorbachev's dream of rebuilding the Soviet economy along noncapitalist lines, see Peter Gowan, "Western Economic Diplomacy and the New Eastern Europe," *New Left Review* 182 (July–August 1990): 63–84.

21. For a discussion of the evolution of a postcapitalist society such as the one to be described here into in "higher communism," see the last chapter of my earlier book *Against Capitalism*.

22. In the first incarnation of my systematic critique of capitalism (my doctoral dissertation), I appealed explicitly to utilitarianism, then the reigning ethical theory in social-political philosophy. (Economic Democracy is likely to promote greater happiness for more people than any form of capitalism.) Shortly thereafter, I wrote an

article arguing that John Rawls, whose *A Theory of Justice* (Cambridge, MA: Harvard University Press, 1971) set out a powerful critique of utilitarianism and proposed a compelling alternative, should also, in light of his own theory, prefer Economic Democracy to capitalism. ("Should Rawls Be a Socialist?" *Social Theory and Practice* 5, no. 1 [Fall 1978]: 1–27.) In *Against Capitalism* I grounded my argument on the widely shared value of "participatory autonomy," the right an individual has "to participate in making those rules to which she must submit and those decisions whose consequences she must bear" (181).

23. Cf. Carol Gilligan, *In a Different Voice* (Cambridge, MA: Harvard University Press, 1982). For a recent, well-argued presentation of the ethic of care that investigates its implications for social and political questions, see Virginia Held, *The Ethic of Care: Personal, Political, and Global* (Oxford: Oxford University Press, 2006).

24. Arlie Hochschild, *Time Bind: When Work Becomes Home and Home Becomes Work* (New York: Metropolitan, 1997).

25. Personal observation during a visit in November, 2006, confirmed by Venezuelan activists with whom I spoke.

26. For a substantive treatment of these issues, see Iris Marion Young, *Inclusion and Democracy* (Oxford: Oxford University Press, 2002).

2. Justifying Capitalism

1. John Bates Clark, *The Distribution of Wealth* (New York: Kelley and Millman, 1956), 4. Originally published in 1899.

2. For the mathematically inclined reader: Euler's Theorem states that if $P(x, y)$ is a smooth homogenous function of order 1, then $P(x, y) = xP_x (x, y) + yP_y (x, y)$. If $P(x, y)$ represents the amount of corn produced by x workers on y acres of land, this total decomposes into the number of workers times the marginal product of labor (partial derivative with respect to x) plus the number of acres times the marginal product of land (partial derivative with respect to y.) Of course in real life, production functions are never "smooth homogeneous of order 1," but economists rarely let realism stand in the way of mathematical elegance.

3. Do we calculate the marginal product of capital by adding one more generic "tool"? But what is a "generic tool"? By adding one more dollar? But dollars aren't material factors of production. This question—what exactly *is* capital?—was the central focus of the celebrated "Cambridge Controversy," which pitted MIT (Cambridge, MA) Nobel laureates Paul Samuelson and Robert Solow against the Cambridge (England) economists Joan Robinson, Piero Sraffa, and others. For the technical details see G. C. Harcourt, "The Cambridge Controversies: Old Ways and New Horizons—or Dead End?" *Oxford Economic Papers* 28 (1976): 25–65. See also "The Capital Theory Controversies," in *Capitalism, Socialism and Post-Keynesianism: Selected Essays*, ed. G. C. Harcourt (Aldershot, UK: Edward Elgar, 1995), 41–45. Harcourt concludes (correctly in my view) that Cambridge (England) won the debate, but this victory was completely ignored by the profession's mainstream. "Thus the current position is an uneasy state of rest, under the foundations of which a time

bomb is ticking away, planted by a small, powerless group of economists who are now either aging or dead" (45).

4. John Kenneth Galbraith, *The New Industrial State* (Boston: Houghton Mifflin, 1967), 394.

5. United States Department of Commerce, Bureau of Economic Analysis, "National Income and Product Accounts," which can be found at www.bea.gov.

6. A fair trial is an example of what is called "imperfect procedural justice," since there is an independent standard by which to judge the outcome—the accused either did or did not commit the crime. The outcome is not always just, but allowing the defendant a fair trial is the best we can do. "Perfect procedural justice" obtains when there is an independent standard to determine a fair outcome *and* a procedure exists that will guarantee that outcome. Game theory's favorite example: to ensure that everyone gets an equal slice of a cake, requires that the person doing the cutting take the last piece.

7. Cf. Garrick Blalock, David Just, and Daniel Simon, "Hitting the Jackpot or Hitting the Skids: Entertainment, Poverty and the Demand for State Lotteries," *American Journal of Economics and Sociology* 66, no. 3 (July 2007): 545–70. This study finds a strong positive correlation between lottery ticket sales and poverty rates. It is interesting to note that Americans spend vastly more on lottery tickets than they do on movie tickets, in some states ten times as much.

8. The notion of a Noble Lie was famously proposed by Plato. The citizens of his ideal republic were to be told that they were born with different metals in their blood—gold for the rulers, silver for the soldiers, bronze for the artisans. Individuals would thus recognize their proper places, and not engage in the fratricidal class struggle so common in the Greek city-states. See Plato, *The Republic*, book 3, 414c–415d.

9. John Maynard Keynes, "Economic Possibilities for Our Grandchildren," in *Essays in Persuasion* (New York: Norton, 1963), 324.

10. Aristotle, *Politics*, 1258 b2–5.

11. Thomas Aquinas, *Summa Theologica*, question 78.

12. Quoted by Elizabeth Johnson, "John Maynard Keynes: Scientist or Politician?" in *After Keynes*, ed. Joan Robinson (New York: Barnes and Noble, 1973), 15.

3. Economic Democracy

1. In *Against Capitalism* (Cambridge: Cambridge University Press, 1993), I criticize both "command socialism" and "marketless participatory socialism" (315–19, 329–34). I elaborate my critique of the former, which is essentially the Soviet model, in Bertell Ollman, ed., *Market Socialism: The Debate among Socialists* (New York: Routledge, 1998). (In this book, James Lawler and I defend market socialism; Hillel Ticktin and Ollman oppose it.) I elaborate my critique of the latter as it is presented by Michael Albert in his book *Parecon: Life after Capitalism* (London: Verso, 2003) in an unpublished essay that became part of an online debate between Albert and me. My essay, "Nonsense on Stilts: Michael Albert's Parecon" is posted by Albert on the Parecon section of the ZNet website, along with Albert's reply, my reply to his reply, and his reply to my reply to his reply.

2. Paul Krugman, "Innovating Our Way to Financial Crisis," *New York Times*, December 3, 2007.

3. For an outline of institutions that would enable an economy to mimic the Japanese model, see Chalmers Johnson, *MITI and the Japanese Miracle: The Growth of Industrial Policy, 1925–1975* (Stanford, CA: Stanford University Press, 1982), 315–19. For a more general analysis that includes South Korea and Taiwan as well as Japan, see Robert Wade, *Governing the Market: Economic Theory and the Role of Government in East Asian Industrialization* (Princeton, NJ: Princeton University Press, 1990).

4. I am indebted to Bruno Jossa of the University of Naples for this justification. The idea of allocating funds for public services on a per capita basis comes more readily to mind to a European than to an American, since European countries tend to allocate educational and health care resources that way, whereas we in the United States (unfortunately) do not.

5. In the earlier version of *After Capitalism*, banks gave out grants instead of loans. But since these grants add to the value of the firm's capital assets, and hence increase the amount of the capital assets tax the firm must pay, while increasing as well the size of the required depreciation set-aside, these grants are essentially equivalent to loans repayable over the lifetime of the purchased assets at an interest rate equivalent to the capital assets tax. In this revised version banks simply loan the funds they have received. Nothing of substance hangs on this change.

6. For an account of these quite vast sums, see David Cay Johnson, *Free Lunch: How the Wealthiest Americans Enrich Themselves at Government Expense (and Stick You with the Bill)* (New York: Portfolio, 2007).

7. Joseph Stiglitz, "Quis Custodiet Ipsos Custodes?" ("Who Will Guard the Guardians?") *Challenge: The Magazine of Economic Affairs* 42, no. 6 (November–December 1999): 27.

8. Data from economywatch.com, compiled from IMF data. In 1989 the purchasing-power-parity per capita income of the Central and Eastern European countries, measured in 2009 dollars, was $10,400, versus $32,400 for the G7 countries (United States, Canada, Japan, United Kingdom, Germany, France, and Italy). In 2009, the figures were $13,800 and $38,700 respectively. The gap has thus widened from $22,000 in 1989 to $24,900 today.

9. Quotations in this paragraph are from U.S. Department of Health, Education, and Welfare, *Work in America* (Cambridge, MA: MIT Press, 1973), 112; and Derek Jones and Jan Svejnar, eds., *Participatory and Self-Managed Firms: Evaluating Economic Performance* (Lexington, MA: Lexington Books, 1982), 11. The Blinder-edited collection is *Paying for Productivity: A Look at the Evidence* (Washington, DC: Brookings, 1990). Especially relevant are the contributions by David Levine and Laura Tyson.

10. For an overview of the Pacific Northwest plywood cooperatives, Mondragon and the Italian cooperatives, see Gregory Dow, *Governing the Firm: Workers' Control in Theory and Practice* (Cambridge: Cambridge University Press, 2003), 50–70.

11. Katrina Berman, "A Cooperative Model for Worker Management," in *The Performance of Labour-Managed Firms*, ed. Frank Stephens (New York: St. Martin's Press, 1982), 80.

12. Hendrik Thomas, "The Performance of the Mondragon Cooperatives in Spain," in Jones and Svenjar, *Participatory and Self-Managed Firms*, 149.

13. Will Bartlett, John Cable, Saul Estrin, and Derek Jones, "Labor-Managed Cooperatives and Private Firms in North Central Italy: An Empirical Comparison," *Industrial and Labor Relations Review* 6, no. 1 (October 1992): 116.

14. Harold Lydall, *Yugoslavia in Crisis* (Oxford: Clarendon Press, 1989), 69 (emphasis mine).

15. Lydall, *Yugoslavia in Crisis*, 96 (emphasis mine). The Yugoslav mechanism for allocating investment funds was also deeply implicated. In essence, each region kept the funds generated there, which led to a widening gap between rich and poor regions—thus exacerbating ethnic tensions.

16. Henry Levin, "Employment and Productivity of Producer Cooperatives," in *Worker Cooperatives in America*, ed. Robert Jackall and Henry Levin (Berkeley: University of California Press, 1984), 28.

17. There is *some* room for doubt. It could be argued that certain kinds of enterprises are unsuited for democratic control, and so head-to-head comparisons are misleading, since the unsuitable kinds are, by definition, not available for comparison. This consideration may explain why Gregory Dow remains agnostic on the efficiency question: "Our knowledge is too primitive to attach a confident positive or negative sign to the efficiency properties of workers' control, which undoubtedly vary with industry characteristics and the specific organizational design one has in mind" (*Governing the Firm*, 262). Dow goes on to argue, however, that, given the *other* benefits of worker self-management, such as the value of democracy itself, the enhancement of the dignity of labor, and the lessening of social stratification within a firm, a case can be made for at least some governmental assistance to workers who want to take control of their firms.

18. John Maynard Keynes, *The General Theory of Employment, Interest, and Money* (New York: Harcourt Brace and World, 1936), 161–62.

19. Amartya Sen, *Resources, Values, and Development* (Cambridge, MA: Harvard University Press, 1984), 103.

20. There have been many books and articles written on this fascinating project. There is also an excellent BBC documentary made in 1979, now available at http://video .google.com (search for "The Mondragon Experiment"). For a good overview of this experiment from its inception to the present, see Alessandra Azevedo and Leda Gitaby, "The Cooperative Movement, Self-Management and Competitiveness: The Case of Mondragon Corporación Cooperativa," *Working USA: The Journal of Labor and Society* 13, no. 1 (March 2010): 5–29. Among the best books: Henk Thomas and Chris Logan, *Mondragon: An Economic Analysis* (London: George Allen & Unwin, 1982); Keith Bradley and Alan Gelb, *Cooperation at Work: The Mondragon Experience* (London: Heinemann Educational Books, 1983); William Foote Whyte and Kathleen King White, *Making Mondragon: The Growth and Dynamics of the Worker Cooperative Complex* (Ithaca, NY: Cornell University Press, 1988); Roy Morrison, *We Build the Road as We Travel* (Philadelphia: New Society Publishers, 1991); and George Cheney, *Values at Work: Employee Participation Meets Market Pressure at Mondragon* (Ithaca, NY: ILR/Cornell University Press, 1999), as well as the works by MacLeod and Kasmir cited below.

21. For current financial data on the Mondragon complex, consult their website at www.mondragon.mcc.es. These figures are for the year 2009.

22. See Jose Mari Luzarraga Monasterio, Dionisio Aranzadi Telleria, and Iñazio Irizar Etxebarria, "Understanding the Mondragon Globalization Process: Local Job Creation through Multi-localization: Facing Globalization Threats to Community Stability," paper presented at the First CIRIEC International Research Conference on Social Economy, Victoria, Canada, 2007. The authors surveyed cooperatives with sixty-five production plants abroad employing 14,000 workers. They argue that these plants were set up as a defensive measure to preserve local jobs and were successful in doing so. In fact, domestic employment in those cooperatives with plants abroad grew by 3,000 between 1999 and 2006.

23. Georgia Kelly and Shaula Massena, "Mondragon Coops: Worker-Operatives Decide How to Ride Out a Downturn," *Yes!*, May 7, Summer 2009.

24. Greg MacLeod, *From Mondragon to America: Experiments in Community Economic Development* (Sidney, NS: University College of Cape Breton Press, 1997), 91.

25. MacLeod, *From Mondragon to America*, 90.

26. Sharryn Kasmir, *The Myth of Mondragon: Cooperatives, Politics, and Working-Class Life in a Basque Town* (Albany: State University of New York Press, 1996).

27. Kasmir, *Myth*, 173.

28. Kasmir, *Myth*, 154.

29. Robert Nozick, *Anarchy, State, and Utopia* (New York: Basic Books, 1974), 163.

30. Both quotes cited by Andre Gunder Frank, *Dependent Accumulation and Underdevelopment* (New York: Monthly Review Press, 1979), 98–99. For a more recent statement of this argument, see Ha-Joon Chang, *Kicking Away the Ladder: Development Strategy in Historical Perspective* (London: Anthem Press, 2002).

31. The language here is from Thomas Palley, *Plenty of Nothing: The Downsizing of the American Dream and the Case for Structural Keynesianism* (Princeton, NJ: Princeton University Press, 1998), 172. Palley suggests the second provision as well, although he does not call his proposal "socialist protectionism."

32. I thank Frank Thompson for this observation, which came up in his discussion of socialist protectionism with Cuban economists.

4. Capitalism or Socialism? Inequality, Unemployment, Overwork, Poverty

1. Jan Pen, *Income Distribution: Facts, Theories, Policies* (New York: Praeger, 1971).

2. The data that follow have been derived from the U.S. Census Bureau, "Current Population Survey (HINC-01): Selected Characteristics of Households by Total Money Income in 2009" (accessible at www.census.gov/hhes/www/cpstables/032010/hhinc/new01_007.htm); Emmanuel Saez, "Striking It Richer: The Evolution of Top Incomes in the United States" (update July 2010), available at Saez's homepage, http://elsa.berkeley.edu/saez/; *Forbes*, September 16, 2010; the AFL-CIO website, "Executive Pay Watch"; and Nelson Schwartz and Louise Story, "Pay of Hedge Fund Managers Roared Back Last Year," *New York Times*, March 31, 2010.

3. David Tepper might not have been the last person to cross the line in 2009, that is, the person with the highest *income*. Individual tax returns are not a matter of public record. We do not know, for example, Bill Gates's income. Gates is calculated by *Forbes* researchers to be the richest person in the United States. If his estimated $54 billion fortune generated a revenue stream in excess of 7.5 percent—rather than the 6 percent return I assigned to the billionaires—Gates's income exceeded Tepper's. So there might be one or more giants even taller than sixty-four miles.

4. Plato, *The Republic*, books 3 and 8.

5. Richard Wilkinson and Kate Pickett, *The Spirit Level: Why Greater Equality Makes Societies Stronger* (New York: Bloomsbury Press, 2009), 33–34. Perhaps even more surprising than the relationship between inequality and health, "economic inequality predicts biodiversity loss"—to quote the title of a paper published recently by three McGill University researchers. They too looked both at countries and at the fifty states of the United States, concluding that "unless current trends toward greater inequality are reversed, it may become increasingly hard to conserve the rich variety of the living world" (Gregory Mikkelson, Andrew Gonzales, and Garry Peterson," Economic Inequality Predicts Biodiversity Loss," *PloS One* 2, no. 5 [May 2007], accessible at www.plosone.org/article/info%3Adoi%2F10.1371%2Fjournal. pone.0000444). The correlations are by no means perfect, but they are, in all cases, statistically significant.

6. Wilkinson and Pickett, *Spirit Level*, 248.

7. Chuck Shepherd, "News of the Weird," *Chicago Reader*, January 14, 1994.

8. International Labour Organization, *Global Employment Trends* (Geneva: ILO, January 2010).

9. Karl Marx and Frederick Engels, *The Communist Manifesto* (London: Verso, 1998), 39.

10. Robert Lucas, "Macroeconomic Priorities," *The American Economic Review* 93, no. 1 (March 2003): 1

11. John Maynard Keynes, *The General Theory of Employment, Interest and Money* (New York: Harcourt Brace, 1936), 129.

12. Paul Krugman, "Defining Prosperity Down," *New York Times*, August 1, 2010.

13. Don Peck, "How a New Jobless Era Will Transform America," *Atlantic*, March 2010, 52.

14. For many suggestions, see Van Jones, *The Green Collar Economy: How One Solution Can Fix Our Two Biggest Problems* (New York: HarperCollins, 2008).

15. Paul Krugman, *The Age of Diminished Expectations: U. S. Economic Policies in the 1990s* (Cambridge, MA: MIT Press, 1990), 52.

16. Thelma Leisner, *Economic Statistics 1900–1983* (New York: Facts on File Publications, 1985), 116.

17. Quoted by Alan Blinder, *Hard Heads, Soft Hearts: Tough-Minded Economics for a Just Society* (Reading, MA: Addison-Wesley, 1987), 46.

18. See Andrew Hacker, *Money: Who Has How Much and Why* (New York: Simon and Schuster, 1997), 46, for the earlier data. For current data, see Andrew Sum and Joseph McGlaughlin, "The Massive Shedding of Jobs in America," *Challenge* 53, no. 6 (November–December 2010): 62–76.

19. Cited in Juliet Schor, *Plentitude* (New York: Penguin Press, 2010), 106.

20. Juliet Schor, *The Overworked American: The Unexpected Decline of Leisure* (New York: Basic Books, 1992), 2.

21. Juliet Schor, *Born to Buy* (New York: Scribner, 2004), 10. Schor notes elsewhere: "Thirty percent of U.S. male college graduates and 20 percent of all full-time male workers are on schedules that usually exceed fifty hours. Schor, *Plenitude*, 105.

22. Data from the Bureau of Labor Statistics and from the International Labour Organization, cited by Lonnie Golden and Deborah Figart, "Doing Something about Long Hours," *Challenge* 43, no. 6 (November–December 2000): 25, 17. For more recent data, see Susan Fleck, "International Comparisons of Hours Worked: An Assessment of the Statistics," *Monthly Labor Review* 132, no. 2 (May 2009): 3–31.

23. U.S. Central Intelligence Agency, *The World Fact Book*, available at www.cia.gov. Cuban per capita income is listed as $9,700 (purchasing-power-parity) in 2009, as compared to $47,000 in the United States.

24. United States Bureau of Justice Statistics, "Total Correctional Population" (2009) (accessible at http://bjs.ojp.usdoj.gov/index.cfm?ty=tp&tid=11).

25. For a powerful account of the pain and suffering unemployment-generated poverty brings to our inner cities, see William Julius Wilson's classic indictment, *When Work Disappears: The World of the New Urban Poor* (New York: Vintage, 1997).

26. Lyndon B. Johnson, "Special Address to Congress," March 16, 1964, in *Public Papers of U.S. Presidents, Lyndon B. Johnson, 1963–1964* (Washington, DC: Government Printing Office, 1965), 1:375–80.

27. Peter Singer, *One World: The Ethics of Globalization* (New Haven, CT: Yale University Press, 2002), 150–51.

28. Thomas Pogge, "Real World Justice," *Journal of Ethics* 9, nos. 1–2 (2005): 31.

29. Whether China still merits the label "market socialist" is a matter of debate. This issue will be examined in chapter 6. What is not debatable is the fact that huge increases in economic well-being for poor Chinese took place in the decade following the market reforms post-1978, when the socialist character of the Chinese economy was not in question. Nor is what happened in the Soviet Union in dispute. As Princeton professor Stephen Cohen has noted, "Since 1991 Russian realities have included the worst peacetime industrial depression of the twentieth century; the degradation of agriculture and livestock herds even worse in some respects than occurred during Stalin's catastrophic collectivization of the peasantry in the 1930s; the impoverishment or near-impoverishment of some 75 percent or more of the nation; and more new orphans than resulted from Russia's almost 30 million casualties in World War II." Stephen Cohen, *Failed Crusade: America and the Tragedy of Post-Communist Russia* (New York: Norton, 2000), 28.

30. Partha Dasgupta, *An Inquiry into Well-Being and Destitution* (Oxford: Clarendon Press, 1993), 80. Extreme poverty, he notes, could be eradicated in four years.

31. For a detailed, provocative analysis of one continent, see Olufemi Taiwo, *How Colonialism Preempted Modernity in Africa* (Bloomington: Indiana University Press, 2010).

32. Karl Marx, *Capital*, vol. 1 (New York: International Publishers, 1967), 751.

33. Marx, *Capital*, 432.

34. For a vivid account by someone involved, see John Perkins, *Confessions of an Economic Hit Man* (San Francisco: Berrett-Koehler, 2004). For another compelling

analysis of this issue, see Noreena Hertz, *The Debt Threat: How Debt Is Destroying the Developing World . . . and Threatening Us All* (New York: HarperCollins, 2004).

35. The World Health Organization *2010 Malaria Report* is decidedly upbeat. Malaria deaths declined from 985,000 in 2000 to 781,000 in 2009. However, according to the report, funding appears to have stagnated, falling far short of the estimated $6 billion per year needed. (The report can be accessed at www.who.int/malaria/world_malaria_report_2010/en/index.html).

36. For a good account of Cuba, see Julia Sweig, *Cuba: What Everyone Needs to Know* (Oxford: Oxford University Press, 2009). For more on Kerala, see Richard Franke and Barbara Chasin, *Kerala: Radical Reform as Development in an Indian State* (San Francisco: Institute for Food and Development, 1989) or Bill McKibben, *Hope, Human and Wild* (St. Paul, MN: Hungry Mind Press, 1995), chap. 3. For a more critical perspective, although one that acknowledges Kerala's well-documented successes, see K. Ravi Raman, ed., *Development, Democracy and the State: Critiquing the Kerala Model of Development* (New York: Routledge, 2010).

37. For a critique of existing aid programs and presentation of an alternative approach, see philosopher/mathematician/World Bank insider David Ellerman's *Helping People Help Themselves: From the World Bank to an Alternative Philosophy of Development Assistance* (Ann Arbor: University of Michigan Press, 2006).

38. Alan Weisman, *Gaviotas: A Village to Reinvent the World—10th Anniversary Edition* (White River Junction, VT: Chelsea Green Publishing Company, 2008). For a nice account of Curitiba, see McKibben, *Hope, Human, and Wild*, chap. 2. See also Steven A. Moore, *Alternative Routes to the Sustainable City: Austin, Curitiba, and Frankfurt* (Lanham, MD: Lexington Books: 2007).

39. U.S. Census Bureau, *Income, Poverty and Health Insurance Coverage in the United States, 2009* (Washington, DC: U.S. Census Bureau, 2010) (accessible at www.census.gov/prod/2010pubs/p60-238.pdf).

40. For a classic statement of this argument, see Milton Friedman, *Capitalism and Freedom* (Chicago: University of Chicago Press, 1962), chap. 7.

41. Here is one blunt appraisal from a journalist who spent time on the ground with Tea Party activists: "A loose definition of the Tea Party might be millions of pissed-off white people sent chasing after Mexicans on Medicaid by the handful of banks and investment firms who advertise on Fox and CNBC. . . . It's not like the Tea Partiers hate black people. It's just that they're shockingly willing to believe the appalling horseshit fantasy about how white people in the age of Obama are some kind of oppressed minority." Matt Taibbi, "Tea and Crackers," *Rolling Stone*, October 1, 2010.

5. Capitalism or Socialism?
Economic Instability, Environmental Degradation, Democracy

1. Paul Krugman, *The Return of Depression Economics and the Crisis of 2008* (New York: Norton, 2009), 10.

2. Karl Marx and Frederick Engels, *The Communist Manifesto* (New York: International Publishers, 1968), 15. (The *Manifesto* was originally published in 1848).

For a recent survey see Carmen Reinhart and Kenneth Rogoff, *This Time Is Different: Eight Centuries of Financial Folly* (Princeton, NJ: Princeton University Press, 2009).

3. Marx and Engels, *Communist Manifesto*, 13–14.

4. Alvin Hansen, *Full Recovery or Stagnation?* (New York: Norton, 1938); Paul Baran and Paul Sweezy, *Monopoly Capital* (New York: Monthly Review Press, 1966).

5. Robert Frank, *Richistan: A Journey through the American Wealth Boom and the Lives of the New Rich* (New York: Crown Publishers, 2007), 151.

6. Bill McKibben, "Happiness Is . . ."*Ecologist*, January 2, 2007, 36.

7. For a detailed analysis, see Robert W. McChesney, John Bellamy Foster, Inger L. Stole, and Hannah Holtman, "The Sales Effort and Monopoly Capital," *Monthly Review* 60, no. 11 (April 2009).

8. Juliet Schor, *Plenitude: The New Economics of True Wealth* (New York: Penguin Press, 2010), 16.

9. Schor, *Plenitude*, 27.

10. Paul Krugman, "Money Can't Buy Happiness. Er, Can It?" *New York Times*, June 1, 1999.

11. A new economic paradigm, "behavioral economics," has developed in recent years, challenging the dominant (complacent) neoclassical paradigm. See, for example, George Akerlof and Robert Shiller, *Animal Spirits: How Human Psychology Drives the Economy, and Why It Matters for Global Capitalism* (Princeton, NJ: Princeton University Press, 2010). Although fierce in their critique of neoclassical economics, Akerlof and Shiller continue to believe that capitalism, suitably regulated, "can give us the best of possible worlds" (173). They do, however, acknowledge, if inadvertently, the deeply nondemocratic nature of a capitalist economy: "The future of any country is in the hands of the business people who decide on investments, and it is in large measure dependent on their psychology" (143).

12. John Cassidy, "What Good Is Wall Street?" *New Yorker*, November 29, 2010, 51. In this excellent article, Cassidy interviews John Wooley, head of the Wooley Centre for the Study of Capital Market Dysfunctionality at the London School of Economics, who asks, "Why on earth should finance be the biggest and most highly paid industry when it's just a utility, like sewage or gas?" In questioning so sacred a cow as finance, Wooley admits, "What we are doing is revolutionary."

13. Paul Krugman, *The Conscience of a Liberal* (New York: Norton, 2007), 124–27.

14. Barry Z. Cynamon and Steven M. Fazzari, "Household Debt in the Consumer Age—Source of Growth, Risk of Collapse," *Capitalism and Society* 3, no. 2 (2008): 18, 8.

15. Paul Krugman, "Back to What Obama Must Do," *Rolling Stone*, January 14, 2009.

16. For an early statement of this argument, see Jeremy Rifkin, *The End of Work: The Decline of the Global Labor Force and the Dawn of the Post-Market Era* (New York: G. P. Putnam's Sons, 1995). For a more recent version see Martin Ford, *The Lights in the Tunnel: Automation, Accelerating Technology and the Economy of the Future* (n.p.: Acculant Publishing, 2009).

17. See Barry Lynn, *Cornered: The New Monopoly Capitalism and the Economics of Destruction* (Hoboken, NJ: John Wiley and Sons, 2010), for a powerful analysis of this little-noted phenomenon.

18. Karl Marx, "Preface to *A Contribution to the Critique of Political Economy*," in *Karl Marx: Selected Writings*, ed. Lawrence Simon (Indianapolis, IN: Hackett, 1994), 211.

19. Lest historical amnesia allow us to think that it was the collapse of communism that saved us, we should remember that it was the huge popular movement for nuclear disarmament, coupled with Mikhail Gorbachev's remarkable proposal to eliminate all nuclear weapons by the year 2000, both occurring in the early 1980s, that called decisively into question the ever-more-dangerous arms race. It now appears that the collapse of the Soviet Union has slowed rather than hastened the disarmament process.

20. Bill McKibben, *Deep Economy* (New York: Henry Holt, 2007), 64. This section draws on chapter 3, "The Year of Eating Locally," of this frightening/inspiring/hopeful book, and on Lester Brown, "Feeding Eight Billion People Well," in *Plan B 4.0: Mobilizing to Save Civilization* (New York: W. W. Norton, 2009), chap. 9.

21. Brown, *Plan B 4.0*, 233.

22. McKibben, *Deep Economy*, 67. For an optimistic assessment of the possibilities of organic agriculture in Africa, see UNEP-UNCTAD Capacity Building Task Force on Trade, Environment and Nations, "Organic Agriculture and Food Security in Africa" (New York: United Nations, 2008), which concludes that "organic agriculture can be more conducive to food security in Africa than most conventional production systems, and is more likely to be sustainable in the long term." See also see Roger Thurow and Scott Kilman, *Enough: Why the World's Poorest Starve in an Age of Plenty* (New York: Public Affairs, 2009), which also pays particular attention to Africa.

23. Intergovernmental Panel on Climate Change, *IPCC/TEAP Special Report on Safeguarding the Ozone Layer and the Global Climate System* (Cambridge: Cambridge University Press, 2005).

24. Figures cited by Bradford Plumer, "Fossil-Fuel Subsidies Still Dominate," *New Republic*, August 3, 2010 (accessible at www.tnr.com/blog/the-vine/76750/fossil-fuel-subsidies-still-dominate) from a report by the International Energy Agency.

25. World Bank, *World Development Report 2010: Development and Climate Change* (Washington, DC: The World Bank, 2010).

26. Seth Dunn, "Decarbonizing the Energy Economy," in *State of the World, 2001*, ed. Lester R. Brown, Christopher Flavin, and Hilary French (New York: W. W. Norton, 2001), 95. See also Brown, *Plan B 4.0*.

27. John H. Cushman Jr., "Industrial Group Plans to Battle Climate Treaty," *New York Times*, April 26, 1998.

28. Hans-Peter Martin and Harald Schumann, *The Global Trap* (London: Zed Books, 1997), 14.

29. Paul Hawken, Amory Lovins, and L. Hunter Lovins, *Natural Capitalism: Creating the Next Industrial Revolution* (Boston: Little, Brown, 1999), 5.

30. Hawkins, Lovins, Lovins, *Natural Capitalism*, 5, 2.

31. Hawken, Lovins, Lovins, *Natural Capitalism*, 1.

32. James Gustave Speth, *The Bridge at the Edge of the World: Capitalism, the Environment, and Crossing from Crisis to Sustainability* (New Haven, CT: Yale University Press, 2008).

33. Speth, *The Bridge at the Edge of the World*, 194. He does say that "the question whether this something new is beyond capitalism or is a reinvented capitalism is largely definitional" (194).

34. Brown, *Plan B 4.0*, 242.

35. It is theoretically possible for a country's overall GDP to grow while its consumption of nonrenewable resources and its contribution to global pollution decline. However, given the sheer magnitude of rich-country consumption, it is wishful thinking bordering on self-delusion to suppose that materials substitution and cleaner technologies will allow rich countries to continue, and even increase, their current levels of consumption while the poorer countries catch up.

36. Herman Daly, *Beyond Growth* (Boston: Beacon Press, 1996), 106. The United States, which contains less than 5 percent of the world's population, generates 20 percent of the world's carbon emissions. If the amount of carbon dioxide released globally into the atmosphere is now at or beyond what is sustainable, the United States is producing more than four times its sustainable share. Thus, with respect to carbon emissions, United States can be said to be overdeveloped by at least a factor of four. China, by way of contrast, although recently surpassing the United States as the leading producer of carbon emissions, is generating only slightly more than its per capita share; India is generating less than half of its share.

37. For two recent, strong defenses of this claim, see Schor, *Plenitude*, and Frances Moore Lappé, *EcoMind: Reframing Six Disempowering Ideas That Keep Us from Aligning with Nature—Even Our Own* (New York: Nation Books, 2010). These are beautiful books, highly recommended.

38. Plato, *The Republic*, book 8.

39. John Stuart Mill, *Considerations on Representative Government* (Indianapolis: Bobbs-Merrill, 1958), 138. Mill insists that everyone should have a voice, but "that everyone should have an equal voice is a totally different proposition" (35).

40. Robert Dahl, *Democracy and Its Critics* (New Haven, CT: Yale University Press, 1989), 220.

41. Gore Vidal, interview, *Playboy*, December 1987, 53.

42. Patrick Yeagle, "Record Breaking Year for Campaign Spending," *Illinois Times* (Springfield), November 4, 2010.

43. Jane Mayer, "Covert Operations: The Billionaire Brothers Who Are Waging War against Obama," *New Yorker*, August 30, 2010, 49.

44. It must be admitted, David Koch, for all his seriousness about shaping politics, has a sense of humor. In addressing the alumni association of his high school alma mater, Deerfield Academy—to which he'd just pledged $25 million, he said:

> You might ask: How does David Koch happen to have the wealth to be so generous? Well, let me tell you a story. It all started when I was a little boy. One day, my father gave me an apple. I soon sold it for five dollars and bought two apples and sold them for ten. Then I bought four apples and sold them for twenty. Well, this went on, day after day, week after week, month after month, year after year, until my father died and left me three-hundred million dollars. (Mayer, "Covert Operations," 48.)

45. *International Herald Tribune*, October 21, 1999. Emphasis mine.

46. Vince Stehle, "Righting Philanthropy," *The Nation* 264, no. 25 (June 30, 1997): 15.

47. Cf. Mayer, "Covert Operations," 44–55.

48. Eric Lichtblau, "Scalia and Thomas' Retreat with Koch," *New York Times*, January 21, 2011.

49. This, to me, rather shocking tidbit was reported by fair.org, in their press release, "Taking the Public Out of Public TV," October 19, 2010. *PBS NewsHour* is produced by MacNeil/Lehrer Productions, a company co-owned by MacNeil, Lehrer, and the media conglomerate Liberty Media Corporation, the latter owning a 65 percent stake in the company. *The Nightly Business Report*, previously produced by a public television station, was recently sold to a private company. For an important treatment of the overall media question, see Robert McChesney's classic, *Rich Media, Poor Democracy* (Champaign: University of Illinois Press, 1999). See also his more recent *The Political Economy of Media: Enduring Issues, Emerging Dilemmas* (New York: Monthly Review Press, 2008).

50. For more details of many of these and more, see Michael Sullivan, *American Adventurism Abroad: 30 Invasions, Interventions and Regime Changes since World War II* (Westport, CT: Praeger, 2004). For a detailed account of U.S. involvement in the coup attempt against Chavez, see Eva Golinger, *The Chavez Code: Cracking U.S. Intervention in Venezuela* (Northhampton, MA: The Olive Branch Press, 2006). See also, if you can, the amazing documentary *The Revolution Will Not Be Televised*, produced by David Power and directed by Kim Bartley and Donnacha O'Briain.

51. Noam Chomsky offers some estimates: 4 million dead in Indochina, 500,000 to 1 million dead in Indonesia, 200,000 dead in Central America since 1978, and 200,000 dead in East Timor since 1975. And that's only a sampling. Noam Chomsky, *On Power and Ideology* (Boston: South End Press, 1987), 24.

6. Getting from Here to There

1. As David Ellerman forcefully points out, "voucher privatization" was pushed for political reasons, when it would have made far more economic sense to allow workers to lease or buy their enterprises from the state. A natural evolution toward something like Economic Democracy was consciously blocked. David Ellerman, "Lessons from Eastern Europe's Voucher Privatization," *Challenge: The Magazine of Economic Affairs* 44, no. 4 (July–August 2001): 14–37.

2. For these and other data on Chinese performance, see Peter Nolan, *China's Rise, Russia's Fall: Politics, Economics, and Planning in the Transition from Stalinism* (New York: St. Martin's Press, 1995), 10–16; and Peter Nolan, *China and the Global Business Revolution* (New York: Palgrave, 2001), 912–16.

3. Central Intelligence Agency, *The CIA Factbook 2010* (New York: Skyhorse Publishing, 2009). Anita Chan, "Strikes in Vietnam and China: Contrasts in Labor Laws and Diverging Industrial Relations Patterns," presentation at the American Bar Association's International Labor and Employment Law Committee meeting, Istanbul, Turkey, May 9–13, 2010, pp. 3, 17.

4. Quoted in "Socialism Works in Cuba," an interview by Yunus Carrim, editor of *Umsebenzi* (the online journal of the South African Communist Party), with Oscar Martinez, deputy head of the International Relations Department of Cuba. *Umsebenzi Online* 9, no. 21 (November 3, 2010). For more details on the Cuban reforms, see the full interview.

5. United Nations Development Programme, "Human Development Indicators," http://hdr.undp.org/en/data/build/

6. Cf. Marta Harnecker, "Latin America and Twenty-first Century Socialism: Inventing to Avoid Mistakes," *Monthly Review* 62, no.3 (July–August 2010): 6.

7. For an account of one such effort, see Dario Azzellini, "Venezuela's Solidarity Economy: Collective Ownership, Expropriation and Workers Self-Management," *Working USA: The Journal of Labor and Society* 12, no. 2 (June 2009): 171–91.

8. For a strong, highly positive appraisal of the importance of Venezuela—and Cuba—in opening up a new path forward, see D. L. Raby, *Democracy and Revolution: Cuba, Venezuela and Socialism Today* (London: Pluto Press, 2006). For a critique of the more moderate left governments and their reform proposals from a more radical left perspective, see Fernando Ignacio Leiva, *Latin American Neostructuralism: Contradictions of Post-Neoliberal Development* (Minneapolis: University of Minnesota Press, 2008). For an assessment of Brazil, see the March/April issue of *NACLA Report on the Americas*, an issue devoted to "Lula's Legacy: Brazil."

9. Cited by Jeffrey Wasserstrom, "Throwing the Book at China," *Miller-McCune*, December 19, 2010, a review of some recent books on China. "Sinophobia has a long history," he observes.

10. Tibet is rather special, controversial case. For opposing views, see Wang Lixiong, "Reflections on Tibet," *New Left Review*, n.s., 14 (March–April 2002), and Tsering Shakya, "Blood in the Snows: Reply to Wang Lixiong," *New Left Review*, n.s., 15 (May–June 2002): 39–60.

11. Andreas Lorenz, "China's Environmental Suicide: A Government Minister Speaks," *Open Democracy*, April 5, 2005.

12. Pew Global Attitudes Project, "China's Optimism: Prosperity Brings Satisfaction—and Hope" (accessible at http://pewglobal.org/reports/) (released November 16, 2005). Poland came in last, only 13 percent satisfied, 82 percent dissatisfied. Russia wasn't much better. Less than a quarter of the Russians are satisfied; nearly three-quarters are dissatisfied.)

13. See gallup.com, articles posted October 6, 2010 (China), December 30, 2010 (Europe), and January 5, 2011 (U.S.).

14. Huang Yasheng, *Capitalism with Chinese Characteristics: Entrepreneurship and the State* (Cambridge: Cambridge University Press, 2008). Huang Yasheng teaches at both MIT's Sloan School of Management and at Tsinghua University in China. For a critique of the book's neoliberal conclusions, see Joel Andreas, "A Shanghai Model: On Capitalism with Chinese Characteristics," *New Left Review*, n.s., 65 (September–October 2010): 63–85. For Huang's reply, see "The Politics of China's Path: A Reply to Joel Andreas," *New Left Review*, n.s., 65 (September–October 2010): 87–91.

15. For a sampling of the debate on the Left, see *China: Socialism, Capitalism, Market: What Now? Where Next?* a special issue of *Science and Society* 73, no. 2 (April 2009), guest edited by Barbara Foley and Bernard Moss.

16. All China Federation of Trade Unions, "Chinese Trade Unions Participate in Democratic Management" (November 19, 2004) (accessible at acftu.org.cn).

17. "Wei Jiangxing Speaks on Democratic Management of Non-Public Enterprises during Inspection in Hebei," *Xinhua Domestic Service*, September 29, 2002.

18. Diana Farrell and Susan Lund, "Putting China's Capital to Work," *Far Eastern Economic Review* 169 (May 2006): 5–10. The authors predictably bemoan these facts and urge neoliberal reform.

19. Gao Xu, "State-Owned Enterprises in China: How Big Are They?" blogs.worldbank.org, January 19, 2010 (accessible at: http://blogs.worldbank.org/eastasiapacific/state-owned-enterprises-in-china-how-big-are-they).

20. Kishore Mahbubani, *Beyond the Age of Innocence: Rebuilding Trust between America and the World* (New York: Public Affairs, 2005), 115. He adds, "Their success is evident. . . . To see the most populous society in the world experiencing the most rapid economic growth is like seeing the fattest boy in the class winning the 100-meter hurdles race."

21. Chan, "Strikes in Vietnam and China," 31. In 2009 some 318,000 cases were brought to court under the new law. (Edward Wong, "Global Crisis Adds to Surge of Labor Disputes in Chinese Courts," *New York Times*, September 15, 2010.)

22. Giovanni Arrighi, *Adam Smith in Beijing: Lineages of the Twenty-first Century* (London: Verso, 2007), 389.

23. Karl Marx and Frederick Engels, *The Communist Manifesto* (London: Verso, 1998), 60.

24. For more on the Mondragon-Steelworkers agreement, see "Steelworkers Form Collaboration with Mondragon, the World's Largest Worker-Owned Cooperative," accessible from the USW homepage, www.usw.org. For more on the U.N. Resolution, see http://social.un.org/coopsyear. The ILO Report, authored by Johnston Birchall and Lou Hammond Ketilson, can be downloaded from the ILO webpage, www.ilo.org. For information on existing worker cooperatives in the United States and much more, consult the excellent website of GEO (Grassroots Economic Organizing): www.geo.coop. For details on how employee-owned firms can be set up, see Stephen Clifford, *An Owner's Guide to Business Succession Planning*, 2nd ed. (Kent, OH: Kent Popular Press, 2008). Kent State University is home to the Ohio Employee Ownership Center, whose website, http://dept.kent.edu/oeoc, is lush with practical information.

25. See Gregory Dow, *Governing the Firm: Workers' Control in Theory and Practice* (Cambridge: Cambridge University Press, 2003), 260–89, for details.

26. Dale Wetzel, "Economy Prompts Fresh Look at ND's Socialist Bank," Associated Press, February 16, 2010. For more information, see various articles on the subject by Ellen Brown in *Yes!* magazine: "Reviving the Local Economy with Publicly Owned Banks" (October 14, 2009); "Whose Bank? Public Investment, Not Private Debt" (February 19, 2010); and "More States May Create Public Banks" (May 13, 2010).

27. Cf. Christopher Helman, "What the Top Corporations Pay in Taxes," *Forbes*, April 1, 2010 and "The Tax Policy Briefing Book," on the Tax Policy Center website,

www.taxpolicycenter.org. Buffet's remark is quoted by Ben Stein in "In Class Warfare, Guess Which Class Is Winning," *New York Times*, November 26, 2006.

28. This tax was originally proposed by Nobel laureate James Tobin, building on a suggestion by Keynes. For a lucid explanation of the benefits of a Tobin tax in reasserting national control over financial policy and in generating significant government revenue, see Thomas Palley, "Destabilizing Speculation and the Case for an International Currency Transactions Tax," *Challenge: The Magazine of Economic Affairs* 44, no. 3 (May–June 2001): 70–89. Also see www.tobintax.org.

29. For details and supporting arguments, see the various working papers on the topic at the Research Center for Full Employment and Price Stability (University of Missouri–Kansas City) at www.cfeps.org, and the Centre of Full Employment and Equity (University of Newcastle) at http://el.newcastle.edu.au/coffee. See also William Mitchell and Joan Muysken, *Full Employment Abandoned: Shifting Sands and Policy Failures* (Cheltenham, UK: Edward Elgar, 2008).

30. Arundhati Roy, *An Ordinary Person's Guide to Empire* (Boston: South End Press, 2004), 3.

31. Paul Krugman, *The Conscience of a Liberal* (New York: Norton, 2007), 18. (There are 400 billionaires now, according to *Forbes* September 16, 2010.)

32. In order to reduce the wealth gap, the tax rate on the income of the superrich must, in general, exceed 100 percent—a rate that most people in a democratic society would likely deem unfair.

33. For a detailed proposal for a 2 percent wealth tax, see Bruce Ackerman and Anne Alstott, "Taxing Wealth," chap. 6 in *The Stakeholder Society* (New Haven, CT: Yale University Press, 1999).

34. Bruce Ackerman and Ian Ayres *Voting with Dollars: A New Paradigm for Campaign Finance* (New Haven, CT: Yale University Press, 2004). I present here only a brief summary, of their detailed, cogently argued proposal.

35. Cited by Robert Reich, "Only 4.2 Billion to Buy This Election?" *Robert Reich's Blog*, October 28, 2010 (accessible at www.readersupportednews.org/opinion2/277-75/3755-only-42-billion-to-buy-this-election). Will was arguing that we needn't be concerned about campaign spending—which is not what is being argued here.

36. There is no restriction on the number of parties or candidates who may open accounts with the FEC. If you can persuade people to donate to your campaign, you can receive their (anonymous) contributions.

37. Peter Landers, "State Solution: Nationalizing Banks May Be Japan's Only Option," *Far Eastern Economic Review* 161, no. 40 (October 1, 1998): 80–81.

38. John Maynard Keynes, *The General Theory of Employment, Interest and Money* (New York: Harcourt, Brace and Company, 1936), 376.

39. John Kenneth Galbraith, *Economics and the Public Purpose* (Boston: Houghton Mifflin, 1973), 271–72.

40. Cf. Robin Blackburn, "Rudolf Meidner, 1914–2005: Visionary Pragmatist," *Counterpunch* (December 22, 2005). See also Jonus Pontusson, *The Limits to Social Democracy: Investment Politics in Sweden* (Ithaca, NY: Cornell University Press, 1992).

41. Marx and Engels, *Manifesto*, 50.

42. Marx and Engels, *Manifesto*, 51, 58, 60.

43. Marx and Engels, *Manifesto*, 60.

44. Brian Barry, *Why Social Justice Matters* (Cambridge: Polity Press, 2005), 272, viii.

45. Paul Hawken, Amory Lovins, and L. Hunter Lovins, *Natural Capitalism: Creating the Next Industrial Revolution* (Boston: Little, Brown, 1999), 1.

46. Karl Marx, "Free Human Production," in *Karl Marx: Selected Writings*, ed. Lawrence Simon (Indianapolis: Hackett, 1994), 52.

47. Karl Marx, *Capital*, vol. 1 (New York: International Publishers, 2003), 454.

48. Karl Marx, *German Ideology*, in Simon, *Karl Marx*, 119

49. Marx, *German Ideology*, 134; *Capital*, 474.

50. Karl Marx, "Private Property and Communism," in Simon, *Karl Marx*, 74.

51. Marx, "Private Property and Communism," 77.

52. Marx, *Capital*, vol. 3.

53. E. F. Schumacher, *Small Is Beautiful: Economics as if People Matter* (Point Roberts, WA: Hartley and Marks Publishers, 1999), 40, 38. This is the twenty-fifth anniversary edition, with an introduction by Paul Hawken and numerous commentaries. *Small Is Beautiful* was first published in 1973.

54. Schumacher, *Small Is Beautiful*, 20

55. Schumacher, *Small Is Beautiful*, 89

56. Schumacher, *Small Is Beautiful*, 45, 91. Mike Davis, *Planet of Slums* (London: Verso, 2007). Nick Reding, *Methland: The Death and Life of an American Small Town* (New York: Bloomsbury, 2010).

57. Schumacher, *Small Is Beautiful*, 47, 53.

58. Schumacher, *Small Is Beautiful*, 20.

59. Schumacher, *Small Is Beautiful*, 49.

60. Schumacher, *Small Is Beautiful*, 125.

61. Keynes, *The General Theory*, 372, 376.

62. John Maynard Keynes, "Economic Possibilities for Our Grandchildren," in *Essays in Persuasion* (New York: Norton, 1963), 368–72.

63. Keynes, "Economic Possibilities," 359.

64. Hannah Arendt, *The Human Condition* (Chicago: University of Chicago Press, 1958), 9.

65. Barry, *Why Social Justice Matters*, 251.

66. My thanks to Todd Wilson (personal communication) for this latter point. He adds, "The more people that make these personal changes, the easier it will be, when the time comes, to make the global changes. People will be more receptive to the proposals, more likely to help them 'go viral,' and more likely to support them when they get a chance to. And people do notice when others around them exhibit common behaviors. So there actually is a concrete sense in which one changes the rest of the world by changing oneself."

67. Frances Moore Lappé, *EcoMind: Reframing Six Disempowering Ideas That Keep Us from Aligning with Nature—Even Our Own* (New York: Nation Books, 2010), 135.

68. Emir Sader and Ken Silverstein, *Without Fear of Being Happy: Lula, the Workers Party and Brazil* (London: Verso, 1991), 106.

69. Sader and Silverstein, *Without Fear of Being Happy*, 107, quoting from a PT document.

70. Maria Helena Moreira Alves, "The Workers Party of Brazil: Building Struggle from the Grassroots," in *The Future of Socialism*, ed. William Tabb (New York: Monthly Review Press, 1990), 234. My account of Partido dos Trabalhadores derives from this article, from Sader and Silverstein, from Gianpaolo Baiocchi, ed., *Radicals in Power: The Workers' Party (PT) and Experiments in Urban Democracy in Brazil* (London: Zed Books, 2003), and from Sue Branford and Bernardo Kucinski, *Lula and the Workers Party in Brazil* (New York: The New Press, 2005).

71. Moisés Naím, "The Havana Obsession, *Newsweek*, June 22, 2009.

72. Karl Marx, "Theses on Feuerbach," in Simon, *Karl Marx: Selected Writings*, 101.

Bibliography

Ackerman, Bruce, and Anne Alstott. *The Stakeholder Society.* New Haven, CT: Yale University Press, 1999.

Ackerman, Bruce, and Ian Ayres. *Voting with Dollars: A New Paradigm for Campaign Finance.* New Haven, CT: Yale University Press, 2004.

Akerlof, George, and Robert Shiller. *Animal Spirits: How Human Psychology Drives the Economy, and Why It Matters for Global Capitalism.* Princeton, NJ: Princeton University Press, 2010.

Albert, Michael. *Parecon: Life After Capitalism.* London: Verso, 2003.

Alves, Maria Helena Moreira. "The Workers Party of Brazil: Building Struggle from the Grassroots." In *The Future of Socialism,* edited by William Tabb. New York: Monthly Review Press, 1990.

Andreas, Joel. "A Shanghai Model? On Capitalism with Chinese Characteristics." *New Left Review,* n.s., 65 (September/October 2010): 63–85.

Arendt, Hannah. *The Human Condition.* Chicago: University of Chicago Press, 1958.

Arrighi, Giovanni. *Adam Smith in Beijing: Lineages of the Twenty-first Century.* London: Verso, 2007.

Azevedo, Alessandra, and Leda Gitaby. "The Cooperative Movement, Self-Management and Competitiveness: The Case of Mondragon Corporación Cooperativa." *Working USA: The Journal of Labor and Society* 13, no. 1 (March 2010): 5–29.

Azzellini, Dario. "Venezuela's Solidarity Economy: Collective Ownership, Expropriation and Workers Self-Management." *Working USA: The Journal of Labor and Society* 12, no. 2 (June 2009): 171–91.

Baiocchi, Gianpaolo, ed. *Radicals in Power: The Workers' Party (PT) and Experiments in Urban Democracy in Brazil.* London: Zed Books, 2003.

Baran, Paul, and Paul Sweezy. *Monopoly Capital.* New York: Monthly Review Press, 1966.

Barber, Benjamin. "Beyond Jihad vs. McWorld." *The Nation* 274, no. 2 (2002).

Barry, Brian. *Why Social Justice Matters.* Cambridge: Polity Press, 2005.

Bartlett, Will, John Cable, Saul Estrin, and Derek Jones. "Labor-Managed Cooperatives and Private Firms in North Central Italy: An Empirical Comparison." *Industrial and Labor Relations Review* 6, no. 1 (October 1992): 103–18.

Benjamin, Walter. *Illuminations.* New York: Schocken Books, 1969.

Berlin, Isaiah. *Russian Thinkers.* New York: Penguin Books, 1978.

Berman, Katrina. "A Cooperative Model for Worker Management." In *The Performance of Labour-Managed Firms*, edited by Frank Stephens. New York: St. Martin's Press, 1982.

Birchall, Johnston, and Lou Hammond Ketilson. "Resilience of the Cooperative Business Model in Times of Crisis." Geneva: International Labour Organization, Sustainable Enterprise Programme, 2009.

Blackburn, Robin. "Rudolf Meidner, 1914–2005: Visionary Pragmatist." *Counterpunch*, December 22, 2005.

Blalock, Garrick, David Just, and Daniel Simon. "Hitting the Jackpot or Hitting the Skids: Entertainment, Poverty and the Demand for State Lotteries." *American Journal of Economics and Sociology* 66, no. 3 (July 2007): 545–70.

Blinder, Alan. *Hard Heads, Soft Hearts: Tough-Minded Economics for a Just Society.* Reading, MA: Addison-Wesley, 1987.

———, ed. *Paying for Productivity: A Look at the Evidence.* Washington, DC: Brookings, 1990.

Bourdieu, Pierre. "A Reasoned Utopia and Economic Fatalism." *New Left Review* 227 (January–February 1998): 125–30.

Bradley, Keith, and Alan Gelb. *Cooperation at Work: The Mondragon Experience.* London: Heinemann Educational Books, 1983.

Branford, Sue, and Bernardo Kucinski. *Lulu and the Workers Party in Brazil.* New York: The New Press, 2005.

Brown, Ellen. "More States May Create Public Banks." *Yes!*, May 13, 2010.

———. "Reviving the Local Economy with Publicly Owned Banks." *Yes!*, October 14, 2009.

———. "Whose Bank? Public Investment, Not Private Debt." *Yes!*, February 19, 2010.

Brown, Lester R. *Plan B 4.0: Mobilizing to Save Civilization.* New York: Norton, 2009.

Brown, Lester R., Christopher Flavin, and Hilary French. *State of the World 2001.* New York: Norton, 2001.

Carrim, Yunus, and Oscar Martinez. "Socialism Works in Cuba." *Umsebenzi Online* 9, no. 21 (November 3, 2010).

Cassidy, John. "What Good Is Wall Street?" *New Yorker*, November 29, 2010.

Chan, Anita. "Strikes in Vietnam and China: Contrasts in Labor Laws and Diverging Industrial Relations Patterns." American Bar Association International Labor and Employment Law Committee presentation, Istanbul, Turkey, May 9–13, 2010.

Cheney, George. *Values at Work: Employee Participation Meets Market Pressure at Mondragon.* Ithaca, NY: ILR/Cornell University Press, 1999.

Chomsky, Noam. *On Power and Ideology: The Managua Lectures.* Boston: South End Press, 1987.

Clark, John Bates. *The Distribution of Wealth*. New York: Kelley and Millman, 1956.

Clifford, Stephen. *An Owner's Guide to Business Succession Planning*, 2nd ed. Kent, OH: Kent Popular Press, 2008.

Cockburn, Alexander, and Jeffrey St. Clair. *Five Days That Shook the World*. London: Verso, 2000.

Cohen, Stephen. *Failed Crusade: America and the Tragedy of Post-Communist Russia*. New York: Norton, 2000.

Cushman, John H., Jr. "Industrial Group Plans to Battle Climate Change Treaty." *New York Times*, April 26, 1998.

Cynamon, Barry Z., and Steven M. Fazzari. "Household Debt in the Consumer Age— Source of Growth, Risk of Collapse." *Capitalism and Society* 3, no. 2 (2008).

Dahl, Robert. *Democracy and Its Critics*. New Haven, CT: Yale University Press, 1989.

Dahl, Robert, and Charles Lindblom. *Politics, Economics, and Welfare*. New York: Harper, 1953.

Daly, Herman. *Beyond Growth*. Boston, MA: Beacon Press, 1996.

Dasgupta, Partha. *An Inquiry into Well-Being and Destitution*. Oxford: Clarendon Press, 1993.

Davis, Mike. *Planet of Slums*. London: Verso, 2007.

Dow, Gregory. *Governing the Firm: Workers' Control in Theory and Practice*. Cambridge: Cambridge University Press, 2003.

Dunn, Seth. "Decarbonizing the Energy Economy." In *State of the World 2001*, edited by Lester R. Brown, Christopher Flavin, and Hilary French. New York: Norton, 2001.

Ellerman, David. *Helping People Help Themselves: From the World Bank to an Alternative Philosophy of Development Assistance*. Ann Arbor: University of Michigan Press, 2006.

———. "Lessons from Eastern Europe's Voucher Privatization." *Challenge: The Magazine of Economic Affairs* 44, no. 4 (July–August 2001): 14–37.

Farrell, Diana, and Susan Lund. "Putting China's Capital to Work." *Far Eastern Economic Review* 169 (May 2006): 5–10.

Fleck, Susan. "International Comparisons of Hours Worked: An Assessment of the Statistics." *Monthly Labor Review* 132, no. 5 (May 2009): 3–31.

Foley, Barbara, and Bernard Moss, eds. "China: Socialism, Capitalism, Market: What Now? Where Next?" *Science and Society* 73, no. 2 (April 2009).

Ford, Martin. *The Lights in the Tunnel: Automation, Accelerating Technology and the Economy of the Future*. N.p.: Acculant Publishing, 2009.

Frank, Andre Gunder. *Dependent Accumulation and Underdevelopment*. New York: Monthly Review Press, 1979.

Frank, Robert. *Richistan: A Journey through the American Wealth Boom and the Lives of the New Rich*. New York: Crown Publishers, 2007.

Franke, Richard, and Barbara Chasin. *Kerala: Radical Reform as Development in an Indian State*. San Francisco: Institute for Food and Development, 1989.

Friedman, Milton. *Capitalism and Freedom*. Chicago: University of Chicago Press, 1962.

Friedman, Robert. "And Darkness Covered the Land: A Report from Israel and Palestine." *The Nation* 273, no. 21 (December 24, 2001).

Fukuyama, Francis. *The End of History and the Last Man.* New York: Free Press, 1992.

Galbraith, John Kenneth. *Economics and the Public Purpose.* Boston: Houghton Mifflin, 1973.

———. *The New Industrial State.* Boston: Houghton Mifflin, 1967.

Gilligan, Carol. *In a Different Voice.* Cambridge, MA: Harvard University Press, 1982.

Golden, Lonnie, and Deborah Figart. "Doing Something about Long Hours." *Challenge: The Magazine of Economic Affairs* 43, no. 6 (November/December 2000).

Golinger, Eva. *The Chavez Code: Cracking U.S. Intervention in Venezuela.* Northhampton, MA: Olive Branch Press, 2006.

Gowan, Peter. "Western Economic Diplomacy and the New Eastern Europe." *New Left Review* 182 (July–August 1990): 63–82.

Hacker, Andrew. *Money: Who Has How Much and Why.* New York: Simon and Schuster, 1997.

Ha-Joon Chang. *Kicking Away the Ladder: Development Strategy in Historical Perspective.* London: Anthem Press, 2002.

Hanson, Alvin. *Full Recovery or Stagnation?* New York: Norton, 1938.

Harcourt, G.C. "The Cambridge Controversies: Old Ways and New Horizons—or Dead End?" *Oxford Economic Papers* 28 (1976).

———. "The Capital Theory Controversies." In *Capitalism, Socialism and Post-Keynesianism: Selected Essays,* edited by G. C. Harcourt. Aldershot, UK: Edward Elgar, 1995.

Harnecker, Marta. "Latin America and Twenty-first Century Socialism: Inventing to Avoid Mistakes." *Monthly Review* 62, no. 3 (July–August 2010).

Hawken, Paul. *Blessed Unrest: How the Largest Movement in the World Came into Being and Why No One Saw It Coming.* New York: Viking, 2008.

Hawkins, Paul, Amory Lovins, and L. Hunter Lovins. *Natural Capitalism: Creating the Next Industrial Revolution.* Boston: Little, Brown, 1999.

Held, Virginia. *The Ethic of Care: Personal, Political, and Global.* Oxford: Oxford University Press, 2006.

Helman, Christopher. "What the Top Corporations Pay in Taxes." *Forbes,* April 1, 2010.

Hendrik, Thomas. "The Performance of the Mondragon Cooperatives in Spain." In *Participatory and Self-Managed Firms,* edited by Derek Jones and Jan Svejnar. Lexington, MA: Lexington Books, 1982.

Hertz, Noreena. *The Debt Threat: How Debt Is Destroying the Developing World . . . and Threatening Us All.* New York: HarperCollins, 2004.

Hochschild, Arlie. *Time Bind: When Work Becomes Home and Home Becomes Work.* New York: Metropolitan Books, 1997.

Holmstrom, Nancy, and Richard Smith. "The Necessity of Gangster Capitalism: Primitive Accumulation in Russia and China." *Monthly Review* 51, no. 9 (February 2000).

Huang Yasheng. *Capitalism with Chinese Characteristics: Entrepreneurship and the State.* Cambridge: Cambridge University Press, 2008.

———. "The Politics of China's Path: A Reply to Joel Andreas." *New Left Review* 65 (September–October 2010).

Intergovernmental Panel on Climate Change. *IPCC/TEAP Special Report on Safe-guarding the Ozone Layer and the Global Climate System.* Cambridge: Cambridge University Press, 2005.

International Labour Organization. *Global Employment Trends.* Geneva: ILO, 2010.

Isaac, Jeffrey. "Marxism and Intellectuals." *New Left Review* 2 (March–April 2000).

Johnson, Chalmers. *MITI and the Japanese Miracle: The Growth of Industrial Policy, 1925–1975.* Stanford, CA: Stanford University Press, 1982.

Johnson, David Cay. *Free Lunch: How the Wealthiest Americans Enrich Themselves at Government Expense (and Stick You with the Bill).* New York: Portfolio, 2007.

Johnson, Elizabeth. "John Maynard Keynes: Scientist or Politician?" In *After Keynes,* edited by Joan Robinson. New York: Barnes and Noble, 1973.

Johnson, Lyndon B. "Special Address to Congress, March 16, 1964." In *Public Papers of U.S. Presidents, Lyndon B. Johnson, 1963–1964.* Washington, DC: Government Printing Office, 1965.

Jones, Derek, and Jan Svejnar, eds. *Participatory and Self-Managed Firms: Evaluating Economic Performance.* Lexington, MA: Lexington Books, 1982.

Jones, Van. *The Green Collar Economy: How One Solution Can Fix Our Two Biggest Problems.* New York: HarperCollins, 2008.

Kasmir, Sharryn. *The Myth of Mondragon: Cooperatives, Politics, and Working-Class Life in a Basque Town.* Albany: SUNY Press, 1996.

Kelly, Georgia, and Shaula Massena. "Mondragon Coops: Worker-Operatives Decide How to Ride Out a Downturn." *Yes!,* May 7, 2009.

Keynes, John Maynard. *Essays in Persuasion.* New York: Norton, 1963.

———. *The General Theory of Employment, Interest, and Money.* New York: Harcourt, Brace and Company, 1936.

Krugman, Paul. *The Age of Diminished Expectations: U.S. Economic Policies in the 1990s.* Cambridge, MA: MIT Press, 1990.

———. "Back to What Obama Must Do." *Rolling Stone,* January 14, 2009.

———. *The Conscience of a Liberal.* New York: Norton, 2007.

———. "Defining Prosperity Down." *New York Times,* August 1, 2010.

———. "Innovating Our Way to Financial Crisis." *New York Times,* December 3, 2007.

———. "Money Can't Buy Happiness. Er, Can It?" *New York Times,* June 1, 1999.

———. *The Return of Depression Economics and the Crisis of 2008.* New York: Norton, 2009.

Landers, Peter. "State Solution: Nationalizing Banks May Be Japan's Only Option." *Far Eastern Economic Review* 161, no. 40 (October 1, 1998).

Lappé, Francis Moore. *EcoMind: Reframing Six Disempowering Ideas That Keep Us from Aligning with Nature—Even Our Own.* New York: Nation Books, 2010.

Lawler, James. "Marx's Theory of Socialisms: Nihilistic and Dialectical." In *Debating Marx,* edited by Louis Pastouras. Lewiston, NY: Edward Mellon Press, 1994.

Leisner, Thelma. *Economic Statistics 1900–1983.* New York: Facts on File Publications, 1985.

Leiva, Fernando Ignacio. *Latin American Neostructuralism: Contradictions of Post-Neoliberal Development.* Minneapolis: University of Minnesota Press, 2008.

Lenin, V.I. *State and Revolution*. New York: International Publishers, 1932.

Levin, Henry. "Employment and Productivity of Producer Cooperatives." In *Worker Cooperatives in America*, edited by Robert Jackall and Henry Levin. Berkeley: University of California Press, 1984.

Lichtblau, Eric. "Scalia and Thomas' Retreat with Koch." *New York Times*, January 21, 2011.

Lorenz, Andreas. "China's Environmental Suicide: A Government Minister Speaks." *Open Democracy*, April 5, 2005.

Lowenstein, Roger. *When Genius Failed: The Rise and Fall of Long-Term Capital Management*. New York: Random House, 2000.

Lucas, Robert. "Macroeconomic Priorities." *The American Economic Review* 93, no. 1 (March 2003).

Lydall, Harold. *Yugoslavia in Crisis*. Oxford: Clarendon Press, 1989.

Lynn, Barry. *Cornered: The New Monopoly Capitalism and the Economics of Destruction*. Hoboken, NJ: John Wiley and Sons, 2010.

MacLeod, Greg. *From Mondragon to America: Experiments in Community Economic Development*. Sidney, Nova Scotia: University College of Cape Breton Press, 1997.

Mahbubani, Kishore. *Beyond the Age of Innocence: Rebuilding Trust between America and the World*. New York: Public Affairs, 2005.

Mann, Michael. "Globalization and September 11." *New Left Review*, n.s., 12 (November–December 2001).

Martin, Hans-Peter, and Harald Schumann. *The Global Trap*. New York: Zed Books, 1997.

Marx, Karl. *Capital*. Vol. 1. New York: International Publishers, 2003.

———. *Capital*. Vol. 3. New York: International Publishers, 1967.

———. *Karl Marx: Selected Writings*. Edited by Lawrence Simon. Indianapolis: Hackett, 1994.

Marx, Karl, and Frederick Engels. *The Communist Manifesto*. London: Verso, 1998.

Mayer, Jane. "Covert Operations: The Billionaire Brothers Who Are Wagin' War against Obama." *New Yorker*, August 30, 2010.

McChesney, Robert W. *The Political Economy of Media: Enduring Issues, Emerging Dilemmas*. New York: Monthly Review Press, 2008.

———. *Rich Media, Poor Democracy*. Champaign: University of Illinois Press, 1999.

McChesney, Robert W., John Bellamy Foster, Inger L. Stole, and Hannah Holtman. "The Sales Effort and Monopoly Capital." *Monthly Review* 60, no. 11 (April 2009).

McKibben, Bill. *Deep Economy*. New York: Henry Holt, 2007.

———. "Happiness Is . . ." *Ecologist* (2 January 2007).

———. *Hope, Human and Wild*. St. Paul, MN: Hungry Mind Press, 1995.

Mikkelson, Gregory, Andrew Gonzales, and Garry Peterson. "Economic Inequality Predicts Biodiversity Loss." *PloS One* 2, no. 5 (May 2007).

Mill, John Stuart. *Considerations of Representative Government*. Indianapolis: Bobbs-Merrill, 1958.

Mitchell, William, and Joan Muysken. *Full Employment Abandoned: Shifting Sands and Policy Failures*. Cheltenham, UK: Edward Elgar, 2008.

Moore, Steven A. *Alternative Routes to the Sustainable City: Austin, Curitiba, and Frankfurt.* Lanham, MD: Lexington Books, 2007.

Morrison, Roy. *We Build the Road as We Travel.* Philadelphia: New Society Publishers, 1991.

Naim, Moisés. "The Havana Obsession." *Newsweek*, June 22, 2009.

Nolan, Peter. *China and the Global Business Revolution.* New York: Palgrave, 2001.

———. *China's Rise, Russia's Fall: Politics, Economics, and Planning in the Transition from Stalinism.* New York: St. Martin's Press, 1995.

Nozick, Robert. *Anarchy, State, and Utopia.* New York: Basic Books, 1974.

Ollman, Bertell, ed. *Market Socialism: The Debate among Socialists.* New York: Routledge, 1998.

Olsen, Mancur, and Hans Landsberg, eds. *The No-Growth Society.* New York: Norton, 1974.

Palley, Thomas. "Destabilizing Speculation and the Case for an International Currency Transactions Tax." *Challenge: The Magazine of Economic Affairs* 44, no. 3 (May–June 2001).

———. *Plenty of Nothing: The Downsizing of the American Dream and the Case for Structural Keynesianism.* Princeton, NJ: Princeton University Press, 1998.

Peck, Don. "How a New Jobless Era Will Transform America." *Atlantic*, March 2010.

Pen, Jan. *Income Distribution: Facts, Theories, Policies.* New York: Praeger, 1971.

Perkins, John. *Confessions of an Economic Hit Man.* San Francisco: Berrett-Koehler, 2004.

Plumer, Bradford. "Fossil-Fuel Subsidies Still Dominate." *New Republic*, August 3, 2010.

Pogge, Thomas. "Real World Justice." *Journal of Ethics* 9, nos. 1–2 (2005).

Pontusson, Jonus. *The Limits to Social Democracy: Investment Politics in Sweden.* Ithaca, NY: Cornell University Press, 1992.

Raby, D. I. *Democracy and Revolution: Cuba, Venezuela and Socialism Today.* London: Pluto Press, 2006.

Rahman, K. Ravi, ed. *Development, Democracy and the State: Critiquing the Kerala Model of Development.* New York: Routledge, 2010.

Rawls, John. *A Theory of Justice.* Cambridge, MA: Harvard University Press, 1971.

Reding, Nick. *Methland: The Death and Life of an American Small Town.* New York: Bloomsbury, 2010.

Reich, Robert. "Only 4.2 Billion to Buy This Election?" *Robert Reich's Blog*, October 28, 2010.

Reinhart, Carmen, and Kenneth Rogoff. *This Time Is Different: Eight Centuries of Financial Folly.* Princeton, NJ: Princeton University Press, 2009.

Rifkin, Jeremy. *The End of Work: The Decline of the Global Labor Force and the Dawn of the Post- Market Era.* New York: G. P. Putnam's Sons, 1995.

Rorty, Richard. "For a More Banal Politics." *Harper's*, May 1992.

Roy, Arundhati. *An Ordinary Person's Guide to Empire.* Boston: South End Press, 2004.

Sader, Emir, and Ken Silverstein. *Without Fear of Being Happy: Lula, the Workers Party and Brazil.* London: Verso, 1991.

Samuelson, Paul. *Economics.* 11th ed. New York: McGraw Hill, 1980.

Schor, Juliet. *Born to Buy.* New York: Scribner, 2004.

———. *The Overworked American: The Unexpected Decline of Leisure.* New York: Basic Books, 1992.

———. *Plentitude: The New Economics of True Wealth.* New York: Penguin Press, 2016.

Schumacher, E. F. *Small Is Beautiful: Economics as if People Matter.* Point Roberts, WA: Hartley and Marks Publishers, 1999.

Schwartz, Nelson, and Louise Story. "Pay of Hedge Fund Managers Roared Back Last Year," *New York Times*, March 31, 2010.

Schweickart, David. *Against Capitalism.* Cambridge: Cambridge University Press, 1993.

———. "Does Historical Materialism Imply Socialism?" In *Reason and Emancipation: Essays on the Philosophy of Kai Nielsen*, edited by Michel Seymour and Matthias Fitsch. Amherst, MA: Humanity Books, 2006.

———. "Should Rawls Be a Socialist?" *Social Theory and Practice* 5, no. 1 (Fall 1978).

Sen, Amartya. "Capitalism Beyond the Crisis." *New York Review of Books*, March 26, 2009.

———. *Development as Freedom* New York: Knopf, 1999,

———. *Resources, Values, and Development.* Cambridge, MA: Harvard University Press, 1984.

Shakya, Tsering. "Blood in the Snows: Reply to Wang Lixiong." *New Left Review* 15 (May–June 2002).

Singer, Peter. *One World: The Ethics of Globalization.* New Haven, CT: Yale University Press, 2002.

Speth, James Gustave. *The Bridge at the Edge of the World: Capitalism, the Environment, and Crossing from Crisis to Sustainability.* New Haven, CT: Yale University Press, 2008.

Stehle, Vince. "Righting Philanthropy." *The Nation* 264, no. 25 (June 30, 1997).

Stein, Ben. "In Class Warfare, Guess Which Class Is Winning?" *New York Times*, November 26, 2006.

Stiglitz, Joseph. "America's Socialism for the Rich." Berkeley Electronic Press, June 2009.

———. "*Quis Custodiet Ipsos Custodes?*" *Challenge: The Magazine of Economic Affairs* 42, no. 6 (November/December 1999).

Sullivan, Michael. *American Adventurism Abroad: 30 Invasions, Interventions and Regime Changes since World War II.* Westport, CT: Praeger, 2004.

Sum, Andrew, and Joseph McGlaughlin. "The Massive Shedding of Jobs in America." *Challenge: The Magazine of Economic Affairs* 53, no. 6 (November–December 2010).

Sweig, Julia. *Cuba: What Everyone Needs to Know.* Oxford: Oxford University Press, 2009.

Taibbi, Matt. "Tea and Crackers." *Rolling Stone*, October 1, 2010.

Taiwo, Olufemi. *How Colonialism Preempted Modernity in Africa.* Bloomington: Indiana University Press, 2010.

Thomas, Henk, and Chris Logan. *Mondragon: An Economic Analysis.* London: George Allen and Unwin, 1982.

Thurow, Roger, and Scott Kilman. *Enough: Why the World's Poorest Starve in an Age of Plenty.* New York: Public Affairs, 2009.

UNEP-UNCTAD Capacity Building Task Force on Trade, Environment and Nations. "Organic Agriculture and Food Security in Africa." New York: United Nations, 2008.

United Nations Development Programme. *Human Development Report 1998.* Oxford: Oxford University Press, 1998.

United States Bureau of Labor Statistics and Bureau of the Census. *CPS Annual Demographic Survey: March 1999 Supplement.* Washington, DC: Government Printing Office, 1999.

United States Census Bureau. *Income, Poverty and Health Insurance Coverage in the United States, 2009.* Washington, DC: U.S. Census Bureau, 2010.

United States Central Intelligence Agency. *The CIA Factbook 2010.* New York: Skyhorse Publishing, 2009.

United States Department of Commerce. *Statistical Abstract of the United States, 1999.* Washington, DC: Government Printing Office, 2000.

United States Department of Health, Education, and Welfare. *Work in America.* Cambridge, MA: MIT Press, 1973.

Wade, Robert. *Governing the Market: Economic Theory and the Role of Government in East Asia Industrialization.* Princeton, NJ: Princeton University Press, 1990.

Wang Lixiong. "Reflections on Tibet." *New Left Review* 14 (March–April 2002).

Wasserstrom, Jeffrey. "Throwing the Book at China." *Miller-McCune,* December 19, 2010.

Wei Jiangxing. "Wei Jiangxing Speaks on Democratic Management of Non-Public Enterprises during Inspection in Hebei." *Xinhaua Domestic Service,* September 29, 2002.

Weisman, Alan. *Gaviotas: A Village to Reinvent the World.* White River Junction, VT: Chelsea Green, 2008.

Wetzel, Dale. "Economy Prompts Fresh Look at ND's Socialist Bank." Associated Press, February 16, 2010.

Whyte, William Foote, and Kathleen King White. *Making Mondragon: The Growth and Dynamics of the Worker Cooperative Complex.* Ithaca, NY: Cornell University Press, 1988.

Wilkinson, Richard, and Kate Pickett. *The Spirit Level: Why Greater Equality Makes Societies Stronger.* New York: Bloomsbury Press, 2009.

Wilson, William Julius. *When Work Disappears: The World of the New Urban Poor.* New York: Vintage, 1997.

Wong, Edward. "Global Crisis Adds to Surge of Labor Disputes in Chinese Court." *New York Times,* September 15, 2010.

World Bank. *World Development Report 2010: Development and Climate Change.* Washington, DC: World Bank, 2010.

World Health Organization. *2010 Malaria Report.*

Yeagle, Patrick. "Record Breaking Year for Campaign Spending." *Illinois Times* (Springfield), November 4, 2010.

Young, Iris Marion. *Inclusion and Democracy.* Oxford: Oxford University Press, 2002.

Žižek, Slavoj. *The Fragile Absolute: Or, Why Is the Christian Legacy Worth Fighting For?* 2nd ed. London: Verso, 2009.

Index

Council on Foreign Relations, 155
counterproject, 5–14, 16, 80, 193–94
Cuba, xxvi, 12, 59, 60, 112, 119, 140,
    161, 162, 170, 171, 173
Czechoslovakia, 200

Dahl, Robert, 152
Daly, Herman, 149
Dasgupta, Partha, 114
Davis, Mike, 200
democracy, 15; classical Greek, 158;
    under Economic Democracy, 18,
    87–89, 158–59; defined in contrast
    to polyarchy, 152–53, 220n40; and
    gender, 16; lack thereof, under capi-
    talism, 48, 151–59. *See also* workplace
    democracy
democratic centralism, 194
democratic socialism, xxi, 15
Democratic Party, 121
Denmark, 200. *See also* Scandinavia
deontology, 98–99
depreciation fund, 50
diminishing returns, 29–30
Dominican Republic, 161
Dow, Gregory, 180, 213n17
Drake, Francis, 42
Dunayevskaya, Raya, 7
Dunn, Seth, 143
DuPont Chemicals, 143-44

Eastern Europe, 12, 26, 46, 59, 98, 152,
    170, 204
East Timor, 162, 221n51
ecology. *See* environment
Economic Democracy, xxi; accumulat-
    ing wealth in, 134; and the alleviation
    of global poverty, 82–83, 117–19;
    arguments for its superiority over
    capitalism, 19–20, 80–81, 88–89,
    133–34; arguments for the viability
    of, 58–66, 67–73; bankruptcy in, 64;
    basic model, 47–49; bureaucracy
    under, 163; capitalists in, 75, 77–80,
    176; care for the elderly in, 17, 73–74,

103; consumption/leisure tradeoff in,
    18, 110; democracy in, 60, 87–88, 90,
    158–59; drawbacks of, 66; efficiency
    of, 63, 213n17; expanded model, 75–
    83; fair-share principle in, 53–55, 64;
    firms in, lack expansionary dynamic,
    102, 150; government as employer-
    of-last-resort in, 75–76, 183, 193;
    home mortgages and other consumer
    loans in, 76–77; inequality within,
    95–97; in one country, 66, 80–83; as
    orienting device, 165–71; origin of
    the model, 48; political liberties in,
    85, 161–62; political parties in, 164;
    public sector in, 55–56; and racism,
    121; raising children in, 73–74, 103;
    small businesses in, 77–79, 176; and
    socialism, 48, 81, *167*; sustainable
    development under, 150–51; trading
    relations with other nations, 80–83;
    and unemployment, 75, 87, 102–4,
    113. *See also* intergenerational soli-
    darity; socialist protectionism
economic growth: export-led, 148; ne-
    cessity of, under capitalism, 147–49;
    pace of, in Economic Democracy,
    149–50; private savings and, 44–46
Ecuador, 173, 174
Egypt, 170
Elizabeth I, 42
Ellerman, David, 217n38, 221n1
El Salvador, 161, 174
emigration, 122
Employee Stock Ownership Plans
    (ESOPs), 180
Engels, Frederick, 1, 7. *See also* Marx, Karl
England, 81
entrepreneurial activity, 34, 38–39, 77,
    176; in Economic Democracy, 34,
    77–79; as justification for capital-
    ism, 34–36, 41–42; and risk, 41; and
    savings, 44
environment: capitalist degradation of,
    110–11, 142–51, 220n35; climate
    change, 141–51, 203; and Economic

About the Author

David Schweickart is professor of philosophy at Loyola University Chicago. He holds PhDs in both mathematics and philosophy. His books include *Against Capitalism*; *Market Socialism: The Debate among Socialists*; and *After Capitalism* (2002; second edition 2011). All three of these works have been translated into Chinese. His work has also been translated into Spanish, French, Slovak, Catalan, and Farsi.